Ernst Denert Award for
Software Engineering 2022

Eric Bodden • Michael Felderer •
Wilhelm Hasselbring • Paula Herber •
Heiko Koziolek • Carola Lilienthal •
Florian Matthes • Lutz Prechelt •
Bernhard Rumpe • Ina Schaefer
Editors

Ernst Denert Award for Software Engineering 2022

Practice Meets Foundations

Editors
Eric Bodden
Secure Software Engineering, Heinz Nixdorf
Institut der Universität Paderborn
Paderborn University and Fraunhofer IEM
Paderborn, Germany

Wilhelm Hasselbring
Software Engineering
Christian-Albrechts-Universität Kiel
Kiel, Germany

Heiko Koziolek
ABB Corporate Research
Ladenburg, Germany

Florian Matthes
Software Engineering of Business Information
Systems, Department of Computer Science (CS)
Technical University of Munich
Garching bei München, Germany

Bernhard Rumpe
Software Engineering
RWTH Aachen
Aachen, Germany

Michael Felderer
Institute for Software Technology
German Aerospace Center (DLR),
University of Cologne
Cologne, Germany

Paula Herber
Embedded Systems Group
University of Münster
Münster, Germany

Carola Lilienthal
WPS - Workplace Solutions GmbH
Hamburg, Germany

Lutz Prechelt
Institut für Informatik
Freie Universität Berlin
Berlin, Germany

Ina Schaefer
Testing, Validation and Analysis of
Software-Intensive Systems (TVA)
Institute for Information Security
and Dependability (KASTEL)
Karlsruhe Institute of Technology (KIT)
Karlsruhe, Germany

ISBN 978-3-031-44414-2   ISBN 978-3-031-44412-8 (eBook)
https://doi.org/10.1007/978-3-031-44412-8

This work was supported by the Gerlind & Ernst Denert-Stiftung.

© The Editor(s) (if applicable) and The Author(s) 2024. This book is an open access publication.
Open Access This book is licensed under the terms of the Creative Commons Attribution 4.0 International License (http://creativecommons.org/licenses/by/4.0/), which permits use, sharing, adaptation, distribution and reproduction in any medium or format, as long as you give appropriate credit to the original author(s) and the source, provide a link to the Creative Commons license and indicate if changes were made.
The images or other third party material in this book are included in the book's Creative Commons license, unless indicated otherwise in a credit line to the material. If material is not included in the book's Creative Commons license and your intended use is not permitted by statutory regulation or exceeds the permitted use, you will need to obtain permission directly from the copyright holder.
The use of general descriptive names, registered names, trademarks, service marks, etc. in this publication does not imply, even in the absence of a specific statement, that such names are exempt from the relevant protective laws and regulations and therefore free for general use.
The publisher, the authors, and the editors are safe to assume that the advice and information in this book are believed to be true and accurate at the date of publication. Neither the publisher nor the authors or the editors give a warranty, expressed or implied, with respect to the material contained herein or for any errors or omissions that may have been made. The publisher remains neutral with regard to jurisdictional claims in published maps and institutional affiliations.

Cover illustration: © 2020 Ernst Denert, all rights reserved.

This Springer imprint is published by the registered company Springer Nature Switzerland AG
The registered company address is: Gewerbestrasse 11, 6330 Cham, Switzerland

Paper in this product is recyclable.

Contents

Ernst Denert Software Engineering Award 2022 1
Eric Bodden, Michael Felderer, Wilhelm Hasselbring, Paula Herber,
Heiko Koziolek, Carola Lilienthal, Florian Matthes, Lutz Prechelt,
Bernhard Rumpe, and Ina Schaefer

**Conditional Statements in Requirements Artifacts: Logical
Interpretation, Use Cases for Automated Software Engineering,
and Fine-Grained Extraction** 9
Jannik Fischbach and Andreas Vogelsang

**From Design to Reality: An Overview of the MontiThings
Ecosystem for Model-Driven IoT Applications** 45
Jörg Christian Kirchhof

Security Compliance in Model-Driven Software Development 73
Sven Peldszus

**Model-Driven Engineering of Microservice Architectures—The
LEMMA Approach** 105
Florian Rademacher, Philip Wizenty, Jonas Sorgalla, Sabine Sachweh,
and Albert Zündorf

**Usefulness of Automatic Static Analysis Tools: Evidence from
Four Case Studies** 149
Alexander Trautsch

Ernst Denert Software Engineering Award 2022

Eric Bodden, Michael Felderer, Wilhelm Hasselbring, Paula Herber, Heiko Koziolek, Carola Lilienthal, Florian Matthes, Lutz Prechelt, Bernhard Rumpe, and Ina Schaefer

---

E. Bodden
Secure Software Engineering, Heinz Nixdorf Institut der Universität Paderborn, Paderborn University and Fraunhofer IEM, Paderborn, Germany
e-mail: eric.bodden@uni-paderborn.de

M. Felderer
Institute for Software Technology, German Aerospace Center (DLR), University of Cologne, Cologne, Germany
e-mail: michael.felderer@uni-koeln.de

W. Hasselbring
Software Engineering, Christian-Albrechts-Universität Kiel, Kiel, Germany
e-mail: hasselbring@email.uni-kiel.de

P. Herber
Embedded Systems Group, University of Münster, Münster, Germany
e-mail: paula.herber@uni-muenster.de

H. Koziolek
ABB Corporate Research, Ladenburg, Germany
e-mail: heiko.koziolek@de.abb.com

C. Lilienthal
WPS - Workplace Solutions GmbH, Hamburg, Germany
e-mail: carola.lilienthal@wps.de

F. Matthes
Software Engineering of Business Information Systems, Department of Computer Science (CS), Technical University of Munich, Garching bei München, Germany
e-mail: matthes@in.tum.de

L. Prechelt
Institut für Informatik, Freie Universität Berlin, Berlin, Germany
e-mail: prechelt@inf.fu-berlin.de

B. Rumpe (✉)
Software Engineering, RWTH Aachen, Aachen, Germany
e-mail: rumpe@se-rwth.de

I. Schaefer
Testing, Validation and Analysis of Software-Intensive Systems (TVA), Institute for Information Security and Dependability (KASTEL), Karlsruhe Institute of Technology (KIT), Karlsruhe, Germany
e-mail: ina.schaefer@kit.edu

© The Author(s) 2024
E. Bodden et al. (eds.), *Ernst Denert Award for Software Engineering 2022*,
https://doi.org/10.1007/978-3-031-44412-8_1

Abstract The Ernst Denert Award is already existing since 1992, which does not only honor the award winners but also the software engineering field in total. Software engineering is a vivid and intensively extending field that regularly spawns new subfields such as *automotive software engineering*, *research software engineering*, or *quantum software engineering*, covering specific needs but also generalizing solutions, methods, and techniques when they become applicable. This is the introductory chapter of the book on the Ernst Denert Software Engineering Award 2022. It provides an overview of the five nominated PhD theses.

1 Introduction

Software-based products, apps, systems, or other services are influencing all areas of our daily life. They are the basis and central driver for digitization and all kinds of innovation. This makes software engineering a core discipline to drive technical and societal innovations in the age of digitization [4].

As of 2023, software engineering operates in many new or significantly changed application domains, such as the Internet of Things (IoT), smart manufacturing, autonomous systems, machine learning, artificial intelligence (AI), and even quantum computing. Surveys argue that more than 90% of research projects use software for gaining new insights, managing their results, understanding the research topic, controlling the physical gadgets, etc. Researchers of nearly all domains are significantly developing software within their research. Model-driven software and systems engineering approaches nowadays support handling the ever-growing complexity of modern systems. Sophisticated static analysis tools identify more and more faults in the code and can mitigate the rising cyber-security challenges by identifying security vulnerabilities early or monitoring the system during runtime for a safe, reliable, robust, and secure operation.

A rather strong recent trend, which affects software engineering practices, is the advent of generative AI, thanks to large language models (LLMs) based on the transformer architecture [10]. These models were popularized in recent months by publicly available, easy-to-use tools (e.g., GitHub CoPilot, ChatGPT, Bard). Such tools can generate source code based on natural language queries but can also interpret, fix, or document existing code. Trained with a vast data set including many popular libraries, such LLMs can potentially relieve software engineers from many accidental complexities and focus on the essential complexities of solving computing problems. Early experiments at Microsoft Research demonstrated a 55% developer productivity increase from using GitHub CoPilot for web programming, signifying promising potential for advancing software development practices [7].

While some authors already pro-claim "the end of programming" [9], the technology is still under development. LLMs sometimes find very helpful sentences and programs but sometimes only hallucinate. Generated source code thus may be partially semantically incorrect or doing something completely wrong. We will have to evaluate the new technology carefully. It will affect software engineering research to utilize generative AI for the development of programs, models, and the understanding of requirements to the fullest. It may be that the new approaches will leverage methods from psychology, where intelligent interrogation allows to reveal how an AI really works.

We see a forthcoming challenging and very interesting future for software engineering research, not only for the application of AI models for software development but also for specific upcoming domains, such as research software engineering [5] or quantum computing [8].

It is important to recall that the *IEEE Standard Glossary of Software Engineering Terminology* [6] defines software engineering as follows:

(1) The application of a systematic, disciplined, quantifiable approach to the development, operation, and maintenance of software; that is, the application of engineering to software.
(2) The study of approaches as in (1).

It defines software engineering as an engineering discipline ("application of engineering to software") with its own methodology ("systematic, disciplined, quantifiable approach") applied to all phases of the software life cycle ("development, operation, and maintenance of software"). The two-part structure of the definition of software engineering also makes the tight integration of software engineering (1) and software engineering research (2) explicit.

Therefore, the Ernst Denert Software Engineering Award specifically rewards researchers who value the practical impact of their work and aim to improve current software engineering practices [3]. Creating tighter feedback loops between professional practitioners and academic researchers is essential to make research ideas ready for industry adoption. Researchers who demonstrate their proposed methods and tools on nontrivial systems under real-world conditions in various phases of the software life cycle shall be supported so that the gap between research and practice can be decreased.

Overall, five PhD theses that were defended between September 1, 2021, and October 31, 2022, were nominated and finally presented during the Software Engineering Conference SE 2023.

All submissions fulfill the ambitious selection criteria of the award defined in detail in the book for the Ernst Denert Software Engineering Award 2019 [2]. These criteria include, among others, practical applicability, usefulness via tools, theoretical or empirical insights, currentness, and contribution to the field. In a nutshell, "The best submissions are those that will be viewed as important steps forward even 15 years from now." [3].

In this introductory chapter, we give an overview of the nominated five PhD theses, present the work of the award winner, and outline the structure of the book.

2 Overview of the Nominated PhD Theses

As previously mentioned, the Ernst Denert Software Engineering Award 2022 committee identified five worthy nominations for PhD theses that were eligible to receive the Ernst Denert Award. These theses encompass a wide range of research in the field of software engineering, highlighting its diverse applications across various domains. They also demonstrate the vibrancy and diversity of the field through the utilization of different research methods, including formal methods, design science, and quantitative and qualitative empirical methods. Furthermore, these theses address various activities in the software life cycle, such as analysis, design, programming, testing, deployment, operation, and maintenance. This section provides a brief overview of the nominated PhD theses. They will be presented in alphabetical order based on the names of the respective nominees, accompanied by a concise summary of the chapters contributed by each thesis to this book.

The chapter of Jannik Fischbach and Andreas Vogelsang entitled "Conditional Statements in Requirements Artifacts: Logical Interpretation, Use Cases for Automated Software Engineering, and Fine-Grained Extraction" provides readers with an understanding of (1) the notion of conditionals in RE artifacts, (2) how to extract them in fine-grained form, and (3) the added value that the extraction of conditionals can provide to RE. Jannik Fischbach is the winner of the Ernst Denert Software Engineering Award 2022, and we present his work in more detail in the next section.

The chapter of Jörg Christian Kirchhof entitled "From Design to Reality: An Overview of the MontiThings Ecosystem for Model-Driven IoT Applications" proposes a model-driven process for rapid development of IoT applications. The chapter gives an overview of how to develop, deploy and analyze distributed IoT applications using MontiThings. MontiThings demonstrates the benefits of a model-driven development approach not only in the initial conceptualization of the application but also in later development phases (e.g., deployment), leading to an app store concept that separates hardware from software development.

The chapter of Sven Peldszus entitled "Security Compliance in Model-Driven Development of Software Systems in Presence of Long-Term Evolution and Variants" provides an approach for tracing and verifying security requirements in the model-driven development of software-intensive systems. Early security considerations based on the principle of security by design are part of many modern development processes, but to ensure the security of the final product, which may even comprise an entire product line, it is essential to check each individual product for compliance with the planned security design. To this end, the thesis investigates the systematic traceability of security requirements throughout the software development life cycle and how this traceability can be used for automated security compliance checking. The individual solutions were validated against 18 objectives, and the overall approach was demonstrated on two open-source case studies.

The chapter of Florian Rademacher et al., entitled "Model-Driven Engineering of Microservice Architectures: The LEMMA Approach", investigates the application of model-driven engineering (MDE) to the design, development, and operation of software systems that are based on microservice architecture (MSA). From a set of well-known challenges in MSA engineering as well as real-world microservice architectures and approaches to the modeling of service-oriented architectures, Rademacher et al. derive a set of integrated, stakeholder-oriented MSA modeling languages. Furthermore, they accompany these languages with a framework for the implementation of model processors that is oriented toward technology-savvy MSA stakeholders without an MDE background. Finally, Rademacher et al. present and discuss the application of their MSA modeling languages and framework for the (i) extensible generation of microservice code; (ii) microservice architecture reconstruction; (iii) quality assessment of microservices; (iv) microservice architecture defect resolution; and (v) establishment of a common architecture understanding among distributed MSA teams.

Finally, the chapter of Alexander Trautsch entitled "Usefulness of Automatic Static Analysis Tools: Evidence from Four Case Studies" presents results from multiple empirical studies in the context of software engineering research. The studies explore an automated static analysis tool and its impact on quality in a broad overview from multiple perspectives. The chapter contains studies that focus on the evolution of static analysis warnings, static analysis warnings in the context of software defects, as well as the context of developer intent.

3 The Work of the Award Winner

We congratulate *Jannik Fischbach*, his advisor *Andreas Vogelsang*, and his alma mater, Universität zu Köln, for winning the Ernst Denert Software Engineering Award 2022 for the PhD thesis "Why and How to Extract Conditional Statements From Natural Language Requirements." Dr. Jannik Fischbach focuses on conditionals (e.g., "If the system detects an error, an error message shall be shown") in requirements and highlights **why** and **how** *requirements engineering* can benefit from the automated extraction of conditionals. Specifically, he makes the following contributions:

1. He presents empirical results on the prevalence and logical interpretation of conditionals in RE artifacts. Jannik Fischbach found that conditionals in requirements mainly occur in explicit, marked form and may include up to three *antecedents* and two *consequents*. Hence, the extraction approach must understand conjunctions, disjunctions, and negations to fully capture the relation between *antecedents* and *consequents*. He also found that conditionals are a source of ambiguity, and there is not just one way to interpret them formally. This affects any automated analysis that builds upon formalized requirements (e.g., inconsistency checking) and may also influence guidelines for writing requirements.

2. Jannik Fischbach presents his tool-supported approach CiRA capable of detecting conditionals in NL requirements and extracting them in fine-grained form. For the detection, CiRA uses syntactically enriched BERT embeddings combined with a softmax classifier and outperforms existing methods. His experiments show that a sigmoid classifier built on RoBERTa embeddings is best suited to extract conditionals in fine-grained form. CiRA is available at http://www.cira.bth.se/demo/.
3. He highlights how extracting conditionals from requirements can help create acceptance tests automatically. Specifically, Jannik Fischbach shows how extracted conditionals can be mapped to a *Cause-Effect-Graph* from which test cases can be derived automatically. He demonstrates the feasibility of his approach in a case study with three industry partners. In his study, out of 578 manually created test cases, 71.8% can be generated automatically. Furthermore, his approach discovered 80 relevant test cases missed in manual test case design.

His findings prove that automated conditional extraction can contribute to implementing automatic acceptance test creation. However, he does not achieve full automation of acceptance test generation mainly due to (1) incomplete requirements and (2) errors of his approach in interpreting conditionals that contain three or more *consequents*. Hence, Jannik Fischbach suggests using CiRA to supplement the existing manual creation process to make test designers aware of all test cases that should be tested from a combinatorial point of view. He hypothesizes that this will help reduce the risk of missed negative test cases significantly. The work of Jannik Fischbach is presented in more detail in Chapter "Conditional Statements in Requirements Artifacts: Logical Interpretation, Use Cases for Automated Software Engineering, and Fine-Grained Extraction" of this book.

4 Structure of the Book

The remainder of the book is structured into five chapters, one for the work of each nominee listed above. Each nominee presents in his chapter

- an overview and the key findings of the work,
- its relevance and applicability to practice and industrial software engineering projects,
- additional information and findings that have only been discovered afterwards, e.g., when applying the results in industry or when continuing research.

The chapters of the nominees are based on their PhD theses and arranged in alphabetic order.

As already highlighted in the introductory book chapter of the Ernst Denert Software Engineering Award 2019 [3] and by Prof. Denert's reflection on the field [1], software engineering is teamwork. Outstanding research with high impact is also always teamwork, which somewhat conflicts with the requirement that a doctoral thesis must be the work of a single author.

4.1 Thanks

We again thank Professor Ernst Denert for all his help in making this award a success and the *Gerlind & Ernst Denert-Stiftung* for the kind donation of the first price and the overall support. We thank the team of the Software Engineering Conference SE 2023, which was organized by Gregor Engels, Stefan Sauer, Regina Hebig and Matthias Tichy at Paderborn University, to host the presentations of the nominees and the award ceremony. We also thank the German, Austrian, and Swiss computer science societies, i.e., the GI, the OCG, and the SI, respectively, for their support in making the Ernst Denert Software Engineering Award 2022 a success. Finally, we thank all the people that helped in its organization, including Christian Kirchhof and Florian Rademacher (both RWTH Aachen University), who supported in the organization of this book.

References

1. Denert, E.: Software engineering. In: Ernst Denert Award for Software Engineering 2019, pp. 11–17. Springer, Berlin (2020)
2. Felderer, M., Hasselbring, W., Koziolek, H., Matthes, F., Prechelt, L., Reussner, R., Rumpe, B., Schaefer, I.: Ernst Denert Award for Software Engineering 2019: Practice Meets Foundations (2020)
3. Felderer, M., Hasselbring, W., Koziolek, H., Matthes, F., Prechelt, L., Reussner, R., Rumpe, B., Schaefer, I.: Ernst denert software engineering awards 2019. In: Ernst Denert Award for Software Engineering 2019, pp. 1–10. Springer, Berlin (2020)
4. Felderer, M., Reussner, R., Rumpe, B.: Software Engineering und Software-Engineering-Forschung im Zeitalter der Digitalisierung. Informatik Spektrum **44**(2), 82–94 (2021)
5. Felderer, M., Goedicke, M., Grunske, L., Hasselbring, W., Lamprecht, A.L., Rumpe, B.: Toward Research Software Engineering Research (2023). https://doi.org/10.5281/zenodo.8020525
6. IEEE: IEEE standard glossary of software engineering terminology. IEEE Std 610.12-1990 pp. 1–84 (1990)
7. Peng, S., Kalliamvakou, E., Cihon, P., Demirer, M.: The impact of AI on developer productivity: Evidence from github copilot (2023). Preprint arXiv:2302.06590
8. Schaefer, I.: Quantum software engineering - quo vadis? In: Engels, G., Hebig, R., Tichy, M. (eds.) Software Engineering 2023, Fachtagung des GI-Fachbereichs Softwaretechnik, 20–24. Februar 2023, Paderborn, LNI, vol. P-332, pp. 19–20. Gesellschaft für Informatik e.V., Luxembourg (2023). https://dl.gi.de/20.500.12116/40069
9. Welsh, M.: The end of programming. Commun. ACM **66**(1), 34–35 (2022)
10. Zhou, C., Li, Q., Li, C., Yu, J., Liu, Y., Wang, G., Zhang, K., Ji, C., Yan, Q., He, L., et al.: A comprehensive survey on pretrained foundation models: A history from bert to chatgpt (2023). Preprint arXiv:2302.09419

Open Access This chapter is licensed under the terms of the Creative Commons Attribution 4.0 International License (http://creativecommons.org/licenses/by/4.0/), which permits use, sharing, adaptation, distribution and reproduction in any medium or format, as long as you give appropriate credit to the original author(s) and the source, provide a link to the Creative Commons licence and indicate if changes were made.

The images or other third party material in this chapter are included in the chapter's Creative Commons licence, unless indicated otherwise in a credit line to the material. If material is not included in the chapter's Creative Commons licence and your intended use is not permitted by statutory regulation or exceeds the permitted use, you will need to obtain permission directly from the copyright holder.

Conditional Statements in Requirements Artifacts: Logical Interpretation, Use Cases for Automated Software Engineering, and Fine-Grained Extraction

Jannik Fischbach and Andreas Vogelsang

Abstract This thesis constitutes the first work in the RE community that studies the potential of extracting conditional statements from requirements. It is intended to stimulate further engagement of researchers and practitioners in the field of conditionals in RE artifacts. In essence, we present fundamental research on the notion of conditionals in requirements as well as methods for their fine-grained extraction. We show that conditionals are prevalent in requirements and mainly occur in explicit, marked form. Further, we reveal that conditionals are a source of ambiguity, and there is not just one way to interpret them formally. This affects any automated analysis that builds upon formalized requirements (e.g., inconsistency checking) and may also influence guidelines for writing requirements. We also present our tool-supported approach CiRA, capable of detecting conditionals in NL requirements and extracting them in fine-grained form. We evaluate our approach in a case study with three industry partners, namely, *Allianz Deutschland AG* (insurance), *Ericsson* (telecommunication), and *Leopold Kostal GmbH & Co. KG* (automotive), and highlight that automated conditional extraction facilitates automated acceptance test creation. CiRA is available at http://www.cira.bth.se/demo/.

J. Fischbach (✉)
Netlight Consulting GmbH and fortiss GmbH, Munich, Germany
e-mail: jafi@netlight.com

A. Vogelsang
University of Cologne, Köln, Germany
e-mail: vogelsang@cs.uni-koeln.de

1 Introduction

Functional requirements often describe system behavior by relating events to each other, e.g., "If the system detects an error (e_1), an error message shall be shown (e_2)." Such conditionals consist of two parts: the *antecedent* (see e_1) and the *consequent* (e_2), which convey strong, semantic information about the intended behavior of a system. Automatically extracting this embedded knowledge enables several analytical disciplines and is already used for *question answering* [1], *event prediction* [2–4], *emergency management* [5], *medical text mining* [6–8], and *information retrieval* [9]. For example, Doan et al. [10] extract conditionals from *Twitter* messages to identify factors causing stress, insomnia, and headache. Radinsky et al. [11] propose an approach capable of identifying conditionals in news articles to predict future events that certain events can cause. We argue that automated conditional extraction can also provide added value to *requirements engineering* (RE) by automating two RE tasks for which sufficient methods and tools are not yet available: "acceptance test creation" (👤 Use Case 1) and "dependency detection between requirements" (👤 Use Case 2). However, the potential of extracting conditionals has not yet been leveraged for RE. We are convinced that this has two principal reasons:

> **Problem 1:** Missing Understanding of the Notion of Conditional Statements in Requirements Artifacts

The extent, form, and complexity of conditional statements in requirements artifacts are poorly understood. We lack empirical evidence on conditionals in traditional RE artifacts (e.g., requirements documents) and agile RE artifacts (e.g., acceptance criteria). Further, we do not know how authors of requirements formulate conditionals and in which complexity the conditionals usually occur: do they tend to specify only the dependency of a single *antecedent* and *consequent*, or do conditionals in RE artifacts include multiple interdependent events? We also do not know whether conditionals in RE artifacts typically occur in *marked* or *unmarked* form. This lack of knowledge hinders the development of approaches capable of extracting conditionals from requirements artifacts. Even more importantly, we do not know how RE practitioners logically interpret conditional statements. For example, we still lack insight into whether RE practitioners perceive *antecedents* only as sufficient or also necessary for the *consequents*. However, reliable knowledge about the logical interpretations of conditionals by RE practitioners is vital since conditionals need always be associated with a formal meaning to process them automatically. Otherwise, we choose a formalization that does not reflect how practitioners interpret conditional sentences, rendering downstream activities error-prone. We would likely derive incomplete test cases or interpret dependencies between the requirements incorrectly.

> **Problem 2:** Missing Tool-Supported Approach for Fine-Grained Extraction of Conditional Statements

The fine-grained extraction of conditionals is necessary to bridge the gap between requirements and test cases. Specifically, we need to consider the combinatorics between *antecedents* and *consequents* and split them into more fine-granular text fragments (e.g., variable and condition), making the extracted conditionals suitable for automatic test case derivation and dependency detection. However, existing approaches cannot extract conditional clauses from *Natural Language* (NL) requirements in fine-grained form (illustrated by Table 1). Some approaches [12–14] extract *antecedents* and *consequents* only on word level (see extracted conditionals c_1 and c_2). Consequently, valuable information about the conditional statement is lost (e.g., the conditions of "input A," "input B," and "the system" are ignored). Recent approaches [15–20] address this problem and identify conditionals on the phrase level. Nevertheless, they only extract *antecedent-consequent* pairs, whereby the combinatorics between the *antecedents* and *consequents* get lost during the extraction (see c_3 and c_4). We must extract the entire embedded conditional statement to make it usable for test case derivation and dependency detection between requirements (see c_5). Thus, we require a new conditional extraction approach to implement our described use cases. This approach should be accompanied by adequate tool support to be easily integrated into testing processes in practice. Building on the two outlined problems, we formulate the following problem statement:

> **ⓘ Problem Statement:**
>
> We need (1) a better understanding of the notion of conditionals in requirements artifacts and (2) a comprehensive method and tool support to extract conditionals in fine-grained form.

We contribute to both areas and establish an understanding of (1) the notion of conditionals in RE artifacts, (2) how to extract them in fine-grained form, and (3) the added value that the extraction of conditionals can provide to RE. The remainder of this chapter is structured as follows: Sect. 2 presents the fundamentals that are needed to comprehend the content of this work. In Sect. 3, we present empirical results on the prevalence and logical interpretation of conditionals in RE artifacts. Section 4 presents our tool-supported approach CiRA, capable of detecting conditionals in NL requirements and extracting them in fine-grained form. CiRA is available at http://www.cira.bth.se/demo/. In Sect. 5, we highlight how extracting conditionals from requirements can help create acceptance tests automatically. Specifically, we show how extracted conditionals can be mapped to a *Cause-Effect-Graph* from which test cases can be derived automatically. We demonstrate the

Table 1 Existing techniques for conditional extraction from NL

	State of the art (excerpt)	Example: If $\underbrace{\text{input A is true}}_{\text{antecedent}_1}$ and $\underbrace{\text{input B is false}}_{\text{antecedent}_2}$, $\underbrace{\text{the system shall show an error message}}_{\text{consequent}_1}$	#
Word	Chang and Choi [12], Rink et al. [13], Khoo et al. [7]	antecedent$_1$ = *true*, consequent$_1$ = *message*	c$_1$
		antecedent$_2$ = *false*, consequent$_1$ = *message*	c$_2$
Phrase	Dasgupta et al. [15], Li et al. [16], Girju [1]	antecedent$_1$ = *input A is true*, consequent$_1$ = *the system shall show an error message*	c$_3$
		antecedent$_2$ = *input B is false*, consequent$_1$ = *the system shall show an error message*	c$_4$
Full	Our Scope	antecedent$_1$ = *input A is true* ∧ antecedent$_2$ = *input B is false*, consequent$_1$ = *the system shall show an error message*	c$_5$

feasibility of our approach in a case study with three industry partners. This chapter is based on ten peer-reviewed publications [21–30] and the PhD thesis [31] of the first author.

2 Theoretical Foundation

Subject of Interest: Conditional Statements
Conditional statements (e.g., "If A and B, then C") are integral to everyday discourse because they allow us to express conditions and their consequences. A conditional statement is a grammatical structure consisting of two parts: an adverbial clause, often referred to as the *antecedent*, and a main clause, also known as the *consequent* [32]. The semantics of conditionals has been intensively discussed in the last decades and has received notable attention in studies of various disciplines, e.g., in psychology [33], linguistics [34–36], and philosophy [37]. These studies demonstrate that conditionals are a complex linguistic pattern that can occur in a variety of forms (e.g., *explicit/implicit* conditionals, *marked/unmarked* conditionals). For example, **Conditional 1.1** (see below) is *marked* since the cue phrases "if" and "then" indicate the dependence between the *antecedent* and the *consequent*. The same relation can also be expressed as an *unmarked* conditional: "A and B occur. C evaluates to true." This conditional is semantically identical to its *marked* form. Still, it spans two sentences and does not contain a cue phrase that signals the relationship of the *antecedent* and *consequent*. Both **Conditional 1.1** and **Conditional 1.2** are *explicit*. Specifically, they contain information about the *antecedent* and the *consequent*. **Conditional 1.3** is *implicit* because the *consequent* that C evaluates to true is not explicitly stated. Rather, the interaction of the *antecedent* and *consequent* is encoded in the predicate (i.e., "leads to" implies that A and B are the triggers for C to occur).

- **Cond. 1.1:** If A and B occur, then C evaluates to true. (marked and explicit)
- **Cond. 1.2:** A and B occur. C evaluates to true. (unmarked and explicit)
- **Cond. 1.3:** The occurrence of A and B leads to C. (marked and explicit)

In everyday language, conditionals like "If A, then B" are often conceived as causal relations. Specifically, *antecedents* are usually understood as causes (see "A") and *consequents* as effects ("B"). Hence, the terms conditionals and causation are often used interchangeably, although they represent completely different concepts. A conditional is a linguistic pattern that describes a dependence between an *antecedent* and a *consequent*. In other words, the *antecedent* and *consequent* are associated [38]. Causation is more specific and represents a distinctive form of association. To turn an association into a causal relationship, three constraints must be satisfied [39, 40]:

- **Constraint 1:** The causing event (cause) must be both *sufficient* and *necessary* for the caused event (effect) [41]. Consequently, the connection between cause

and effect is counterfactual: If the cause did not occur, then the effect could not have occurred either [42].
- **Constraint 2:** The effect occurs either simultaneously with or after the cause [43].
- **Constraint 3:** The cause must occur independently (i.e., no confounder influences the cause and effect and incorrectly implies causation) [44].

One sees immediately that a conditional describes any relationship between an *antecedent* and a *consequent*. At the same time, causation is a specific type of relationship for which several constraints must be met. Hence, we can conclude that a conditional does not imply causation: conditionals can arise in the presence (i.e., "A" causes "B") or absence (i.e., "A" and "B" have a common cause) of a causal relationship [45]. It is, therefore, misleading to always interpret *antecedents* as causes and *consequents* as effects when analyzing the meaning of a conditional. We explicitly do not deal with causation in the context of our work but rather more fundamentally with conditionals in RE artifacts. However, we argue that causation is often the main focus when formulating conditionals in RE artifacts [22]. As a requirements author, I want to formulate the system behavior precisely by defining an *antecedent* as both the sufficient and necessary reason for the occurrence of a *consequent* (see **Constraint 1**). In other words, if "A" occurs, "B" should also occur, and if "A" does not evaluate to true, then "B" should also not occur. In practice, it is common to formulate several requirements that describe the same *consequent* (e.g., "When C occurs, then B"). In this context, we assume that each requirement describes a separate case in which the *consequent* should occur and link their *antecedents* with disjunctions (i.e., $A \vee C \Leftrightarrow B$).

Logical Interpretation of Conditional Statements
As outlined in the previous section, there are many ways to express conditional statements in NL. Hence, the syntax can vary greatly among conditionals. Multiple studies [46–48] demonstrate that conditionals can also be associated with different semantic meanings, which makes them a source of ambiguity. We investigate the logical interpretations of conditionals by RE practitioners concerning two dimensions: *necessity* and *temporality*. This section demarcates both dimensions and introduces suitable formal languages that can be used to formalize the interpretations appropriately. We use the following conditional as a running example: "If the system detects an error (e_1), an error message shall be shown (e_2)."

Necessity The relationship between an *antecedent* and *consequent* can be interpreted logically in two different ways. First, through an implication as $e_1 \Rightarrow e_2$, in which e_1 is a *sufficient* condition for e_2. Interpreting the running example as an implication requires the system to display an error message if e_1 is true. However, it is not specified what the system should do if e_1 is false. The implication allows both the occurrence of e_2 and its absence if e_1 is false. In contrast, the relationship of *antecedent* and *consequent* can also be understood as a logical equivalence, where e_1 is both a *sufficient* and *necessary* condition for e_2 (i.e., $e_1 \Leftrightarrow e_2$). Interpreting the running example as an equivalence requires the system to display an error message *if and only if* it detects an error. Consequently, if e_1 is false, then e_2 should also be false. Interpreting conditionals as an implication or equivalence significantly influences further development activities. For example, a test designer who interprets conditionals rather as implications than equivalences might only add positive test cases to a test suite. This may lead to a misalignment of tests and requirements if the business analyst intended to express an equivalence.

Temporality The temporal relation between an *antecedent* and *consequent* can be interpreted in three different ways: (1) the *consequent* occurs simultaneous with the *antecedent*, (2) the *consequent* occurs immediately after the *antecedent*, and (3) the *consequent* occurs at some indefinite point after the *antecedent*. *Propositional logic* (PL) does not consider the temporal ordering of events and is therefore not expressive enough to model temporal relationships. In contrast, we require temporal logic (e.g., LTL), which considers temporal ordering by defining the behavior σ of a system as an infinite sequence of states $\langle s_0, \ldots \rangle$, where s_n is a state of the system at "time" n [49]. Accordingly, requirements are understood as constraints on σ. The desired system behavior is defined as an LTL formula F, where next to the usual PL operators, also temporal operators like $\Box$ (*always*), $\Diamond$ (*eventually*), and $\bigcirc$ (*next state*) are used.

Formalization Matrix To distinguish the logical interpretations of practitioners and their formalization, we constructed a formalization matrix (see Fig. 1). It defines a conditional statement of F and G along the two dimensions (*Necessity* and *Temporality*), each divided on a nominal scale. Specifically, the dimension *Necessity* has two levels: F is only *sufficient* or also *necessary* for G. The dimension *Temporality* has four levels: *during*, *next state*, *eventually*, and temporal ordering is not relevant. Each 2-tuple of characteristics can be mapped to an entry in the formalization matrix. For example, the LTL formula $\Box(F \Rightarrow \bigcirc G)$ formalizes a conditional statement, in which F is only *sufficient* and G occurs in the *next state*. To define F as both *sufficient* and *necessary* for G, we replace the implication by equivalence and rephrase the LTL formula as follows: $\Box(F \Leftrightarrow \bigcirc G)$. However, the equivalence operator is inadequate in cases where G will be caused *eventually*. Specifically, the formula $\Box(F \Leftrightarrow \Diamond G)$ would define that as soon as F evaluates

Necessity	Temporality			
	Temporal Ordering Relevant			VI. Temporal Ordering Not Relevant
	III. G is caused *during* F is true	IV. G will be caused in the *next state*	V. G will be caused *eventually*	
I. F is only *sufficient*	$\Box(F \Rightarrow G)$	$\Box(F \Rightarrow \bigcirc G)$	$\Box(F \Rightarrow \Diamond G)$	$F \Rightarrow G$
II. F is also *necessary*	$\Box(F \Leftrightarrow G)$	$\Box(F \Leftrightarrow \bigcirc G)$	$\Diamond G \Rightarrow (\neg G \mathcal{U} F)$	$F \Leftrightarrow G$

Fig. 1 Formalization matrix defining a conditional of F and G along the two dimensions, *Necessity* and *Temporality*

to false, G is locked permanently. We argue that this formula does not represent the behavior we want to express since there may also be scenarios in which F is initially false but turns true at a later state and leads to the occurrence of G. Therefore, we want to specify that as soon as G occurs, F must have occurred concurrently or at a previous state (i.e., F is a *necessary* condition for an occurrence of G). To this end, we build on the *precedence relation* introduced by Dwyer et al. [50]: $\Diamond G \Rightarrow (\neg G \; \mathcal{U} \; (F \wedge \neg G))$. The core element of the *precedence relation* is the until $\mathcal{U}$ operator. Literally, the *precedence relation* can be interpreted as "If G occurs eventually, then G has been false until the state in which F occurs without G occurring concurrently." Hence, in its original form, the *precedence relation* defines F as a *necessary* pre-condition of G. Since the *eventually* operator allows that G and F occur simultaneously, we adapt the *precedence relation* as follows: $\Diamond G \Rightarrow (\neg G \; \mathcal{U} \; F)$.

3 Understanding of Conditional Statements in Requirements Artifacts

We conduct two empirical studies to address the first problem of the thesis, namely, "the missing understanding of the notion of conditionals in RE artifacts." In the first study (see Sect. 3.1), we analyze the extent, form, and complexity of conditionals in requirements rooted in 14,983 sentences and emerging from 53 requirement documents. In the second study (see Sect. 3.2), we study how 104 RE practitioners interpret 12 different conditional clauses in requirements.

3.1 Prevalence, Form, and Complexity of Conditionals in Requirements Artifacts

Reliable knowledge about the distribution of conditionals in requirements artifacts is necessary to develop efficient approaches for their automated extraction. However, empirical evidence on conditionals in requirements artifacts is presently still weak. We address this research gap and analyze conditional statements' prevalence, form, and complexity in requirements artifacts. Based on the terminology introduced in Sect. 2, we investigate the following research questions (RQ):

- **RQ 1:** To which degree do conditionals occur in requirement documents?
- **RQ 2:** How often do the relations *cause*, *enable*, and *prevent* occur?
- **RQ 3:** In which form do conditional statements occur in requirement documents?
  - **RQ 3a:** How often do *marked* and *unmarked* conditionals occur?
  - **RQ 3b:** How often do *explicit* and *implicit* conditionals occur?

- **RQ 3c:** Which cue phrases are used? Are they mainly *ambiguous* or *non-ambiguous*?
- **RQ 4:** At which complexity do conditional statements occur in requirement documents?
    - **RQ 4a:** How often do multiple *antecedents* occur?
    - **RQ 4b:** How often do multiple *consequents* occur?
    - **RQ 4c:** How often do two-sentence conditionals occur?
    - **RQ 4d:** How often do *event chains* occur?
- **RQ 5:** Is the distribution of labels in all categories domain-independent?

3.1.1 Study Design

Study Objects We created a new large gold standard corpus of requirements [22] by collecting publicly available requirements specifications employing a web search. We queried *Google* and libraries as *Everyspec* to retrieve documents from different domains. We only considered documents in PDF format, have at least ten pages, are written in English, and do contain requirements. We conducted a brief manual review of each document to verify the latter. After pre-processing, our data set contains 212,186 complete sentences.[1] To the best of our knowledge, this data set is currently the most extensive collection of requirements available to the research community. We randomly selected 53 documents from the data set to analyze the prevalence of conditionals in RE artifacts. Hence, our study focuses on 14,983 sentences from 18 domains.

Data Annotation We annotate the sentences in our data set concerning eight categories: ⬥Conditional Present, ⬥Explicit, ⬥Marked, ⬥Single Sentence, ⬥Single Antecedent, ⬥Single Consequent, ⬥Event Chain, and ⬥Relationship. To answer RQ 5, we perform a stratified analysis for each category using the domains as strata. Due to the imbalanced data set concerning the domains the requirements sentences originate from, we formulate the following null hypothesis for each category X: "sentences from different domains have the same distribution of values in category X."

3.1.2 Study Results

Figure 2 presents the analysis results for each labeled category. When interpreting the values, it is important to note that we analyze entire requirement documents in our study. Consequently, our data set contains records with different contents that

---

[1] Available at https://figshare.com/s/725309c06b9dc82aa4a1. Due to the terms of use of some sources, we can only share the URLs of the collected documents. We attached a script to download the data set automatically.

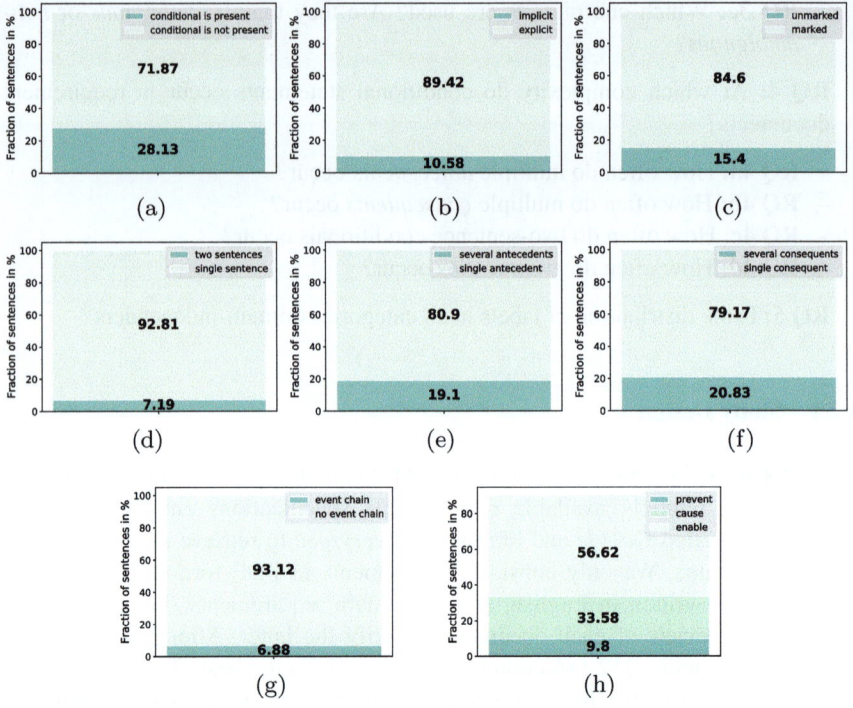

Fig. 2 Annotation results per category. The Y axis of the bar plot for the category ✎ Conditional Present refers to the total number of analyzed sentences. The other bar plots are only related to the sentences that contain a conditional. (**a**) Conditional present. (**b**) Explicit. (**c**) Marked. (**d**) Single sentence. (**e**) Single antecedent. (**f**) Single consequent. (**g**) Event chain. (**h**) Relationship

do not represent all functional requirements. For example, requirement documents also contain non-functional requirements, phrases for content structuring, purpose statements, etc. Hence, the results of our analysis do not only refer to functional requirements but in general to the content of requirement documents.

Answer to RQ 1 Figure 2 highlights that conditional statements occur in requirement documents. About 28% of the analyzed sentences contain a conditional. Therefore, conditionals are a major linguistic element of requirement documents since almost one-third of all sentences describe a dependence between an *antecedent* and *consequent*.

Answer to RQ 2 The majority (56%) of conditionals contained in requirement documents express an *enable* relationship between certain events. Only about 10% of the conditionals indicate a *prevent* relationship. *Cause* relationships are found in about 34% of the annotated data.

Answer to RQ 3a Figure 2 shows that the majority of conditionals contain one or more cue phrases to indicate the relationship between certain events. *Unmarked* conditionals occur only in about 15% of the analyzed sentences.

Answer to RQ 3b Most conditionals are *explicit*, i.e., they contain information about both the *antecedent* and the *consequent*. Only about 10% of conditionals in the investigated requirements documents are *implicit*.

Answer to RQ 3c To assess the ambiguity of a cue phrase x, we formulate a binary classification task: consider all sentences as the sample space. The conditionals of that sample space represent the relevant elements. The precision of cue phrase x as a selection criterion for conditionals is the conditional probability that a sentence from the sample space contains a conditional given that it contains cue phrase x and hence reflects the ambiguity of the cue phrase. A high precision value indicates a *non-ambiguous* cue phrase, i.e., the occurrence of the cue phrase in a sentence is a strong indicator for the sentence containing a conditional. In contrast, low values indicate strongly *ambiguous* cue phrases. Our analysis demonstrates that several different cue phrases are used to express conditionals in requirement documents. Not surprisingly, cue phrases like "if," "because," and "therefore" show precision values of more than 90%. However, a variety of cue phrases indicate conditionals in some sentences but also occur in other contexts. This is especially evident in the case of pronouns. Relative sentences can indicate conditionals, but not in every case, which is reflected by the low precision value of, for example, "which." A similar pattern emerges concerning the used verbs. Only a few verbs (e.g., "leads to, degrade," and "enhance") show a high precision value. Consequently, most used pronouns and verbs do not necessarily indicate a conditional if they are present in a sentence.

Answer to RQ 4a Figure 2 illustrates that a conditional in requirement documents often includes only a single *antecedent*. Multiple *antecedents* occur in only 19.1% of analyzed conditionals. The exact number of *antecedents* was not documented during the annotation process. However, the participating annotators reported consistently that in the case of complex conditional statements, two to three *antecedents* were usually included. More than three *antecedents* were rare.

Answer to RQ 4b Interestingly, the distribution of *consequents* is similar to that of *antecedents*. Likewise, single *consequents* occur significantly more often than multiple *consequents*. According to the annotators, the number of *consequents* in case of complex conditionals is limited to two *consequents*. Three or more *consequents* occur rarely.

Answer to RQ 4c Most conditionals can be found in single sentences. Relations where *antecedent* and *consequent* are distributed over several sentences occur only in about 7% of the analyzed data. The annotators reported that most often, the cue phrase "therefore" was used to express two-sentence conditionals.

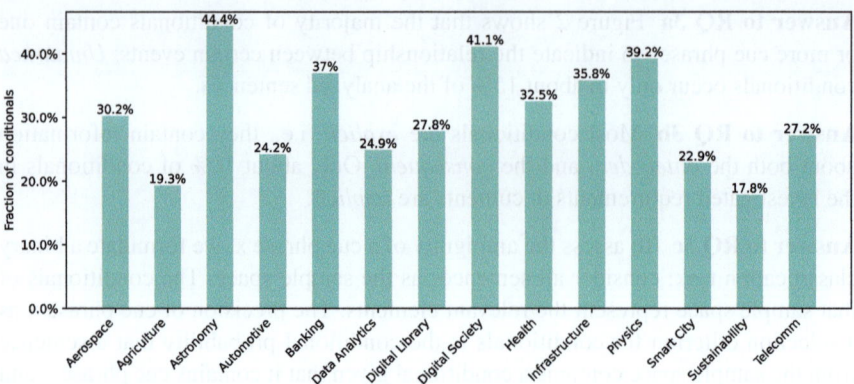

Fig. 3 Distribution of conditional statements among domains

Answer to RQ 4d Figure 2 shows that *event chains* are rarely used in requirement documents. Most conditionals contain isolated relations between *antecedent* and *consequent* and only a few *event chains*.

Answer to RQ 5 Figure 3 visualizes the distribution of conditionals among all domains represented with more than 100 sentences. As conditionals' percentages range from 17.8% up to 44.4%, we can assume that conditional statements occur in all eligible domains. Our Chi-squared test suggests rejecting the null hypothesis for domain-independence for 10 out of 14 eligible domains considering the Bonferroni-corrected significance level. We can conclude that conditionals are a phenomenon observable independent of the domain from which requirements originate, but the extent to which conditionals occur differs with statistical significance.

The Chi-squared test of independence does not suggest rejecting the null hypothesis for the categories ▼ Single Antecedent and ▼ Event Chain, but the distribution of two out of the eligible nine domains in the category ▼ Marked and ▼ Single Sentence is significantly different. We can conclude that the distribution of values in all categories is domain-independent to a certain degree. While the complexity of conditionals is mostly domain-independent, the distribution of marked conditionals and conditionals contained in single sentences differs significantly for about a fourth of the eligible domains.

Our stratified analysis for RQ 3c shows considerable differences in the usage of cue phrases in the domains but also a degree of overlap: the cue phrase "if" is among the five most frequent cue phrases in all domains, closely followed by the cue phrases "when" and "where". Our stratified frequencies lead to the assumption that the distribution of cue phrases is mostly domain independent. When looking at the most precise cue phrases per domain and the least precise cue phrases per domain, the cue phrases also reflect the findings from the overall distribution: precise cue phrases like "if", "when", and "because" as well as infrequent but precise causative verbs are equally represented in the domains just as imprecise cue phrases like "for" or "by". Despite slight domain-specific variations, the results for RQ 3c are also domain-independent.[2]

3.1.3 Concluding Discussion

Conditionals are prevalent in requirements artifacts and therefore matter in requirements engineering, which motivates the necessity of an effective and reliable approach for the automatic extraction of conditionals in requirements. The complexity of conditional statements is confined since they usually consist of a single *antecedent* and *consequent* relationship in all observed, eligible domains. However, for an approach that aims to extract conditionals to be applicable in practice, it needs to comprehend also more complex relations containing at least two to three and at best an arbitrary number of *antecedents* and *consequents*. Understanding conjunctions, disjunctions, and negations is consequently imperative to fully capture the relationships between *antecedents* and *consequents* and ensure the applicability of a detection and extraction approach. *Two-sentence conditionals* and *event chains* occur only rarely. Thus, both aspects can initially be neglected in developing the approaches and preserve coverage of more than 92% of the analyzed sentences. The dominance of *explicit* over *implicit* conditionals in the observed sentences simplifies the detection and extraction of conditionals. The information about both *antecedent* and *consequent* is embedded directly in the sentences so that an approach requires little or no *implicit* knowledge. The analysis of the precision values reveals that most of the used cue phrases are ambiguous. Consequently, automatic extraction methods require a deep understanding of language, as certain cue phrases are insufficient to indicate conditionals. Instead, a combination of the sentence's syntax and semantics must be considered to detect conditional statements reliably.

3.2 Logical Interpretation of Conditionals in Requirements Artifacts

The interpretation of the semantics of conditionals affects all activities carried out based on documented requirements such as manual reviews, implementation, or test case generations. Even more, a correct interpretation is essential for all automatic analyses of requirements that consider the semantics of sentences, for instance, automatic quality analysis like smell detection [51], test case derivation [21, 52], and dependency detection [22]. Consequently, conditionals should always be associated with a formal meaning to process them automatically. However, determining a suitable formal interpretation is challenging because conditional statements in NL

---

[2] More extensive tables reporting on the frequency and precision of cue phrases in eligible domains are included in our replication package: https://doi.org/10.5281/zenodo.5596668.

tend to be ambiguous. We aim to understand and (logically) formalize the interpretation of conditionals in requirements by RE practitioners in software development projects. To this end, we conducted a survey following the guidelines by Ciolkowski et al. [53]. The expected outcome of our survey is a better understanding of how practitioners logically interpret conditional clauses in requirements. Further, we aim to determine which elements in our formalization matrix (introduced in Sect. 2) match their logical interpretations. We derived three research questions (RQ) from our survey goal.

- **RQ 1:** How do practitioners logically interpret conditionals in requirements?
- **RQ 2:** Which factors influence the logical interpretation of conditionals in requirements?
- **RQ 3:** Which (if any) cue phrases promote (un)ambiguous interpretation?

3.2.1 Study Design

Target Population and Sampling The selection of survey participants was driven by a purposeful sampling strategy [54] along with the following criteria: (a) they elicit, maintain, implement, or verify requirements, and (b) they work in industry and not exclusively in academia. Each author prepared a list of potential participants using their personal or second-degree contacts (convenience sampling [55]). From this list, the research team jointly selected suitable participants based on their adequacy for the study. To increase the sample size further, we asked each participant for other relevant contacts after the survey (snowball sampling). Our survey was started by 168 participants, of which 104 completed the survey. All figures in this section refer to the 104 participants that completed the survey.

Study Objects To conduct the survey and answer the RQs, we used three data sets (DS), each from a different domain. DS 1 contains conditionals from a requirements document describing the behavior of an automatic door in the automotive domain. We argue that all participants understand how an automatic car door is expected to work, so all participants should have the required domain knowledge. DS 2 contains conditionals from *Aerospace* systems. We hypothesize that no or only a few participants have deeper knowledge in this domain, making DS 2 well suited for analyzing the impact of domain knowledge on logical interpretations. DS 3 contains abstract conditionals (e.g., "If event A and event B, then event C"). Thus, they are free from any domain-induced interpretation bias. To address RQ 3, we focused on four cue phrases in the conditionals: "if", "while", "after", and "when". To avoid researcher bias, we created the data sets by randomly extracting conditionals from existing practice requirement documents. The conditionals in DS 1 are taken from a requirements document written by *Mercedes-Benz Passenger Car Development* [56]. The conditionals contained in DS 2 originate from three

> **Q1**: F does not occur. What happens consequently?
> - **R1.1**: G occurs nevertheless. (sanity check)
> - **R1.2**: G does not occur. ($\rightarrow$ II)
> - **R1.3**: Not defined in the statement. ($\rightarrow$ I)
>
> **Q2**: When does G occur?
> - **R2.1**: Simultaneously with F. ($\rightarrow$ III)
> - **R2.2**: Immediately after F. ($\rightarrow$ IV)
> - **R2.3**: At some indefinite point after F. ($\rightarrow$ V)
> - **R2.3**: Temporal ordering is irrelevant in the statement. ($\rightarrow$ VI)

Fig. 4 Questionnaire template. The note after each answer option (e.g., $\rightarrow$ IV) indicates the matching characteristic in the formalization matrix. If a participant selects R1.2, for example, they implicitly interpret F as *necessary* for G. The notes were not included in the questionnaire

requirements documents published by NASA and one by ESA.[3] The conditionals in DS 3 are syntactically identical to those in DS 1, except that we replace the names of the events with abstract names. DS 1–3 contain 4 conditionals each, resulting in 12 study objects. Each cue phrase occurs exactly once in each DS.

Questionnaire Design We chose an online questionnaire as our data collection instrument to gather quantitative data on our research questions. Since our research goal is descriptive, most questions are closed-ended. We designed three questions (Q) addressing the two dimensions and prepared a distinct set of responses (R), among which the participants can choose. Each of these responses can be mapped to a characteristic in the formalization matrix and thus allows us to determine which characteristic the practitioners interpret as being reflected by a conditional. We build the questionnaire for each study object (e.g., "If F then G") according to a predefined template (see Fig. 4). The template is structured as follows: The first question (**Q 1**) investigates the dimension of *Necessity*: if event G cannot occur without event F, then F is not only *sufficient*, but also necessary for G. We add "nevertheless" as a third response option (see R1.1 in Fig. 4) to perform a sanity check on the answers of the respondents. We argue that interpreting that the *consequent* should occur although the *antecedent* does not occur indicates that the sentence has not been read carefully. The second question (**Q 2**) covers the temporal ordering of the events. In this context, we explicitly ask for the three temporal relations *eventually*, *always*, and *next state* described in Sect. 2. Should a participant perceive temporal ordering as irrelevant for interpreting a certain conditional, we can conclude that PL is sufficient for its formalization. We ask **Q 1–2** for each of the 12 study objects, resulting in 24 questions. To get an overview of the background

---
[3] We retrieved these documents from our gold standard corpus of requirements presented in Sect. 3.1. We are referring to the documents: REQ-DOC-22, REQ-DOC-26, REQ-DOC-27, and REQ-DOC-30.

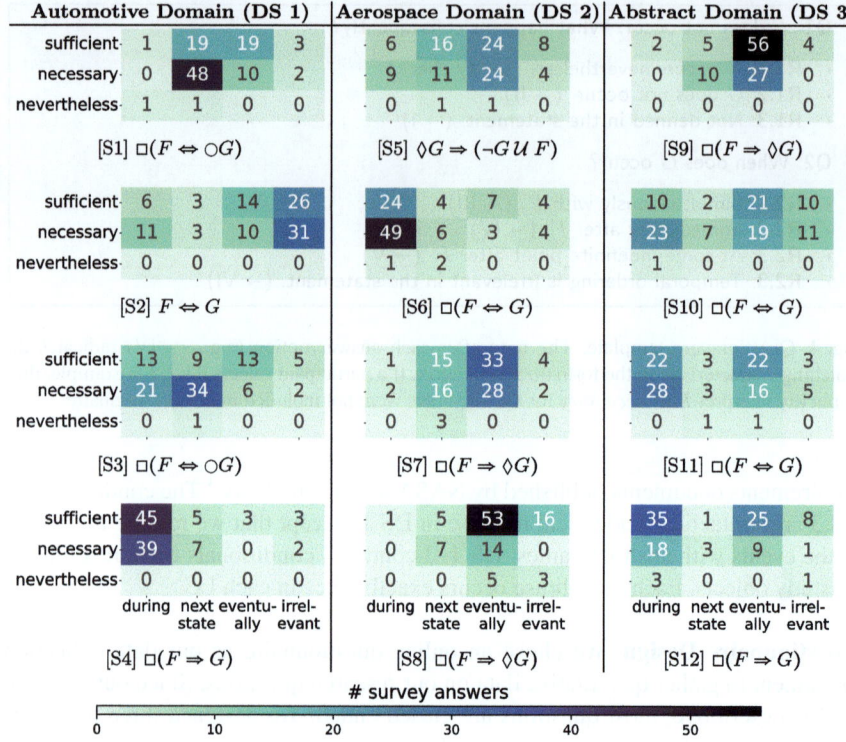

Fig. 5 Heatmaps visualizing the interpretations of the participants

of our respondents, we also integrated five demographic questions. In total, our final questionnaire consists of 29 questions and can also be found in our replication package.[4]

3.2.2 Study Results

3.2.3 RQ 1: How Do Practitioners Logically Interpret Conditionals in Requirements?

To answer RQ 1, we first look at the total number of answers for each dimension across all data sets. Secondly, we analyze the ratings distribution based on our constructed heatmaps (see Fig. 5).

---

[4] Our replication package contains (1) our final questionnaire, (2) the survey protocol, and (3) the survey responses. It can be found at https://doi.org/10.5281/zenodo.5070235.

Necessity Our participants did not have a clear tendency whether an *antecedent* is only *sufficient* or also *necessary* for the *consequent*. Among the total of 1,248 answers, 2.1% correspond to the level "nevertheless," 46.9% to "also necessary," and 51% for "only sufficient". That means that more than half of the respondents stated that the conditional does not cover how the system is expected to work if the *antecedent* does not occur (i.e., the negative case is not specified).

Temporality We found that time plays a major role in the interpretation of conditionals in requirements. Among the 1,248 answers, only 13% were "temporal ordering is irrelevant" for the interpretation. This indicates that conditionals in requirements require temporal logics for a suitable formalization. For some study objects, the exact temporal relationship between *antecedent* and *consequent* was ambiguous. For S3, 34 participants selected "during," 43 "next state," and 19 "eventually". Similarly, we observed divergent temporal interpretations for S2, S5, S7, S10, S11, and S12. In contrast, the respondents widely agreed on the temporal relationship of S1 (67 survey answers for "next state"), S4 (84 survey answers for "during"), S6 (73 survey answers for "during"), S8 (67 survey answers for "eventually"), and S9 (83 survey answers for "eventually"). Across all study objects, 29.8% of survey answers were given for the level "during", 20.1% for "next state," and 37.1% for "eventually".

Agreement Our heatmaps illustrate that there are only a few study objects for which more than half of the respondents agreed on a 2-tuple (see Fig. 5). This trend is evident across all data sets. The presence or absence of domain knowledge does not seem to have an impact on a consistent interpretation. The greatest agreement was achieved in the case of S1 (48 survey answers for ⟨necessary, next state⟩), S6 (49 survey answers for ⟨necessary, during⟩), S8 (53 survey answers for ⟨sufficient, eventually⟩), and S9 (56 survey answers for ⟨sufficient, eventually⟩). However, for the majority of study objects, there was no clear agreement on a specific 2-tuple. For S5, two 2-tuples were selected equally often, and for S10, the two most frequent 2-tuples differed by only two survey answers.

Generally Valid Formalization? Mapping the most frequent 2-tuples in the heatmaps to our constructed formalization matrix reveals that all study objects cannot be formalized in the same way. The most frequent 2-tuples for each study object yield the following six patterns:

- **Pattern 1:** ⟨necessary, next state⟩: S1, S3
- **Pattern 2:** ⟨necessary, irrelevant⟩: S2
- **Pattern 3:** ⟨necessary, during⟩: S6, S10, S11
- **Pattern 4:** ⟨necessary, eventually⟩: (S5)
- **Pattern 5:** ⟨sufficient, eventually⟩: (S5), S7, S8, S9
- **Pattern 6:** ⟨sufficient, during⟩: S4, S12

One sees immediately that it is not possible to derive a formalization for conditionals in general. Especially the temporal interpretations differed between the conditionals and the used cue phrases. However, it can be concluded that, except for S2, the interpretations of all study objects can be represented by LTL.

3.2.4 RQ 2: Which Factors Influence the Logical Interpretation of Conditional Clauses in Requirements?

This section reports the results of our chi-square tests. In our contingency tables, no more than 20% of the expected counts are <5. Hence, we satisfy the assumption of enough observations per category for the chi-square test [57]. In the following, we explain the relationships where the chi-square test indicated a dependency between the logical interpretation and a factor.

The Logical Interpretation Regarding Temporality Depends on RE Experience In the group with less than 1 year of experience, there is a tendency to perceive the temporal relationship between the events as "during" (36.4%). In the group of participants with 4–10 years of experience, most of the respondents rated the temporal relationship as "eventually" (41.3%). The χ^2 test reveals that the distribution of ratings differs between the experience levels. The calculated Θ value indicates that the strength of the relationship is low.

The Logical Interpretation Regarding Temporality Is Dependent on How a Practitioner Interacts With Requirements Our contingency table reveals that the distribution of ratings differs between the interaction levels. Practitioners who implement requirements fluctuate mainly between "during" and "eventually," while they rarely selected the other two *Temporality* levels. A different pattern emerges for practitioners who maintain and verify requirements. Across all study objects, they choose the levels "during", "next state," and "eventually" equally often. A χ^2 test indicates a dependency between both variables. The calculated ϕ value indicates that the strength of the relationship is high.

The Logical Interpretation Regarding Necessity Is Dependent on Domain Knowledge The disagreement about whether an *antecedent* is only *sufficient* or also *necessary* holds regardless of domain knowledge. However, the trend differs between the data sets with respect to the *Necessity* levels. In the case of DS 1 (domain knowledge assumed), more answers were given for "also necessary" (54.3%) than for "only sufficient" (45%). In contrast, more ratings were given for "only sufficient" in the case of DS 2 (53.1%) and DS 3 (55%). The slight difference in the distribution of the ratings regarding *Necessity* is supported by the χ^2 test. However, the strength of the relationships is low.

The Logical Interpretation Regarding Temporality Is Dependent on Domain Knowledge Our contingency table shows that the distribution of ratings regarding *Temporality* differs between the data sets. In the case of DS 1, ratings were mainly given for "during" (32.9%) and "next state" (31.3%). In the case of the unknown domain (DS 2), ratings were mainly assigned to "eventually" (46.2%), while only 20.7% were given to "next state" and 22.4% to "during." In DS 3, where no domain knowledge is necessary for the understanding of the conditionals, most ratings were given to "during" (34.1%) and "eventually" (47.1%). A χ^2 test shows that there is a statistically significant dependency between both variables. According to the calculated ϕ value, the strength of the relationship is medium.

3.2.5 RQ 3: Which (if Any) Cue Phrases Promote (Un)Ambiguous Interpretation?

Our analysis reveals that the logical interpretation regarding *Temporality* depends on the cue phrase used to express a conditional. For study objects containing "while" (S4, S6, and S12), the respondents largely agreed that the *consequent* occurs simultaneously with the *antecedent*. In contrast, almost no respondent associated simultaneous events in the study objects with the cue phrase "after". Instead, the respondents vacillated between the temporal levels "next state" and "eventually". The largest disagreement, though, was found in the interpretations of the conditionals "if" or "when". Especially in the case of "when", there was no clear agreement across S3, S5, and S11 on whether *antecedent* and *consequent* are in a "during", "next state," or "eventually" temporal relationship. Regarding *Necessity*, we observe that the practitioners, irrespective of the used cue phrase, disagree whether the *antecedent* is only *sufficient* or also *necessary* for the *consequent*. We found one outlier in our histograms (S8), where an 80% agreement for the level "sufficient" could be achieved. For the remaining study objects, however, there is a balanced number of survey answers for both levels.

3.2.6 Concluding Discussion

We show that conditionals are interpreted ambiguously by RE practitioners. In particular, there is disagreement (1) about whether an *antecedent* is only *sufficient* or also *necessary* for a *consequent* and (2) about the temporal occurrence of *antecedent* and *consequent* when different cue phrases (such as "when" or "if") are used. Thus, a generic formalization of conditionals will inevitably fail at least some practitioner's interpretation. We see two immediate implications in practice:

Implications for Automatic Methods Especially (if not limited) for automated test case generation, it is vital to understand which behavior is desired if the *antecedent* does not occur. The evidence presented in this chapter refutes the prevailing assumption (cf. [22, 58]) that *antecedents* can always be treated as *necessary* conditions. Hence, we propose that future methods should display the automatically generated positive and negative test cases to practitioners and explicitly verify the following: "Is the negative case of your conditional also valid?" This will foster the discussion within project teams about the expected system behavior and enables to resolve misunderstandings at an early stage. We consider this finding when developing our approach for the automatic generation of acceptance tests and integrated it into the *User Interface* of our tool (see Sect. 4.2).

Implications for Requirements Authors It should be incorporated into RE writing guidelines that it does matter which cue phrase is used for the formulation of a conditional. "While" is interpreted consistently, but "if" and "when" cause misunderstandings about the temporal interpretation of *antecedent* and *consequent*. This poses a problem especially in the implementation of requirements and eventually leads to discrepancies between actual and expected system behavior. Project teams should therefore agree early on how they want to interpret the different cue phrases to avoid ambiguities. Additionally, our findings provide empirical evidence for the claim by Berry et al. [59] and Rosadini et al. [60] that requirements authors should always specify the negative case (e.g., by using an else-statement) to prevent confusion about the necessity of *antecedents*.

4 Extracting Conditionals from Requirements Artifacts

This section addresses the second problem of the thesis, namely, "the missing method and tool support to extract conditionals in fine-grained form". We present our tool-supported approach named CiRA (*Conditionals in Requirements Artifacts*), capable of detecting conditionals in NL requirements and extracting them in fine-grained form.

4.1 The CiRA Pipeline

CiRA consists of two steps: It first detects whether an NL requirement contains a conditional. Second, it extracts the conditional in fine-grained form. Specifically, CiRA considers the combinatorics between *antecedents* and *consequents* and splits them into more granular text fragments (e.g., variable and condition), making the extracted conditionals suitable for automatic test case derivation. We have implemented and compared different methods for both steps and incorporated the best-performing methods into the pipeline of CiRA. We describe the functionality of CiRA using the following requirement: "If A is valid and B is false, then C is true."

Step 1: Detection of Conditionals Our experiments showed that enriching input sequences with dependency tags leads to a better performance of our conditional detection approach. Therefore, in the first step, we use *spaCy* to assign dependency tags to the individual tokens in the sentence. This allows our conditional classifier to take into account not only the content of the tokens themselves but also the grammatical structure of the sentence when categorizing a sentence into the two classes `🔖 Conditional Present` and `🔖 Conditional Not Present`. In the case of our exemplary requirement, the token "If" is assigned the dependency tag *mark*, indicating that "If" introduces a clause subordinate to another clause. After allocating appropriate dependency tags to each token in the sentence, the sentence is decomposed using the *WordPiece* tokenizer and enriched with additional synthetic tokens such as the CLS token. Finally, we feed each token into the BERT model to generate word embeddings. Since we perform conditional detection at the sentence level, we only pass the CLS token into the softmax classifier, which computes the probability of whether the input sequence contains a conditional. The classifier calculates a confidence of 91% that our exemplary requirement contains a conditional. With only 9% confidence, our classifier assumes that the input sequence does not contain a conditional. Our approach selects the category with the highest confidence and classifies our example correctly as [● Conditional Present]. The detected conditional is passed to the next step of the pipeline.

Step 2: Fine-grained Extraction of Conditionals In the second step, we utilize the *Byte-Pair Encoding* (BPE) tokenizer to convert the detected conditional statement into a form that can be processed by RoBERTa. After decomposing the input sequence into individual tokens, we pass each token into the RoBERTa model to create word embeddings. Since we perform conditional extraction at the token level, we feed the embeddings of all tokens into our sigmoid classifier. Our classifier calculates the probability for each class whether a given token should be assigned to that class. Since we differentiate between twelve classes, the sigmoid classifier calculates twelve probabilities accordingly. We select the classes with a probability ≥ 0.5 as the final classification result. In the case of our exemplary requirement, the "If" token is classified as [● Not Relevant] with the confidence of 99.6%. The token "A" is assigned to two classes: On the bottom annotation layer, "A" is correctly marked as a [● Variable]. On the top annotation layer, "A" is identified as belonging to [● Antecedent 1]. The synthetically added tokens by the BPE tokenizer like "<s>" and "<pad>" are correctly identified as [● Not Relevant]. We follow the classifications of our sigmoid classifier and assign the corresponding labels to each token of the input sequence. The output of the CiRA pipeline thus represents a list of top-layer and bottom-layer labels, allowing us to annotate the conditional in fine-grained form.

4.2 Tool Support

We implemented a corresponding tool support to facilitate easy interaction with CiRA. We invite fellow researchers and interested practitioners to employ CiRA at www.cira.bth.se/demo/. Our tool does not only allow the use of CiRA for the fine-grained extraction of conditionals from NL sentences, but also enables the automatic derivation of acceptance tests based on the extracted conditionals. Specifically, our tool realizes [▲ Use Case 1] by combining CiRA with *Cause-Effect-Graphing* to create acceptance tests automatically. As shown in Fig. 6, we produce

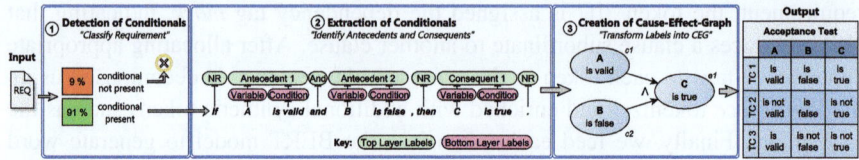

Fig. 6 Overview of our approach consisting of three steps: (1) detection of conditionals, (2) fine-grained extraction of conditionals, and (3) CEG creation. Processed REQ: "If A is valid and B is false, then C is true"

a CEG based on the extracted *antecedents* and *consequents* by CiRA. Our web application is built as a restful node.js server utilizing the *Express* framework. The backend's main purpose is executing a *Python* script, which is a wrapper around our conditional classifier and conditional extraction algorithm. Our tool-supported approach consists of four components: (1) *detection of conditionals*, (2) *extraction of conditionals*, (3) *creation of cause-effect graph*, and (4) *creation of acceptance test*. We outline all four components below and use the following requirement as our running example: "If the temperature change is requested, then the determine heating/cooling mode process is activated and makes a heating/cooling request."

Detection of Conditionals The UI provides a text input field in which an arbitrary NL sentence can be entered. Upon pressing the "classify"-button, the sentence is sent to the backend, where it is processed by the aforementioned wrapped conditional classifier. On return of the REST call, the classification and confidence of the model are rendered in the UI. The user may confirm or correct the classifier's choice. The entered sentence and the optional user confirmation or correction are then stored in the backend to (1) display the five most recently entered sentences, (2) provide preliminary insight into the performance of the classifier on unseen sentences, and (3) preserve sentences for future training of the classifier. At this point, we support batch learning and plan to implement an online learning algorithm in future research to leverage the collected data directly for enhancing our conditional classifier. Our exemplary requirement is classified as `Conditional Present` with confidence of 98.72%. After confirming this correct classification, the user is forwarded to the second step.

Extraction of Conditionals In the second step, our pre-trained binary-file conditional extractor is loaded and used to annotate the entered sentence according to our fine-grained labeling scheme (see Fig. 7). The predicted labels per token are rendered in the UI. We explain each label at the bottom of the UI to inform users about the meaning of the labels. For example, the expression "the temperature change is requested" is labeled as `Antecedent 1`. On the lower annotation layer, "the temperature" is labeled as `Variable` and "is requested" is labeled as `Condition`. Further, our extractor has correctly detected that `Consequent 1` and `Consequent 2` are connected by a conjunction. In total, CiRA assigned nine labels to the entered sentence.

Conditional Statements in Requirements Artifacts

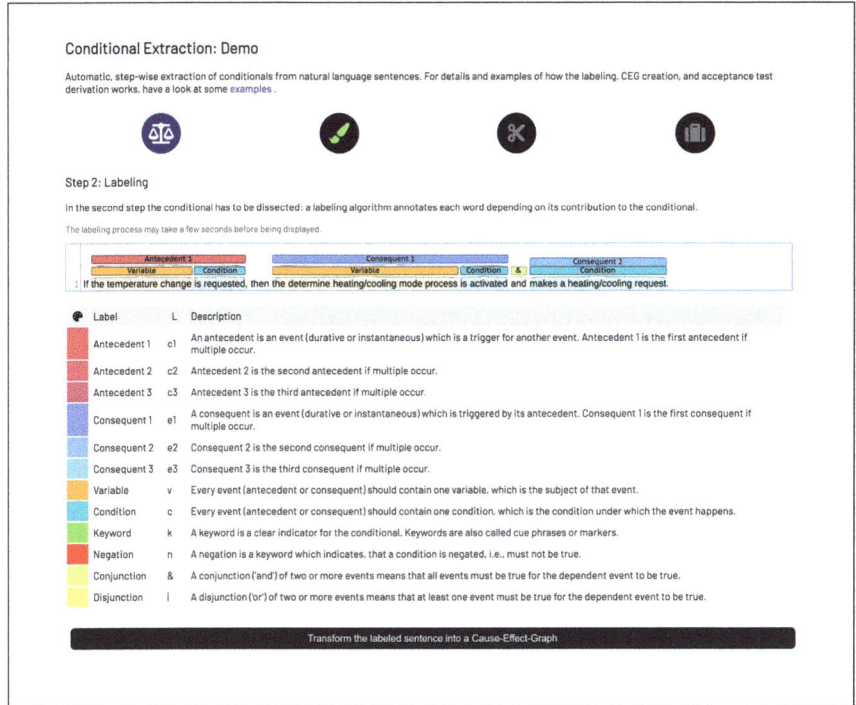

Fig. 7 Overview of the user interface provided by CiRA

Creation of Cause-Effect Graph In the third step, we create a CEG based on the annotated conditional. Specifically, we represent *antecedents* as cause nodes and *consequents* as effect nodes and relate them to each other using edges. Creating the CEG is not a trivial, potentially error-prone task. We integrated a model editor into the tool to enable the user to correct potential errors manually or to modify the CEG for other reasons. This allows users to add new nodes using simple drag and drop or to adjust existing nodes and their edges. Pressing the DEL key can remove elements from the CEG. The auto-layout function supports the user in arranging the nodes to ensure clarity of the CEG. In the simplest case, *antecedents* and *consequents* encompass both a variable and condition in the lower annotation layer. We then fill the created cause and effect nodes with the corresponding information. If either of the two labels is missing, we need to extract the information from the nearest referent to correct incomplete nodes. In the given example, the variable of [Consequent 2] is not included in the entered sentence. Hence, we enrich its corresponding effect node with the variable of [Consequent 1].

Creation of Acceptance Test In the last step, we automatically derive the minimum number of test cases required to fully check the entered requirement from the created CEG. For this purpose, we consider the findings of our study on the logical interpretation of conditionals by RE practitioners. The user can choose whether s/he perceives *antecedents* to be both sufficient and necessary conditions for *consequents* or not (see checkbox below the test case specification). Depending on the selection, we filter the derived test cases and display the acceptance test corresponding to the user's interpretation. In the given example, we perceive the *antecedent* as a necessary condition for both *consequents*. Accordingly, our approach derived two test cases from the created CEG.

5 Industrial Application: Leveraging Conditional Extraction for Automatic Acceptance Test Creation

We aim to investigate whether our approach is suitable for the automatic generation of acceptance tests in practice. Specifically, we study the following research questions (RQ):

- **RQ 1:** Can our automated approach create the same test cases as the manual approach?
- **RQ 2:** What are the reasons for deviating test cases?

RQ 1 and RQ 2 inspect the impact of our approach: does it achieve the status quo or even lead to an improvement of the manual test case derivation? To this end, we conduct a case study with three industry partners in an exploratory fashion and compare automatically created test cases with existing, manually created test cases. For our study, we follow the guidelines by Runeson and Höst [61] for conducting case study research.

5.1 Study Design

Case Sampling and Study Objects We apply purposive case sampling augmented with convenience sampling [62]. Specifically, we approached some of our industry contacts inquiring whether they are interested in exploring the potential of CiRA. We were provided with data from three companies operating in different domains: *Allianz Deutschland AG* (insurance), *Ericsson* (telecommunication), and *Leopold Kostal GmbH & Co. KG* (automotive). Since the data is subject to non-disclosure agreements, we are unable to share the provided requirements and test cases.

Allianz Data We analyze 219 *Acceptance Criteria* (ACC) describing the functionality of a business information system used for vehicle insurance. 127 of these ACC contain conditionals and are therefore suitable for assessing CiRA. The remaining ACC specify the expected functionality based on process flows (16 criteria) or in a static way (76 criteria). We analyze the acceptance tests that were manually created for each of the ACC including conditionals. In total, 309 test cases were designed, which corresponds to about 2.43 test cases per acceptance test.

Conditional Statements in Requirements Artifacts

Ericsson Data We analyze 109 requirements derived from five *Business Use Cases* (BUCs), which are feature-level units of development at *Ericsson*. The BUCs originate from different functional topics. 49 of these 109 requirements contain conditionals, while the remaining requirements are expressed in a static way. In total, 65 test cases were manually generated for the 49 requirements containing conditionals, which corresponds to about 1.33 test cases per acceptance test.

Kostal Data We analyze a requirements specification describing a plug interlock function, which prevents a charging plug from being disconnected during an active charging process of an electric car. The specification includes 135 functional requirements. 79 of these functional requirements contain conditionals, while 56 requirements describe the functional behavior in a static way: "The signal `signalName` shall be set to `InitValue`". In our case study, we focus only on the acceptance tests that were manually created for the 79 requirements that contain conditionals. In total, 204 test cases were designed, which corresponds to about 2.58 test cases per acceptance test.

We pass all study objects through our pipeline and compare the automatically created acceptance tests with the manually created acceptance tests (see Fig. 8). Specifically, we investigate five different categories of test cases:

- *Identical*: A test case created manually by the test designer and automatically by our approach.
- $AA \land rel$: A test case that has been missed in manual test design and should be included in the acceptance test.
- $AA \land \neg rel$: A superfluous test case that is correctly not included in the manually created acceptance test.
- $MA \land rel$: A test case that has been missed by our approach and should be included in the acceptance test.
- $MA \land \neg rel$: A superfluous test case that is correctly not included in the automatically created acceptance test.

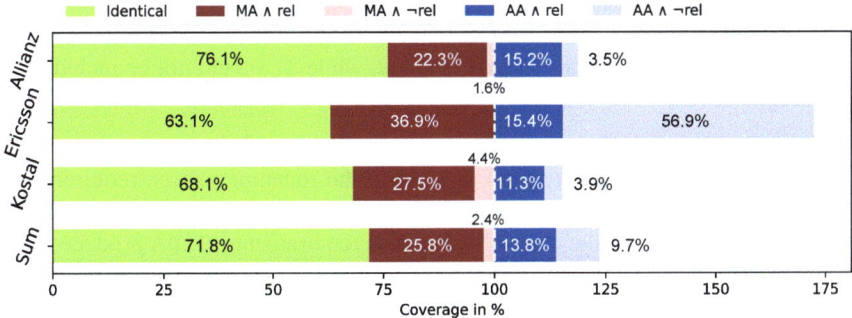

Fig. 8 Case study results. Comparison of manually and automatically created test cases

5.2 Study Results

5.2.1 RQ 1: Can CiRA Create the Same Test Cases as the Manual Approach?

Findings at Allianz CiRA detected 90.55% of the conditionals in the acceptance criteria. Consequently, no test cases were created for the 12 missed criteria containing conditionals. For the correctly classified criteria, our approach generated 314 test cases. This corresponds to about 2.73 test cases per acceptance test. We were able to draw a one-to-one relationship between 224 manually and automatically created test cases. Additionally, we observed a one-to-many relationship between eleven manually created test cases and 32 automatically created test cases. Thus, 76.05% of the manually created test cases could be automatically generated. However, 74 test cases were not created by our approach, of which 27 test cases are related to criteria that were incorrectly identified as ⬥ Conditional Not Present . According to the test designers, the remaining 47 MA test cases can be classified as follows: 42 are necessary to fully test the system functionality, while 5 test cases are superfluous. A comparison of the automatically created test cases with the manually created test cases highlights that 58 test cases have not yet been considered in the manual test design. According to the test designer, these 58 AA test cases can be clustered as follows: 47 are indeed *relevant*, while 11 should not be included in the acceptance test.

Findings at Ericsson CiRA correctly classified 79.6% of the conditionals in requirements but failed to do so for ten requirements. 91 test cases were automatically generated based on these identified requirements, which corresponds to about 2.33 test cases per acceptance test. 28 manual test cases were automatically created by our approach in a one-to-one, 13 more in a one-to-many relationship, resulting in an automatic generation of 41 of 65 test cases (63.1%). However, 24 test cases were not created by our approach, of which 7 test cases are related to criteria that were incorrectly identified as ⬥ Conditional Not Present . According to the test designer, the remaining 17 MA test cases are all necessary to fully test the system's functionality. A comparison of the automatically created test cases with the manually created test cases highlights that 47 test cases have not yet been considered in the manual test design. According to the test designer, these 47 AA test cases can be clustered as follows: 10 are indeed *relevant*, while 37 should not be included in the acceptance test.

Findings at Kostal CiRA correctly assigned the label ⬥ Conditional Present to 72 requirements. However, it failed to identify the remaining seven requirements containing conditionals. Hence, no test cases were ultimately created for these requirements. Regarding the correctly classified requirements, CiRA produced 194 test cases. This corresponds to about 2.69 test cases per acceptance test. We found a one-to-one relationship between 122 manually and automatically created test cases. In addition, we could draw a one-to-many relationship between 17 manual test cases and 41 automatically created test cases. Thus, 68.14% of the manually created test cases could be created automatically. Nevertheless, 65 manually created test cases are not included in the automated test cases. Sixteen of these exclusively manually created test cases refer to the conditionals in requirements that CiRA missed. In the case of the other 49 test cases, we ask test designers at *Kostal* about their relevance. In fact, 81.63% of the exclusively manually created test cases are deemed *relevant*. According to the test designers, nine test cases are superfluous and can be removed from the test set. Examining the automatically created test cases, we observe that 31 test cases have not been considered in the manual creation so far. Interestingly, the test designers confirmed that 74.19% of these test cases were indeed missed in the manual process. However, eight exclusively automatically created test cases are not *relevant* and thus correctly not included in the manual set.

> **ⓘ Answer to RQ 1:**
>
> Across all case companies, our approach automatically created 71.8% of the 578 manually created test cases. Our approach further identified 136 test cases missed in manual test design. In fact, 58.8% of these exclusively automatically generated test cases are indeed relevant and should be included in the acceptance test. We conclude that our approach can automatically create a significant amount of relevant (known and new) test cases.

5.2.2 RQ 2: What Are the Reasons for Deviating Test Cases?

Incomplete Requirements We found that the main reason for test cases that could not be created automatically lies in the poor information available in the requirements. The interviewed test designers confirmed that domain knowledge is often required to determine all relevant test cases. In the case of *Kostal*, 19 out of 79 requirements were incomplete. We found that our approach could not generate 37 $MA \wedge rel$ test cases due to lack of information in these requirements. At *Allianz*, 16 out of 127 conditionals in acceptance criteria lack information. Our analysis shows that our approach could not generate 31 $MA \wedge rel$ test cases due to incomplete acceptance criteria. At *Ericsson*, 17 $MA \wedge rel$ test cases could not be generated due to underspecified or missing requirements.

Incorrect Combinatorics We noticed that some of the exclusively manually created test cases are superfluous—they can be merged or are already covered by other test cases. The interviews revealed that in these cases, the combinatorics of the input and output parameters were interpreted incorrectly. According to the test designers, this stems mainly from the fact that test cases are often not created systematically but rather based on past experience. Unsystematic test design may not only result in superfluous test cases but can also lead to necessary test cases being ignored. We observed that test designers tend to create positive cases and neglect negative cases. At *Kostal*, 21 of the 23 $AA \wedge rel$ test cases were actually negative cases. Only two positive cases were overlooked in the manual process. At *Allianz*, 36 of the 47 $AA \wedge rel$ test cases were actually negative cases. 11 positive cases were missed by the test designers. In the case of *Ericsson*, all ten $AA \wedge rel$ test cases were overlooked negative test cases.

Infeasible Test Cases Our analysis shows that some of the exclusively automatically created test cases cannot occur in practice. According to the test designers, this problem arises mainly for negative test cases where certain scenarios are tested that can only occur theoretically. For example, some parameters cannot take the value false at the same time, even if this case should be checked from a combinatorial point of view. In the case of *Kostal*, we found that three of the eight $AA \wedge \neg rel$ test cases cannot be checked in practice. At *Allianz*, five of the eleven $AA \wedge \neg rel$ test cases can only occur theoretically. At *Ericsson*, 28 of 37 $AA \wedge \neg rel$ test cases fell into this category.

Errors in Our Pipeline Our approach produced not only errors in the detection of the conditionals but also failed in some cases to extract and translate them into the CEG. At *Kostal*, our approach failed to generate three $MA \wedge rel$ test cases and instead created five $AA \wedge \neg rel$ test cases, because the generated CEG reflected a wrong conditional statement. In the case of *Allianz*, we failed to create eleven $MA \wedge rel$ test cases and instead generated six $AA \wedge \neg rel$ test cases. In the case of *Ericsson*, our approach produced nine $AA \wedge \neg rel$ test cases due to incorrect interpretation of the conditional. We found that these errors occurred mainly when the conditionals contained three or more *consequents*.

> **ⓘ Answer to RQ 2:**
>
> In our setting, we observed four reasons for deviating test cases: incomplete requirements, incorrect combinatorics, infeasible test cases, and errors in our pipeline. We found that incomplete requirements are the main reason for test cases that our approach could not create automatically.

5.3 Concluding Discussion

Our case study demonstrates that our approach is able to support practitioners in deriving relevant test cases from conditionals. Across all industry partners, our approach automatically generates more than 70% of the manually created test cases. However, our approach does not achieve full automation of acceptance test creation, mainly due to incomplete requirements. Our approach is heavily dependent on the information contained in the requirements and consequently unable to create test cases for which additional domain knowledge is required. Thus, our case study confirms the findings of Mendez et al. [63] that incompleteness is still a major problem in practice and hinders the automatic processing of requirements.

> **❶ 1. Key Take-away:**
>
> In fact, our approach can help to generate acceptance tests automatically. However, our approach does not substitute a test designer since domain knowledge is often necessary to identify all required test cases.

According to the test designers, the main benefit of our approach is its ability to create test cases automatically based on heuristics. Hence, it is independent of human bias and able to identify test cases that may be missed in the manual process. We argue that our approach should always be used as a supplement to the existing manual process to highlight all test cases that should be tested from a combinatorial point of view, in particular negative test cases that were proportionally more often overlooked than positive test cases. The automatically generated set of test cases may then be manually extended by test cases that require domain knowledge. At *Ericsson*, we observed that a large amount of automatically generated test cases were irrelevant since they can only occur theoretically. Hence, when utilizing our approach as a supplement to manual test design, test designers need to filter the automatically generated test cases. However, we argue that it is easier to discard infeasible test cases than to manually identify undetected relevant test cases.

> **❶ 2. Key Take-Away:**
>
> Our approach is particularly useful for automatically identifying negative test cases, which are often overlooked in the manual creation process. However, not all test cases created by our approach are necessarily relevant, requiring subsequent manual review of the automatically created test specifications.

Since CiRA decomposes each sentence using subword tokenization and labels each token individually, it is much more robust against grammar errors and is also able to process *Out-Of-Vocabulary* (OOV) words. Nevertheless, studies [64] reveal that language models such as BERT show significant performance degradation with increasing amounts of noisy data. As a result, we hypothesize that the robustness of CiRA against grammatical mistakes is limited to a few errors in a sentence. We therefore propose to combine CiRA with requirements smell checkers [65] in the future to automatically verify the linguistic quality of requirements before passing them into the CiRA pipeline.

> **ⓘ 3. Key Take-Away:**
>
> Fully automated acceptance test generation is difficult to achieve because requirements often suffer from poor quality. RE teams should therefore first check the quality of the requirements before processing them with `cira`.

CiRA is limited to single-sentence conditionals and is not able to extract conditional statements that span multiple sentences. However, two-sentence conditionals may arise in practice (e.g., indicated by "therefore", "hence"), requiring us to extend CiRA in future work. According to the test designers, a further challenge in the extraction of conditionals relates to the handling of *event chains* (i.e., linked requirements, in which the *consequent* of a conditional represents a *antecedent* in another conditional). In such cases, it is no longer sufficient to create a single CEG. Rather, we must create several *Cause-Effect Graphs* and connect them to each other. Currently, CiRA only allows the creation of acceptance tests for requirements that contain conditionals. For full automation of test case design, however, we also require approaches capable of processing static requirements and process flows.

> **ⓘ 4. Key Take-Away:**
>
> So far, the feasibility of `cira` is limited to conditionals that span a single sentence. As a consequence, we still need to develop methods for the automatic generation of test cases from static requirements and process flows.

Our case study focuses on a quantitative comparison between manually and automatically created test cases. However, several other metrics are available to benchmark test cases [66]. For example, structural criteria like *test understandability* investigate whether a test is easy to understand in terms of its internal and external descriptions. We plan to extend our study to obtain further insights into the quality of the test cases generated by CiRA.

6 Summary and Outlook

Authors of requirements often use conditionals to specify the desired system behavior. Therefore, conditionals contain rich semantic information about potential system inputs and expected system outputs. Automatically extracting conditionals bears a high potential for *requirements engineering* as it contributes to an increased automation of specific RE tasks. Our study with three industry partners proved that automated conditional extraction can help extract acceptance tests automatically. Further, besides assisting in automating RE tasks, automatic conditional extraction helps identify and reduce misunderstandings in project teams. Since conditionals are interpreted differently by RE practitioners, teams must decide whether they consider *antecedents* to be only *sufficient* or also *necessary* for the *consequent*. We argue that automatically extracting conditionals from requirements and explicitly displaying corresponding positive and negative test cases to users can help foster the discussion among practitioners.

Automated extraction of conditionals is not a trivial task. Shallow rule-based systems are not suitable for extracting conditionals as they can be expressed in many different forms that are difficult to cover with patterns. Our studies proved that ML-based and TL-based approaches are better suited for determining conditionals in NL sentences and extracting them in fine-gained form. However, simply using ML and TL does not automatically lead to a solution of an NLP problem. Rather, the choice of an adequate ML and TL model is dependent on the context and the complexity of the problem that needs to be solved. This is particularly evident in our comparison of ML and TL models for the detection of conditionals. We did not observe a great deviation in performance between the best ML model and our best TL model in solving this binary classification problem. The benefits of *Transfer Learning* were most noticeable when dealing with the considerably more complex problem of conditional extraction. Owing to pre-training on large corpora, the TL models acquired a strong language understanding and are therefore capable of reliably extracting conditionals in fine-grained form. Our tool-supported approach CiRA combines our best-performing TL models and is capable of detecting conditionals in NL requirements and extracting them in fine-grained form. CiRA is available at http://www.cira.bth.se/demo/.

References

1. Girju, R.: Automatic detection of causal relations for question answering. In: Proceedings of the ACL 2003 Workshop on Multilingual Summarization and Question Answering - Volume 12, MultiSumQA '03, (USA), pp. 76–83. Association for Computational Linguistics, Toronto (2003)
2. Silverstein, C., Brin, S., Motwani, R., Ullman, J.: Scalable techniques for mining causal structures. Data Mining Knowl. Discovery **4**, 163–192 (2000)
3. Riaz, M., Girju, R.: Another look at causality: Discovering scenario-specific contingency relationships with no supervision. In: 2010 IEEE Fourth International Conference on Semantic Computing, pp. 361–368 (2010)
4. Hashimoto, C., Torisawa, K., Kloetzer, J., Sano, M., Varga, I., Oh, J.-H., Kidawara, Y.: Toward future scenario generation: Extracting event causality exploiting semantic relation, context, and association features. In: Proceedings of the 52nd Annual Meeting of the Association for Computational Linguistics (Volume 1: Long Papers), (Baltimore, Maryland), pp. 987–997. Association for Computational Linguistics, Toronto (2014)
5. Qiu, J., Xu, L., Zhai, J., Luo, L.: Extracting causal relations from emergency cases based on conditional random fields. Procedia Comput. Sci. **112**, 1623–1632 (2017). Knowledge-Based and Intelligent Information & Engineering Systems: Proceedings of the 21st International Conference, KES-20176-8 September 2017, Marseille, France
6. Bui, Q.-C., Nualláin, B.Ó., Boucher, C.A., Sloot, P.M.: Extracting causal relations on hiv drug resistance from literature. BMC Bioinformat. **11**, 101 (2010)

7. Khoo, C.S.G., Chan, S., Niu, Y.: Extracting causal knowledge from a medical database using graphical patterns. In: Proceedings of the 38th Annual Meeting on Association for Computational Linguistics, ACL '00 (USA), pp. 336–343. Association for Computational Linguistics, Toronto (2000)
8. Mihăilă, C., Ananiadou, S.: Semi-supervised learning of causal relations in biomedical scientific discourse. BioMed. Eng. OnLine **13**, S1 (2014)
9. Khoo, C.S., Myaeng, S.H., Oddy, R.N.: Using cause-effect relations in text to improve information retrieval precision. Informat. Process. Manag. **37**(1), 119–145 (2001)
10. Doan, S., Yang, E.W., Tilak, S.S., Li, P.W., Zisook, D.S., Torii, M.: Extracting health-related causality from twitter messages using natural language processing. BMC Med. Informat. Decision Making **19**, 71–77 (2019)
11. Radinsky, K., Davidovich, S., Markovitch, S.: Learning causality for news events prediction. In: Proceedings of the 21st International Conference on World Wide Web, WWW '12, (New York, NY, USA), pp.. 909–918. Association for Computing Machinery, New York (2012)
12. Chang, D.-S., Choi, K.-S.: Causal relation extraction using cue phrase and lexical pair probabilities. In: Natural Language Processing – IJCNLP 2004, Su, K.-Y., Tsujii, J., Lee, J.-H., Kwong, O.Y. (eds.), pp. 61–70. Springer, Berlin (2004)
13. Rink, B., Harabagiu, S.: UTD: Classifying semantic relations by combining lexical and semantic resources. In: Proceedings of the 5th International Workshop on Semantic Evaluation, (Uppsala, Sweden), pp. 256–259. Association for Computational Linguistics, Toronto (2010)
14. Khoo, C.S.G., Kornfilt, J., Oddy, R.N., Myaeng, S.H.: Automatic extraction of cause-effect information from newspaper text without knowledge-based inferencing. Literary Linguistic Comput. **13**(4), 177–186 (1998)
15. Dasgupta, T., Saha, R., Dey, L., Naskar, A.: Automatic extraction of causal relations from text using linguistically informed deep neural networks. In: Proceedings of the 19th Annual SIGdial Meeting on Discourse and Dialogue, (Melbourne, Australia), pp. 306–316. Association for Computational Linguistics, Toronto (2018)
16. Li, Z., Li, Q., Zou, X., Ren, J.: Causality extraction based on self-attentive BiLSTM-CRF with transferred embeddings. CoRR **vol. abs/1904.07629** (2019)
17. Cui, S., Sheng, J., Cong, X., Li, Q., Liu, T., Shi, J.: Event causality extraction with event argument correlations. In: Proceedings of the 29th International Conference on Computational Linguistics, (Gyeongju, Republic of Korea), pp. 2300–2312. International Committee on Computational Linguistics, New York (2022)
18. Tran Phu, M., Nguyen, T.H.: Graph convolutional networks for event causality identification with rich document-level structures. In: Proceedings of the 2021 Conference of the North American Chapter of the Association for Computational Linguistics: Human Language Technologies, (Online), pp. 3480–3490. Association for Computational Linguistics, Toronto (2021)
19. Zuo, X., Cao, P., Chen, Y., Liu, K., Zhao, J., Peng, W., Chen, Y.: Improving event causality identification via self-supervised representation learning on external causal statement. In: Findings of the Association for Computational Linguistics: ACL-IJCNLP 2021, (Online), pp. 2162–2172. Association for Computational Linguistics, Toronto (2021)
20. Cao, P., Zuo, X., Chen, Y., Liu, K., Zhao, J., Chen, Y., Peng, W.: Knowledge-enriched event causality identification via latent structure induction networks. In: Proceedings of the 59th Annual Meeting of the Association for Computational Linguistics and the 11th International Joint Conference on Natural Language Processing (Volume 1: Long Papers), (Online), pp. 4862–4872. Association for Computational Linguistics, Toronto (2021)
21. Fischbach, J., Vogelsang, A., Spies, D., Wehrle, A., Junker, M., Freudenstein, D.: Specmate: Automated creation of test cases from acceptance criteria. In: 2020 IEEE 13th International Conference on Software Testing, Validation and Verification (ICST), pp. 321–331 (2020)
22. Fischbach, J., Hauptmann, B., Konwitschny, L., Spies, D., Vogelsang, A.: Towards causality extraction from requirements. In: 2020 IEEE 28th International Requirements Engineering Conference (RE), pp. 388–393 (2020)

23. Fischbach, J., Femmer, H., Mendez, D., Fucci, D., Vogelsang, A.: What makes agile test artifacts useful? an activity-based quality model from a practitioners' perspective. In: Proceedings of the 14th ACM / IEEE International Symposium on Empirical Software Engineering and Measurement (ESEM), ESEM '20, (New York, NY, USA). Association for Computing Machinery, New York (2020)
24. Fischbach, J., Frattini, J., Spaans, A., Kummeth, M., Vogelsang, A., Mendez, D., Unterkalmsteiner, M.: Automatic detection of causality in requirement artifacts: The cira approach. In: Requirements Engineering: Foundation for Software Quality, Dalpiaz, F., Spoletini, P. (eds.), pp. 19–36. Springer International Publishing, Cham (2021)
25. Fischbach, J., Frattini, J., Mendez, D., Unterkalmsteiner, M., Femmer, H., Vogelsang, A.: How do practitioners interpret conditionals in requirements?. In: Product-Focused Software Process Improvement, Ardito, L., Jedlitschka, A., Morisio, M., Torchiano, M. (eds.), pp. 85–102. Springer International Publishing, Cham (2021)
26. Fischbach, J., Springer, T., Frattini, J., Femmer, H., Vogelsang, A., Mendez, D.: Fine-grained causality extraction from natural language requirements using recursive neural tensor networks. In: 2021 IEEE 29th International Requirements Engineering Conference Workshops (REW), pp. 60–69 (2021)
27. Frattini, J., Fischbach, J., Mendez, D., Unterkalmsteiner, M., Vogelsang, A., Wnuk, K.: Causality in requirements artifacts: prevalence, detection, and impact. Requirem. Eng. **28**(1), 49–74 (2023)
28. Wiecher, C., Fischbach, J., Greenyer, J., Vogelsang, A., Wolff, C., Dumitrescu, R.: Integrated and iterative requirements analysis and test specification: A case study at kostal. In: 2021 ACM/IEEE 24th International Conference on Model Driven Engineering Languages and Systems (MODELS), pp. 112–122 (2021)
29. Jadallah, N., Fischbach, J., Frattini, J., Vogelsang, A.: Cate: Causality tree extractor from natural language requirements. In: 2021 IEEE 29th International Requirements Engineering Conference Workshops (REW), pp. 77–79 (2021)
30. Fischbach, J., Frattini, J., Vogelsang, A., Mendez, D., Unterkalmsteiner, M., Wehrle, A., Henao, P.R., Yousefi, P., Juricic, T., Radduenz, J., Wiecher, C.: Automatic creation of acceptance tests by extracting conditionals from requirements: Nlp approach and case study. J. Syst. Softw. **197**, 111549 (2023)
31. Fischbach, J.: Why and How to Extract Conditional Statements From Natural Language Requirements. PhD Thesis, Universität zu Köln (2022)
32. Bhatt, R., Pancheva, R.: Conditionals, Ch. 16, pp. 638–687. Wiley, Hoboken (2006)
33. Johnson-Laird, P., Byrne, R.M.J.: Conditionals: A theory of meaning, pragmatics, and inference. Psychol. Rev. **109**(4), 646–678 (2002)
34. Fintel, K.: Exceptive conditionals: The meaning of unless. In: North East Linguistics Society, vol. 22 (1992)
35. Declerck, R., Reed, S.: Conditionals: A Comprehensive Empirical Analysis. Mouton de Gruyter, Berlin; New York (2001)
36. Quirk, R., Greenbaum, S., Leech, G., Svartvik, J.: A Grammar of Contemporary English. Longman, London (1972)
37. Jackson, F.: On assertion and indicative conditionals. Philosoph. Rev. **88**(4), 565–589 (1979)
38. Altman, N., Krzywinski, M.: Association, correlation and causation. Nat. Methods **12**, 899–900 (2015)
39. Holland, P.W.: Statistics and causal inference. J. Amer. Statist. Assoc. **81**(396), 945–960 (1986)
40. Check, J., Schutt, R.K.: Causation and Experimental Design, ch. 5, pp. 116–144. SAGE Publications, Thousand Oaks (2012)
41. Dul, J.: Necessary condition analysis (NCA): Logic and methodology of "necessary but not sufficient" causality. Organizat. Res. Methods **19**, 10–52 (2016)
42. Lewis, D.: Counterfactuals. Blackwell Publishers, Oxford (1973)
43. Sassower, R.: Causality and Correlation, pp. 1–4. American Cancer Society, Atlanta (2017)
44. Simon, H.A.: Spurious correlation: A causal interpretation. J. Amer. Statist. Assoc. **49**(267), 467–479 (1954)

45. Puga, J., Krzywinski, M., Altman, N.: Points of significance: Bayesian networks. Nature Methods, vol. 12, pp. 799–800 (2015). Copyright: Copyright 2015 Elsevier B.V., All rights Reserved
46. Taplin, J.E., Staudenmayer, H.: Interpretation of abstract conditional sentences in deductive reasoning. J. Verbal Learn. Verbal Behavior **12**(5), 530–542 (1973)
47. Marcus, S.L., Rips, L.J.: Conditional reasoning. J. Verbal Learn. Verbal Behavior **18**(2), 199–223 (1979)
48. Staudenmayer, H.: Understanding Conditional Reasoning with Meaningful Propositions, pp. 55–79. Psychology Press, London (1975)
49. Lamport, L.: The temporal logic of actions. ACM Trans. Programm. Languag. Syst. **16**, 872–923 (1994)
50. Dwyer, M.B., Avrunin, G.S., Corbett, J.C.: Patterns in property specifications for finite-state verification. In: Proceedings of the 21st International Conference on Software Engineering, ICSE '99 (New York, NY, USA), pp. 411–420. Association for Computing Machinery, New York (1999)
51. Femmer, H., Méndez Fernández, D., Wagner, S., Eder, S.: Rapid quality assurance with requirements smells. J. Syst. Softw. **123**, 190–213 (2017)
52. Frattini, J., Junker, M., Unterkalmsteiner, M., Mendez, D.: Automatic extraction of cause-effect-relations from requirements artifacts. In: 2020 35th IEEE/ACM International Conference on Automated Software Engineering (ASE), pp. 561–572 (2020)
53. Ciolkowski, M., Laitenberger, O., Vegas, S., Biffl, S.: Practical Experiences in the Design and Conduct of Surveys in Empirical Software Engineering, pp. 104–128. Springer, Berlin (2003)
54. Baltes, S., Ralph, P.: Sampling in software engineering research: A critical review and guidelines. Empir. Softw. Eng. **27**(4), 94 (2022)
55. Wohlin, C., Runeson, P., Hst, M., Ohlsson, M.C., Regnell, B., Wessln, A.: Experimentation in Software Engineering. Springer Publishing Company, Incorporated, Cham (2012)
56. Dalpiaz, F., Ferrari, A., Franch, X., Palomares, C.: Nlp tool showcase at nlp4re. In: Requirements Engineering: Foundation for Software Quality (2019)
57. Yates, D., Moore, D., McCabe, G.: The Practice of Statistics. W. H. Freeman, New York City (1999)
58. Mavin, A., Wilkinson, P., Harwood, A., Novak, M.: Easy approach to requirements syntax (ears). In: 2009 17th IEEE International Requirements Engineering Conference, pp. 317–322 (2009)
59. Berry, D.M., Krieger, M.M.: From contract drafting to software specification: Linguistic sources of ambiguity - a handbook version 1.0 (2000)
60. Rosadini, B., Ferrari, A., Gori, G., Fantechi, A., Gnesi, S., Trotta, I., Bacherini, S.: Using nlp to detect requirements defects: An industrial experience in the railway domain. In: Requirements Engineering: Foundation for Software Quality, Grünbacher, P., Perini, A. (eds.), pp. 344–360. Springer International Publishing, Cham (2017)
61. Runeson, P., Höst, M.: Guidelines for conducting and reporting case study research in software engineering. Empir. Softw. Eng. **14**, 131–164 (2009)
62. Kitchenham, B., Pfleeger, S.L.: Principles of survey research: Part 5: Populations and samples. SIGSOFT Softw. Eng. Notes **27**(5), 17–20 (2002)
63. Fernández, D.M., Wagner, S., Kalinowski, M., Felderer, M., Mafra, P., Vetrò, A., Conte, T., Christiansson, M.T., Greer, D., Lassenius, C., Männistö, T., Nayabi, M., Oivo, M., Penzenstadler, B., Pfahl, D., Prikladnicki, R., Ruhe, G., Schekelmann, A., Sen, S., Spinola, R., Tuzcu, A., De La Vara, J.L., Wieringa, R.: Naming the pain in requirements engineering. Empirical Softw. Engg. **22**(5), 2298–2338 (2017)
64. Kumar, A., Makhija, P., Gupta, A.: Noisy text data: Achilles' heel of BERT. In: W-NUT, pp. 16–21 (2020).
65. Femmer, H., Méndez Fernández, D., Wagner, S., Eder, S.: Rapid quality assurance with requirements smells. J. Syst. Softw. **123**, 190–213 (2017)
66. Tran, H.K.V., Unterkalmsteiner, M., Börstler, J., Ali, N.b.: Assessing test artifact quality–a tertiary study. Inf. Softw. Technol. **139**, 106620 (2021)

Open Access This chapter is licensed under the terms of the Creative Commons Attribution 4.0 International License (http://creativecommons.org/licenses/by/4.0/), which permits use, sharing, adaptation, distribution and reproduction in any medium or format, as long as you give appropriate credit to the original author(s) and the source, provide a link to the Creative Commons licence and indicate if changes were made.

The images or other third party material in this chapter are included in the chapter's Creative Commons licence, unless indicated otherwise in a credit line to the material. If material is not included in the chapter's Creative Commons licence and your intended use is not permitted by statutory regulation or exceeds the permitted use, you will need to obtain permission directly from the copyright holder.

Open Access This chapter is licensed under the terms of the Creative Commons Attribution 4.0 International License (http://creativecommons.org/licenses/by/4.0/), which permits use, sharing, adaptation, distribution and reproduction in any medium or format, as long as you give appropriate credit to the original author(s) and the source, provide a link to the Creative Commons license and indicate if changes were made.

The images or other third party material in this chapter are included in the chapter's Creative Commons license, unless indicated otherwise in a credit line to the material. If material is not included in the chapter's Creative Commons license and your intended use is not permitted by statutory regulation or exceeds the permitted use, you will need to obtain permission directly from the copyright holder.

From Design to Reality: An Overview of the MontiThings Ecosystem for Model-Driven IoT Applications

Jörg Christian Kirchhof

Abstract The Internet of Things (IoT) networks everyday objects that can perceive and influence their environment using sensors and actuators. Since IoT systems are inherently distributed systems, often built on fault-prone hardware and exposed to harsh environmental conditions such as vibration or humidity, developing such systems is challenging. In recent years, some DSLs for IoT system development have been introduced, yet they only slightly improve IoT system development. This chapter provides an overview of *MontiThings*, an ecosystem for model-driven development of IoT systems that covers the life cycle of IoT systems from design in the form of Component and connector (C&C) models, through (dynamic) deployment, to failure analysis. MontiThings is designed to handle different classes of errors and failures. By being able to make counter-suggestions to device owners, the requirement-based deployment algorithm enables device owners to customize their IoT systems to their needs. MontiThings also offers an app store concept to decouple hardware development from software development in order to prospectively reduce problems such as e-waste and security issues that result from too close a coupling. Overall, MontiThings demonstrates an end-to-end model-driven approach to IoT system development.

Note This chapter summarizes the thesis [16]. Thus, the content of this chapter is taken from [16]. In particular, all illustrations were taken from the dissertation and the respective papers the dissertation is based on.

J. C. Kirchhof (✉)
Software Engineering, RWTH Aachen University, Aachen, Germany
e-mail: kirchhof@se-rwth.de

1 Introduction

The Internet of Things (IoT) networks everyday objects. Sensors and actuators enable them to perceive and influence their environment. The data obtained from the sensors is often used to automate processes with the help of the actuators. For example, in a smart home, the heating can be switched off automatically as soon as the window is opened. Because IoT devices belong to real-world objects, IoT systems are inherently distributed systems. The programming languages with which such systems are mostly developed today are often the same General-purpose programming languages (GPLs) such as C++ or Python with which all other types of systems are developed, according to an analysis of GitHub projects [7] and developer surveys [10]. These GPLs were not designed with the (primary) goal of improving the development of IoT applications. Accordingly, these GPLs are not well suited to address the challenges of developing IoT systems [32]. According to [32], the differences to programming traditional applications like web applications include, among other things, multidevice programming, the always-on nature of the system, heterogeneity, and the need to write fault-tolerant software.

In contrast to GPLs, domain-specific (modelling) languages often focus on solving a specific problem. Such modelling languages raise the level of abstraction, allowing certain aspects of development to be solved systematically in a way that GPLs cannot, since they must provide a certain level of generality. In the last decade, quite a few modelling and programming languages have been published for the development of IoT applications, including ThingML [13, 24], Ericsson's Calvin [3, 28, 29], Eclipse Mita [11], CapeCode [4], FRASAD [26], and Node-RED [27]. However, these languages often offer only a low level of abstraction [9], ultimately leaving the complexity of challenges such as multidevice programming to developers or focus only on early development phases and mostly neglect deployment.

In this chapter, we present *MontiThings*, an ecosystem for the model-driven IoT application development that covers the life cycle from initial prototypes to deployment on IoT devices to analysis of deployed applications. MontiThings consists of several modelling languages that clearly separate the business logic from the technical aspects of development. In doing so, MontiThings supports developers through various mechanisms in the development of error-resilient applications. In the event that errors do occur, MontiThings offers various analysis procedures. Since different instances of an IoT system can differ greatly from each other, MontiThings offers device owners the possibility to influence the deployment. In its app store concept, MontiThings also decouples the software from the hardware development, thus perspectively avoiding e-waste and security problems caused by outdated software or required cloud services discontinued by the manufacturer.

Figure 1 provides a brief overview of the MontiThings ecosystem. At design time, the IoT developers are developing various artifacts. Through MontiThings C&C architectures, the business logic of the application can be defined. Data structures are specified using class diagrams. If the MontiThings C&C language

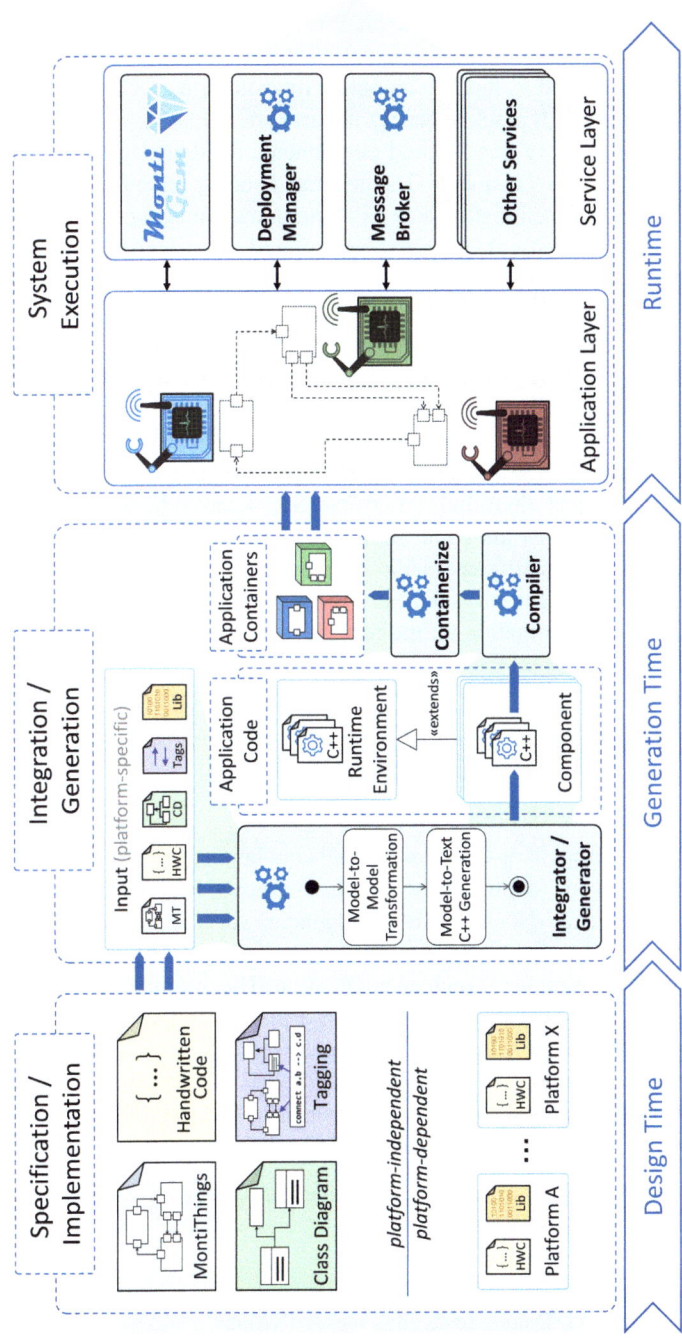

Fig. 1 Overview of the MontiThings ecosystem for model-driven IoT development. Models and code are used to generate C++ code, which is containerized and then downloaded by IoT devices. Multiple services interact with the devices to offer, e.g., communication and digital twins. Figure taken from [22]

is unsuitable to express a certain behavior, handwritten code in a GPL can be used as a supplement. Tagging languages can be used to define additional functionalities such as digital twins. In addition to these platform-independent artifacts, platform-specific artifacts, e.g., certain libraries for controlling a sensor, can also be used. All these artifacts are uploaded as input to an online repository (e.g., GitLab). There, a Continuous integration (CI) pipeline checks the artifacts, performs model-to-model transformations if necessary (e.g., to add components for digital twins), and then generates C++ code from the models. The generated code is linked against an RTE that provides common functionality such as communication between components. The generated code is then containerized and offered via a registry. From there, the IoT devices download the container images relevant to them. The Deployment Manager decides which images are relevant in each case. The Deployment Manager is one of several additional services that are operated at runtime alongside the actual application. These additional services enable communication between the components, provide digital twins, or offer analysis services, for example.

The rest of this chapter presents some parts of MontiThings in more detail: Sec. 2 first introduces the MontiThings language family. Sec. 3 then explains MontiThings' deployment algorithm. After that, Sec. 4 shows how tagging can be used to add digital twins to the application. Sec. 5 introduces MontiThings' app store concept. Sec. 6 shows different methods for error handling and analysis. Sec. 7 concludes. The MontiThings ecosystem can only be briefly described in this chapter. Please find additional information on the respective papers [6, 17–20, 20, 22] and dissertation [16].

2 The MontiThings Language Family

The core of MontiThings is a C&C language. This language is used to describe the business logic of IoT applications. For this purpose, IoT developers specify components that exchange data with other components via typed and directed ports. Instances of the components are connected to each other via connectors.

Figure 2 shows an example of such an application. The example shows a section of a fire alarm system. MontiThings uses both a textual and a graphical syntax. However, only the textual models are actually processed. The graphical models exist only for better understanding. Thus, the top two models are therefore two different representations of the same `FireAlarm` component.

The behavior of a component can be defined in four different ways:

1. By instantiating subcomponents and connecting them to the ports of the component instantiating them,
2. through a Java-like behavior language,
3. using statecharts,
4. using handwritten GPL code (e.g., in C++ or Python).

An Overview of the MontiThings Ecosystem for Model-Driven IoT Applications

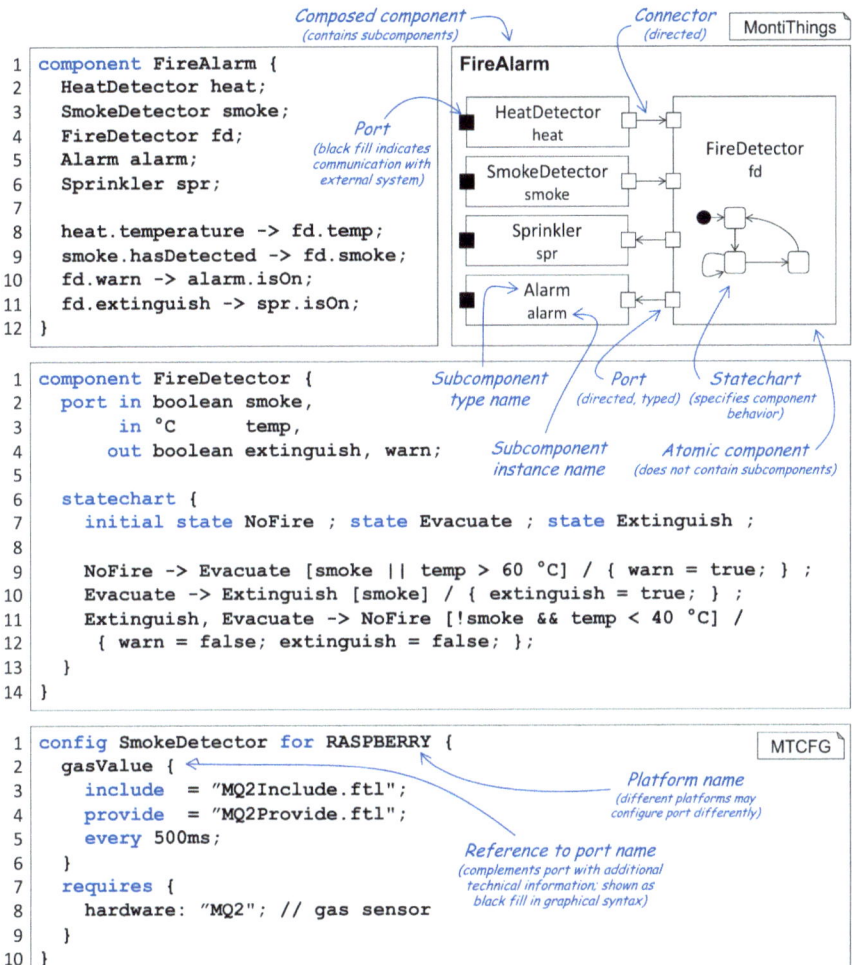

Fig. 2 An example of the graphical and textual syntax of MontiThings. The graphical syntax is only for better comprehensibility. Only the textual version is parsed. Figure adapted from [20]

Components that define their behavior through subcomponents are also called composed components. Components that describe their behavior via one of the other three methods are also called atomic components.

In the graphical syntax, one can see a difference between black and white ports. White ports represent a port that exchanges data with other components. Black ports represent a port for which the IoT developers have stored handwritten code. This handwritten code enables the port to access the hardware (e.g., a sensor). In the textual syntax, however, there is no difference between black and white ports. This makes it possible to use an override mechanism similar to that used by object-oriented languages to override base class methods in subclasses. If a port for which

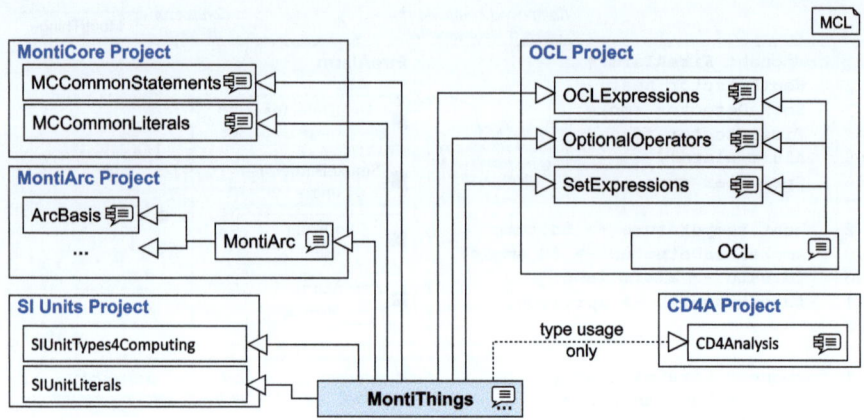

Fig. 3 Overview of languages from the MontiVerse incorporated by MontiThings' core language. Figure taken from [19]

handwritten code exists is connected using a connector, the handwritten code is automatically ignored, and only the connector is considered. This mechanism makes it easier to reuse components in different contexts. For example, a component that accesses hardware can be connected in the context of a test case with mock components that take on the role of the real hardware for the test.

MontiThings also serves as an example of how the MontiCore language workbench [15] can be used to build large languages. In total, MontiThings combines 46 grammars from the MontiCore language library in addition to its own grammars. An overview can be found in Fig. 3. Besides MontiArc, which is the basis for MontiThings, the type system and the expressions are especially worth mentioning. MontiThings reuses the primitive types of MontiCore. They are extended by the types of the International System of Units (SI) Units language. Hereby, it is possible to use SI Units like primitive data types. This can be seen, for example, in the middle model of Fig. 2, where °C is used like a normal data type. If two compatible but different types are to be converted into each other (e.g., km/h and m/s), MontiThings can automatically convert the values into each other in the background. This makes components more flexible to use, since the types of connected ports do not have to match but only have to be compatible to each other. If more complex data types are to be used, they can be defined via class diagrams of the Class diagrams for analysis (CD4A) project. MontiThings can import the symbols of such class diagrams and thus make them available to the components. These types can be instantiated using an object diagram-like syntax similar to Go's composite literals.[1]

Furthermore, MontiThings uses the Object constraint language (OCL) for expressions. The main use case here is to enable IoT developers to describe pre- and postconditions for component behavior. If an error is detected, the execution can

---

[1] https://go.dev/ref/spec.

An Overview of the MontiThings Ecosystem for Model-Driven IoT Applications 51

either be aborted at this point or a behavior can be defined to handle the exception. For example, a default value or the last measured value could be used if a sensor value deviates too much from the expected range. Parts of the OCL can also be used within the Java-like behavioral language at points where Boolean expressions are provided. For example, an if condition can be specified using the OCL.

Further language features of MontiThings' core language such as the definition of initial behavior, periodic behavior, or dynamics can be found in [16].

Besides the C&C language, the MontiThings project consists of other languages. The MontiThings Configuration Language (MTCFG, bottom model of Fig. 2) is a tagging language that can be used to customize components depending on their target platform. For example, different code templates can be selected for different platforms (e.g., Arduino vs. Raspberry Pi). Technical requirements can also be specified here (cf. Sec. 3).

Furthermore, MontiThings includes a language for specifying test cases based on [14]. Figure 4 gives an example of this language. Again, the graphical syntax is only for easier comprehension. MontiThings only parses textual models. Technically, MontiThings uses the test models to generate C++ tests written against the GoogleTest framework. Based on MontiCore's sequence diagram language, the

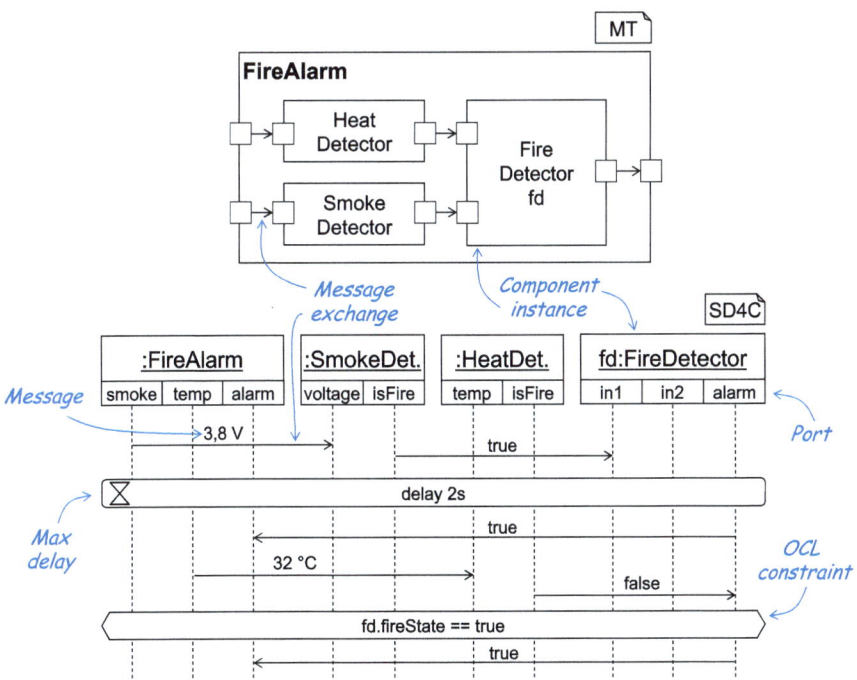

Fig. 4 White box test cases can be specified in the form of sequence diagrams that describe the message exchange between component instances. The graphical syntax of placing ports below components is taken from [14]. Figure taken from [16]

desired interaction between subcomponent instances of a composed component is represented in a sequence diagram. Of course, it is also possible to omit the specification of the inner workings and define a pure blackbox test where only the inputs and outputs are specified. In the depicted example, a smoke detector senses a voltage of 3.8 V and decides based on this voltage that there is a fire and informs the `FireDetector`'s `in1` port about it. After a maximum delay of 2 s, the `FireDetector` must have sent a message to the `alarm` port of the `FireAlarm` component. Then the temperature sensor detects a temperature of 32 °C and informs the `FireDetector` about this. Nevertheless, the `FireDetector` does not change its decision as it still has sufficient evidence of a fire based on the `SmokeDetector`'s earlier message.

3 Requirement-Based Self-Adaptive Deployment

IoT applications are often distributed applications. Partial applications must be deployed to a large number of IoT devices. In the same way, parts of applications can also be deployed to a cloud. The interaction of the IoT devices and the cloud results in the overall business logic. Furthermore, IoT applications can also include user interfaces via which the data of the application can be viewed or commands can be sent to the application. Such graphical user interfaces are not considered in this chapter.

IoT devices can be very different from each other. In addition to different computing power, they can also have different sensors and actuators. Consequently, the sub-applications cannot be deployed arbitrarily on the IoT devices. Instead, deployment requires precise planning of which devices should run which software. In addition to the purely technical framework conditions, the personal wishes of the device owners also play a role. For example, a device owner may wish not to install camera software provided by a social network on the devices in his bathroom. Legal requirements can also play a role. For example, in some countries, it is necessary to install a fire alarm in certain living spaces. A requirement could therefore be to install a fire alarm in every room, for example.

Furthermore, the deployment of IoT applications is not necessarily static. One reason for this is that IoT devices—unlike a television, for example, which is sold as a complete product—are often sold in extensible form. Many people initially buy a small number of IoT devices. If these devices prove successful, more devices are purchased. In this way, the IoT system is continuously expanded. The deployment of the software must adapt to these changes in the hardware accordingly. On the other hand, IoT devices can also fail. IoT devices often consist of inexpensive hardware and are often exposed to harsh environmental conditions. These and other factors favor a failure of the devices. Furthermore, IoT devices can of course also be deliberately removed by their owners. If an IoT device leaves the system, the deployment may have to be adjusted accordingly.

An Overview of the MontiThings Ecosystem for Model-Driven IoT Applications

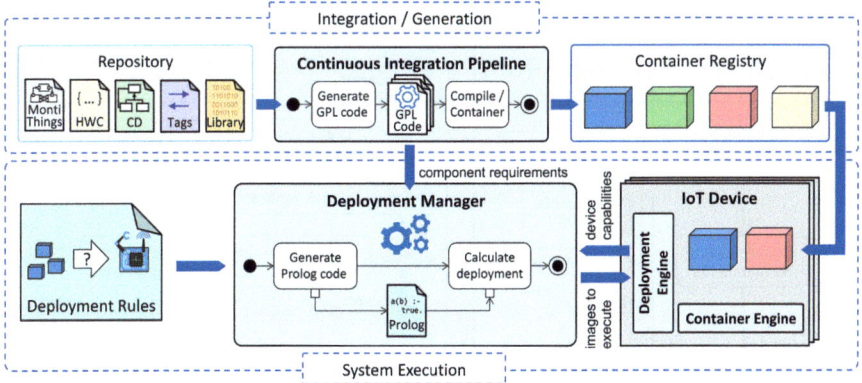

Fig. 5 The deployment manager generates Prolog code that calculates which IoT devices execute which images from the container registry based on technical requirements of the components, requirements of the device owners, and information about the IoT devices. Figure taken from [22]

MontiThings relies on a requirement-based deployment process. Figure 5 gives an overview of this deployment process. MontiThings distinguishes between technical requirements and local requirements. Technical requirements define the properties that a component must technically fulfill in order to be able to execute a component. They are defined by the IoT developers at design time. Local requirements, on the other hand, refer to the locality in which a component is executed. These requirements can be different for each instance of an application. They are defined by the device owners.

The technical and local requirements are merged in the Deployment Manager. In addition, the Deployment Manager receives information about the devices used in an IoT system. The Deployment Manager uses all this information to generate Prolog code that can be used to calculate a distribution of the software components to the IoT devices. In the process, Prolog facts are generated from the information about the IoT devices, and queries are generated from the requirements. A special feature here is that the generated Prolog code can not only calculate a distribution of the software components to the IoT devices but can also make counterproposals in the case of unfulfillable requirements. In particular, the purchase of new IoT devices and the modification (i.e., weakening) of the requirements can be suggested. Once a deployment is agreed upon with the device owner, the Deployment Manager communicates it to the IoT devices, which then download the (Docker) containers assigned to them according to the deployment.

Figure 6 shows the deployment process in more detail. First, IoT developers model their IoT components using MontiThings. In particular, they also specify the technical requirements of the components. If necessary, they also implement handwritten code to implement the behavior of the components. The IoT developers then upload all these artifacts to an online repository. There, a CI pipeline distributes the uploaded artifacts. First, the artifacts are checked for validity. If errors are

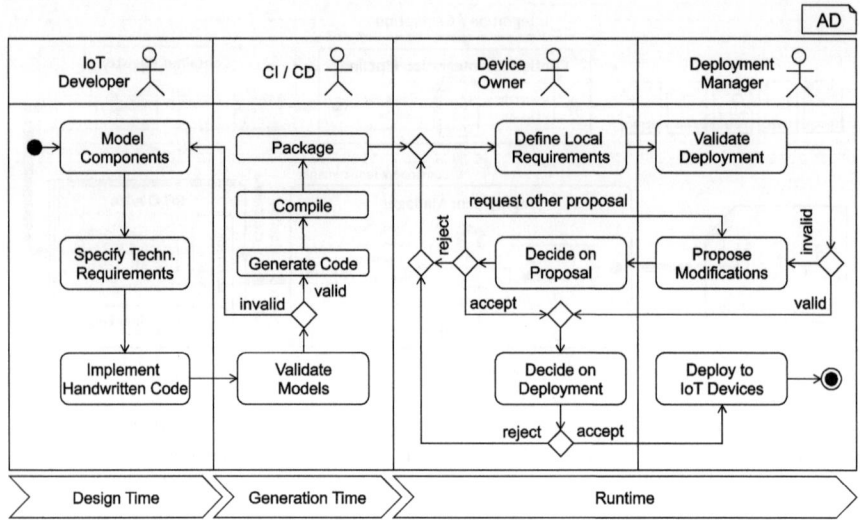

Fig. 6 Deployment process. The artifacts of the IoT developers are checked and provided by a CI/CD pipeline. The device owners negotiate with the deployment manager which devices should run which software. Figure taken from [20]

found, the IoT developers are asked to correct the errors with a corresponding error message. If the artifacts are accepted as valid, they are then used for code generation. The generated code is compiled and packaged into containers.

The device owners who want to deploy the application on their infrastructure must first specify their local requirements. MontiThings currently supports the following four types of local requirements:

1. A component shall (not) be deployed at a specific location,
2. A location requires a (minimum, maximum, or exact) number of components to be deployed there,
3. Two components may not be deployed to the same device,
4. A component requires a certain number of components (optionally in a similar location, i.e., the same room, floor, or building).

The Deployment Manager first validates these local requirements. If a valid deployment can be found taking into account the requirements, the device owners can decide whether they want to install this deployment on their devices. If no deployment can be found, the Deployment Manager suggests changes to the device owners. It is always possible to reject the proposed changes. In this case, the Deployment Manager calculates another proposal. In order not to overload the device owners with very similar proposals, the proposals are filtered so that the rejection of a proposal automatically counts as a rejection of all supersets of this proposal. For example, if the device owners refuse to buy a new fire alarm for the bathroom, a theoretically possible proposal to buy one fire alarm for the bathroom and one for the kitchen is automatically rejected.

An Overview of the MontiThings Ecosystem for Model-Driven IoT Applications

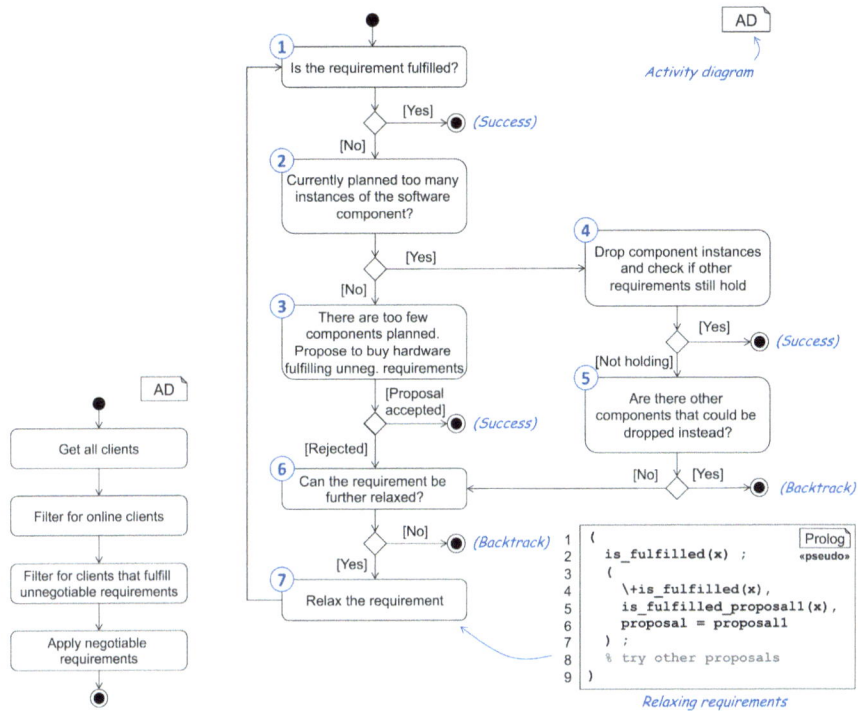

Fig. 7 Overview of the Prolog code generated by Deployment Manager. Left: high-level workflow. Right: applying a single negotiable requirement. Figure taken from [20]

The process of how the automatically generated Prolog code processes the requirements is shown in more detail in Fig. 7. First, Prolog searches the list of all known IoT devices for the devices that are currently online and thus available for deployment. Based on this list, it then identifies the devices that meet the technical requirements. Since the IoT developers are not involved in the deployment process, their technical requirements are considered non-negotiable in the process. If a device does not meet the technical requirements of a component, it cannot execute the component. Device owners cannot overrule this decision. After applying the non-negotiable requirements, the local requirements are checked. These are assumed to be negotiable because the equipment owners are involved in the deployment process and can respond to counterproposals. The reaction includes in particular the possibility to reject all counterproposals and to cancel the deployment, i.e., to consider the local requirements as non-negotiable as well.

When Prolog considers a local requirement, it first checks whether the requirement is already satisfied by the current allocation of components to IoT devices (1 in Fig. 7). If this is the case, one can proceed to the next requirement. If the requirement is not fulfilled, it is first checked whether too many IoT devices are currently executing the corresponding component (2). This can occur, for example, if device owners require a particular component to be deployed *a maximum of 5 times*. If this is the case, components are removed from IoT devices using backtracking, and it is checked whether the requirement can be fulfilled in this way while complying with the previously processed requirements (4 and 5). If the component is not scheduled too often, it is handled that a component is not yet scheduled frequently enough. In this case, it is first checked whether the requirement can be met by purchasing more hardware (3). Only if this is not the case is it suggested that requirements be reduced (6 and 7). In order not to overload the device owners with requests that may not have any influence on the ultimate fulfillment of the deployment later in the process, the modification proposals are first collected before they are presented to the device owners until a theoretically valid deployment is found. The Deployment Manager implicitly assumes that all change requests are accepted. Should a valid deployment be found with this, the proposed changes will be offered to the device owners in a bundle.

Creating local requirements requires some knowledge of the software components of the IoT system. This is not desirable in some cases. On the one hand, because it requires IoT developers to disclose their software architecture to a certain extent and, on the other hand, because it requires training from device owners. Therefore, to increase the level of abstraction, MontiThings also offers an approach based on feature diagrams. Here, IoT developers create a feature diagram that models the features they envision in their application and their dependencies on each other. They use tagging to relate the features to the software components. This is illustrated in Fig. 8. This enables device owners to select the desired features based on the abstract feature diagram. Furthermore, device owners can run automatic analyses through which feature configurations are automatically calculated. For example, the largest possible feature configuration can be calculated or the largest possible feature configuration that can be deployed with the existing IoT devices. Behind the feature analyses lies the previously described requirements-based mechanism, which generates Prolog code from requirements.

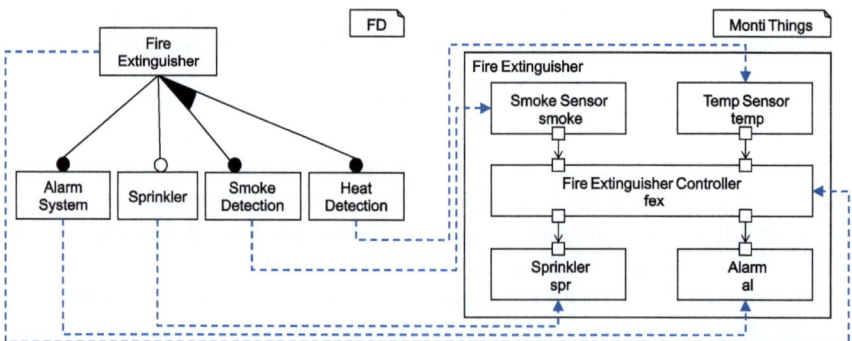

Fig. 8 Feature Diagrams can be used to tag architecture models. In this way, multiple components can be combined into a common feature. Device owners can thus select the desired features at a higher level of abstraction. Figure taken from [6]

For this purpose, requirements are generated from the feature configurations, e.g., that a certain component must be deployed in the system so that a certain feature is fulfilled.

4 Synthesizing Digital Twins

Once the components are deployed to the target infrastructure, the next challenge is to observe or influence the system. For this purpose, digital twins can be created. In this chapter, we will refer to the definition of digital twins that the Chair of Software Engineering has developed through several years of discussions and a systematic literature review [8]:

Definition 1 "Digital Twin, V2.1
 A *digital twin* of a system consists of

- a set of models of the system and
- a set of digital shadows, both of which are purposefully updated on a regular basis, and
- provides a set of services to use both purposefully with respect to the original system.

The digital twin interacts with the original system by

- providing useful information about the system's context and
- sending it control commands." [30]

MontiThings offers the possibility to create digital twins based on class diagrams and C&C architecture models. The class diagram represents the data structure of a Digital twin information system (DTIS). In the actual implementation, the business logic of the system is created as usual with MontiThings. The information system is created with the help of MontiGem [1, 12], a tool for the model-driven creation of web applications. Figure 9 gives an overview of the process of synthesizing digital twins. After the IoT applications and the web application, and thus MontiThings models and class diagrams, have been developed (step 1 and 2 in Fig. 9), a system integrator connects the models together (step 3). For this purpose, he connects attributes of the class diagram with ports of the MontiThings architecture by means of tagging.

For this purpose, let's look at exemplary models of a fire extinguishing system in Fig. 10. The associated tagging model that the system integrator uses to connect the two models is shown in Fig. 11. First, the integrator uses the `identify` keyword to distinguish the different IoT devices from the web system. This can be done either by an entry in the database (especially if the digital twin is created before the real system) (ll. 1–5) or by the system automatically assigning identifiers to the IoT devices and storing them in the database (ll. 6–8). After that, the ports of the architecture models are connected to the attributes of the class diagram. The direction plays a role here. On the one hand, the real system can have data sent to its

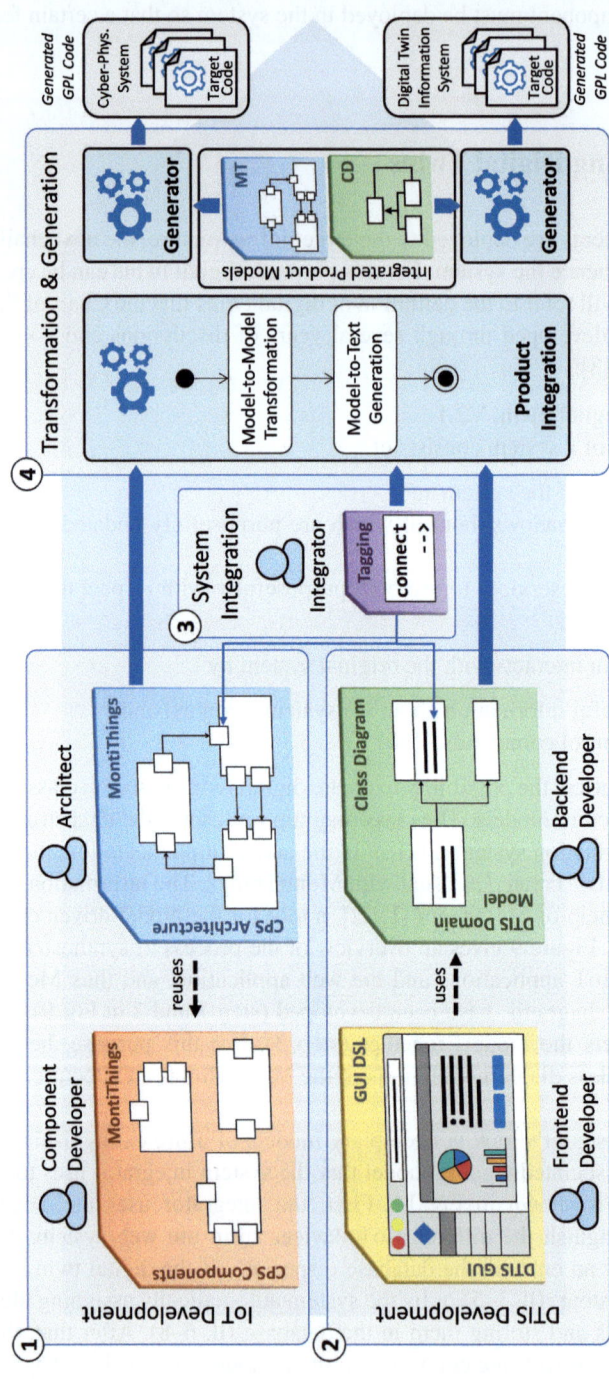

Fig. 9 Tagging allows MontiThings models to be associated with class diagrams that define the data structure of a web application. Via model-to-model transformation, the necessary model elements are added that keep the web system as a digital twin in sync with the IoT system. Figure adapted from [17]

An Overview of the MontiThings Ecosystem for Model-Driven IoT Applications 59

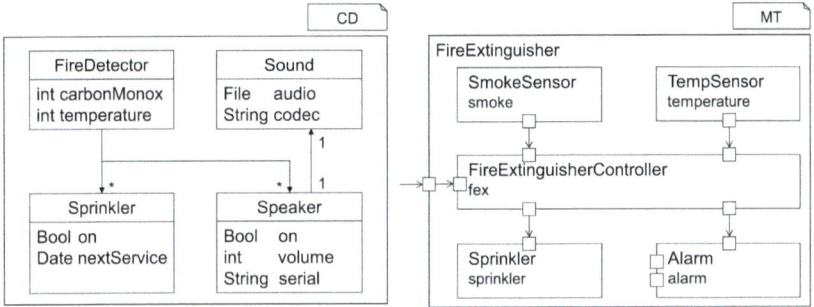

Fig. 10 An example of a fire alarm application. Left: the data structure of the web application. Right: the model of the IoT application. Figure taken from [17]

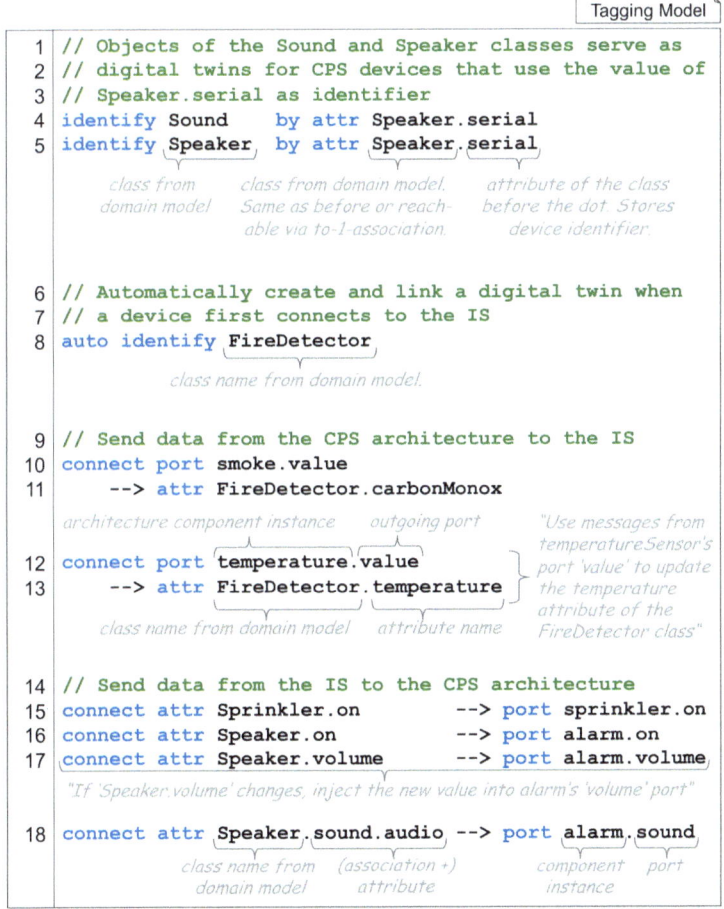

Fig. 11 The tagging language associates attributes of a class diagram with ports of a C&C architecture (ll. 9-18). Additionally, it defines how the IoT devices identify themselves to the web application (ll. 1-8). Figure taken from [17]

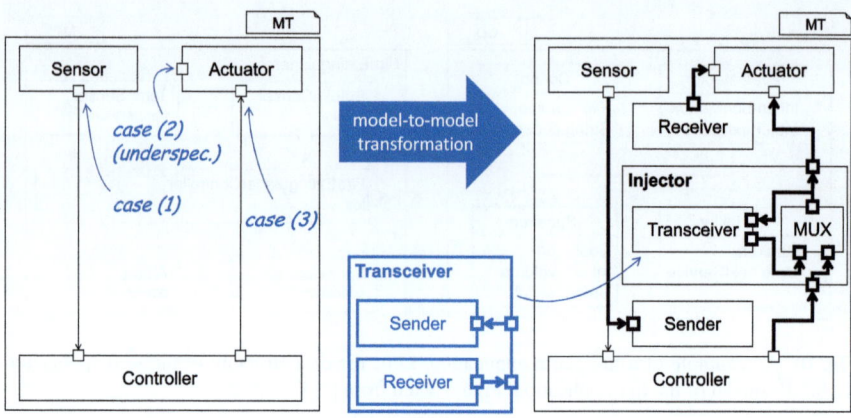

Fig. 12 Model-to-model transformations add components to the C&C architecture that synchronize with the digital twin. Elements created by model-to-model transformations are shown in bold. Figure adapted from [17]

digital twin by sending data from the port to the attribute in the class diagram (and thus to the database generated from it) (ll. 9–13). On the other hand, the digital twin can send data to its real counterpart by defining the reverse direction in the tagging (ll. 14–18).

Once the models are connected, the next step is to process them through model-to-model transformations (step 4 in Fig. 9). The transformations give the models additional elements that keep the real system and its twin in sync with each other. In the following, we will look at the transformations of the architecture. Interested readers can find a more detailed explanation of the method and the transformations of the web system in [17]. Figure 12 gives an overview of the architecture transformations. We distinguish three cases:

1. Connecting an outgoing port
2. Connecting an incoming port that currently has no incoming connectors
3. Connecting an incoming port that already has an incoming connector

In the first case, we add a new component via transformation that receives all data sent through the port and forwards it to the digital twin. In the second case, we do the reverse and add a component that receives data from the digital twin and forwards it to the port. In the third case, the already-existing connector must be resolved. We replace it with a new Injector component. On the one hand, this contains a Transceiver component that can both forward data to the digital twin and receive data from it. The situation can arise here that the value of the digital twin does not correspond to the value that the component receives via the connector replaced by the transformation. To resolve this situation, the Injector component includes a MUX that decides whether to use the data from the digital twin or from the real system. Users can control this MUX in the web interface. It enables them to prevent their desired values from being overwritten by the real system in the next moment. For example, in our fire alarm, a test alarm can be triggered even if the sensors report that there is no fire, and the alarm should therefore be switched off.

5 IoT App Store Concept

When IoT devices are sold today, they are usually sold as a single product consisting of hardware and software. This gives the provider a great degree of control over the IoT devices. Users are usually not free to install new software on their IoT devices. If the manufacturer of the IoT devices now decides to change the rules of the game after the devices have been purchased, e.g., to introduce a subscription model, the user usually has little recourse against this. If the device manufacturer decides to shut down the cloud services required to operate the devices or simply goes bankrupt, the devices can become electronic waste. This practice is neither economically nor ecologically sustainable.

One way to solve this problem is to introduce an app store that would allow software to be installed independently of the hardware manufacturer. Such an IoT app store has already been proposed by various scientists, e.g., [2, 5, 25]. Consequently, MontiThings also includes a concept for an app store. Figure 13 shows an overview of MontiThings' app store concept. This concept is mainly based on the deployment algorithm already presented. A key feature of the concept is the clear separation between hardware and software development. The software developer specifies his application as previously introduced by C&C architecture models. In addition, their hardware requirements are specified for each component. The hardware requirements are specified thereby with the help of OCL. Thus, for example, also ranges of hardware requirements can be defined, e.g., a camera with at least 4 megapixels (instead of *exactly* 4 megapixels). Optionally, other models such as a feature diagram can be used to define high-level features. The applications specified in this way are transformed into executable container images by a CI/Continuous deployment (CD) pipeline.

On the hardware side, device developers develop their IoT devices and the corresponding drivers to access their devices. In addition, they specify the properties of their IoT devices in the form of an object diagram. On the software side, the IoT devices have the following software stack: A container engine executes the containers of the actual IoT application as specified by the deployment algorithm. A message broker enables the device-internal communication between the application containers and the hardware drivers. The hardware access manager coordinates which application containers access which sensors and actuators. This is particularly relevant if there is more than one instance of a hardware component, e.g., *four weight sensors*. It ensures that the application containers do not conflict with each other. The hardware access manager tells the application containers on which topics they can communicate with the requested hardware. The hardware access manager is then no longer involved in the subsequent data exchange.

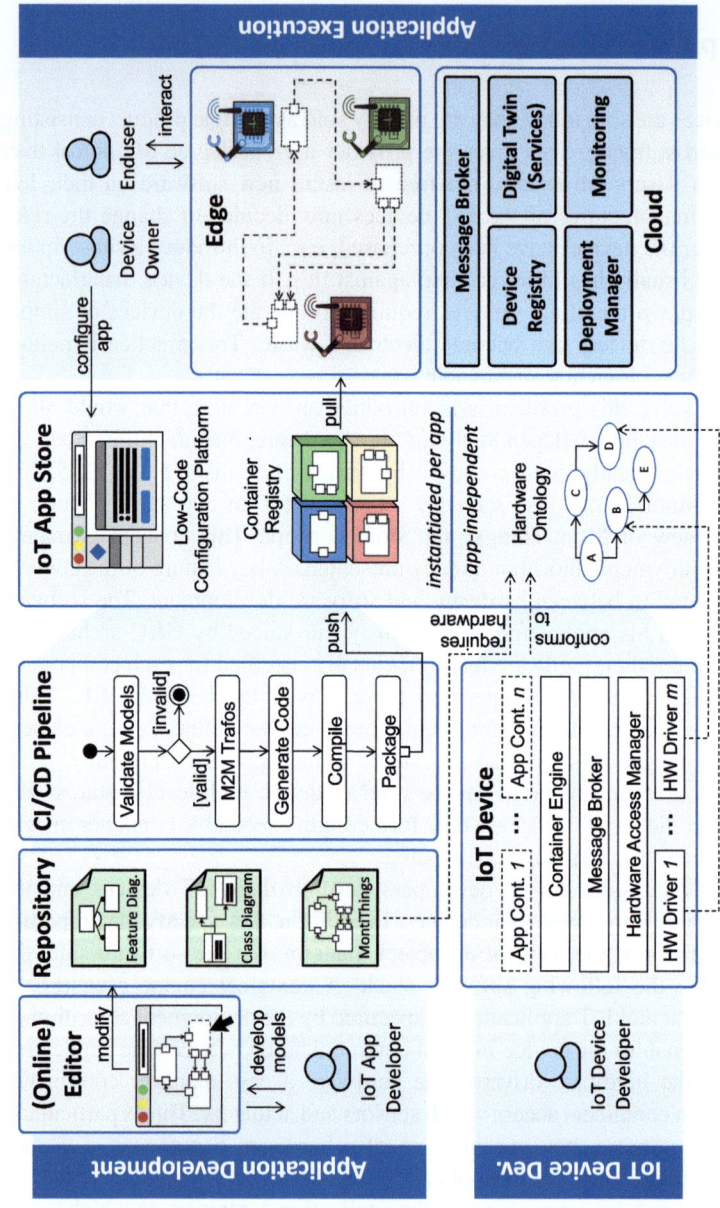

Fig. 13 MontiThings' app store concept decouples hardware and software development. Software developers specify technical requirements for components in OCL. Hardware developers describe technical properties of their devices via object diagrams. A hardware ontology provided by the app store harmonizes the requirements and device properties. Figure taken from [6]

To determine which hardware can execute which software components, the deployment algorithm must now check the OCL requirements of the software against the object diagrams that describe the hardware. For integration into our deployment algorithm, both are transformed into Prolog. The details can be found in [6]. To enable the software and hardware developers to match OCL and object diagrams in the end, even if the developers do not know each other, the app store provides a hardware ontology in the form of a class diagram. This class diagram specifies which types of hardware the app store expects in principle and which properties must be defined for such hardware. For example, it can be defined that cameras are a type of sensor and a width and height in pixels must be specified for each of the images shot. The rest of the deployment process then takes place as usual, i.e., device owners can specify additional local rules in a web interface. The deployment algorithm then decides which IoT devices should execute which software components and the IoT devices download the software accordingly from a container registry.

6 Failure Handling in MontiThings Applications

IoT devices are often based on low-cost hardware. One disadvantage of this hardware is that it is not particularly protected against failures or errors. IoT software must therefore be able to deal with the fact that errors occur. Such errors range from incorrect sensor values to completely failing devices.

MontiThings' C&C models describe the business logic of IoT applications. Technical details are not visible at this level of abstraction. Figure 14 shows an example of this. Even if the application has been modeled correctly in itself, various errors can occur at runtime due to unreliable hardware. Sensors can provide incorrect readings, affecting the flow of the system. Similarly, software errors such as incorrectly set clocks can affect the system. Network problems can delay or completely prevent the delivery of messages. This is especially noticeable on mobile devices that must rely on a cellular connection.

Frameworks for developing IoT applications must therefore be able to handle errors. Thus, MontiThings provides several mechanisms for analyzing and handling errors, which are summarized in the remainder of this section.

6.1 *Record and Replay for Handling Failing Devices*

The strongest form of failure of an IoT device is its complete failure. MontiThings deployment algorithm can detect failing devices by missing heartbeat messages. When a device fails, the components that the device was executing before its failure (if possible) are reassigned to another IoT device. However, this new device is not in the same state as the failed device before its failure.

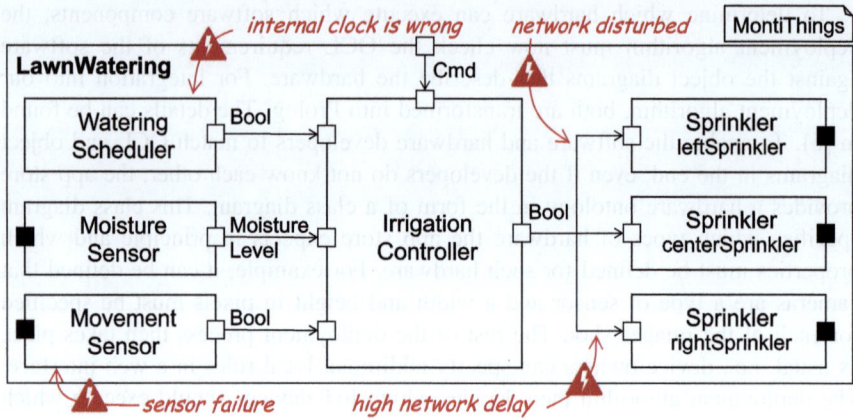

Fig. 14 (Hardware) errors that are not caused by the business logic may not be detected directly in the C&C architecture. Figure taken from [18]

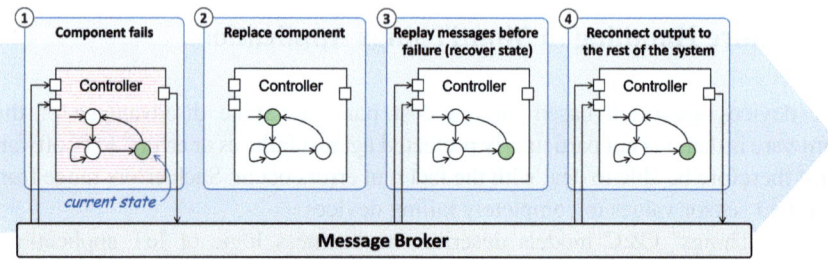

Fig. 15 If components fail (due to hardware defects), the components that replace them are not necessarily in the same state. MontiThings restores the state of the failed component by resending messages sent to the failed component to the new component. Figure taken from [22]

To address the issue of complete hardware failure, MontiThings uses record-and-replay. Figure 15 shows an overview of this. MontiThings continuously records the messages exchanged between the devices during runtime. If one device fails, the deployment algorithm starts the component on another device. When the new component is launched, incoming connectors are first connected to a replayer. The recorded messages are then used to put the new component in the state of the failed component. The replayer plays back the recorded messages. Once the messages are replayed and thus the state is restored, the ports are connected to the rest. In particular, the outgoing ports are connected only now, so that the messages sent as a by-product during state recovery do not affect the rest of the system.

This procedure has a complexity of $\mathcal{O}(n)$, where n is the number of messages. To improve this, components can periodically serialize their state and store it in the record-and-replay system. If a component fails, only the constant number of messages since the last state serialization has to be replayed. Thus the complexity sinks to $\mathcal{O}(1)$.

6.2 Recording and Transformation-Based Replaying

In less severe failure cases, only parts of the IoT system fail or misbehave. One problem in analyzing such errors is that they often cannot be reproduced under laboratory conditions. To analyze such faults, MontiThings therefore offers the possibility to record the behavior of the system and reproduce it later under deterministic conditions. Figure 16 shows an overview of this procedure. The procedure consists of the following steps:

1. IoT developers model their application through a C&C architecture as usual.
2. the developers' models are used to generate (C++) code that is executed by the IoT devices.
3. during the runtime of the system, a recorder records all messages exchanged between the devices. Metadata is also recorded. This includes, for example, what time elapsed between sending and receiving a message. As a result, system traces are created that contain the recorded system behavior.
4. a transformation engine uses the architecture models originally used by the generator and the system traces to create a new architecture model, the reproduction model. This model is a modified form of the original model that allows the replay of the system traces.
5. from the reproduction model, a new (non-distributed) application and (C++) code are created. Unlike the original version of the application, this is not a distributed application but a single binary. We call this application Reproduction Executable.
6. the Reproduction Executable can now be analyzed by the IoT developer using the usual debugging tools such as *gdb*. In particular, he now also has the possibility, for example, to set breakpoints and thus stop the entire system. Inspecting the global state of the system like this is not easily possible in a distributed system [31].

In step 4, the reproduction model was created from the architecture and system traces. Figure 17 gives a detailed insight into the relationship between the original model and the reproduction model. The transformation engine looks for places in the original model where the hardware or the environment affects the execution of the IoT system. At these points, the corresponding model elements are replaced or extended in such a way that the influences are removed and deterministically reproduced for the reproduction. In particular, sensors and actuators are replaced by components. By the mechanism described in Sec. 2, it is sufficient to insert new components and connect their ports to the black ports for this purpose. The new components then mock the real hardware by, for example, replaying recorded sensor values at the right time. Where components are connected, new components are introduced that simulate the recorded network properties. This means in particular delaying or losing messages. Where components execute a computation (atomic components), a wrapper is introduced around the components, which maps the

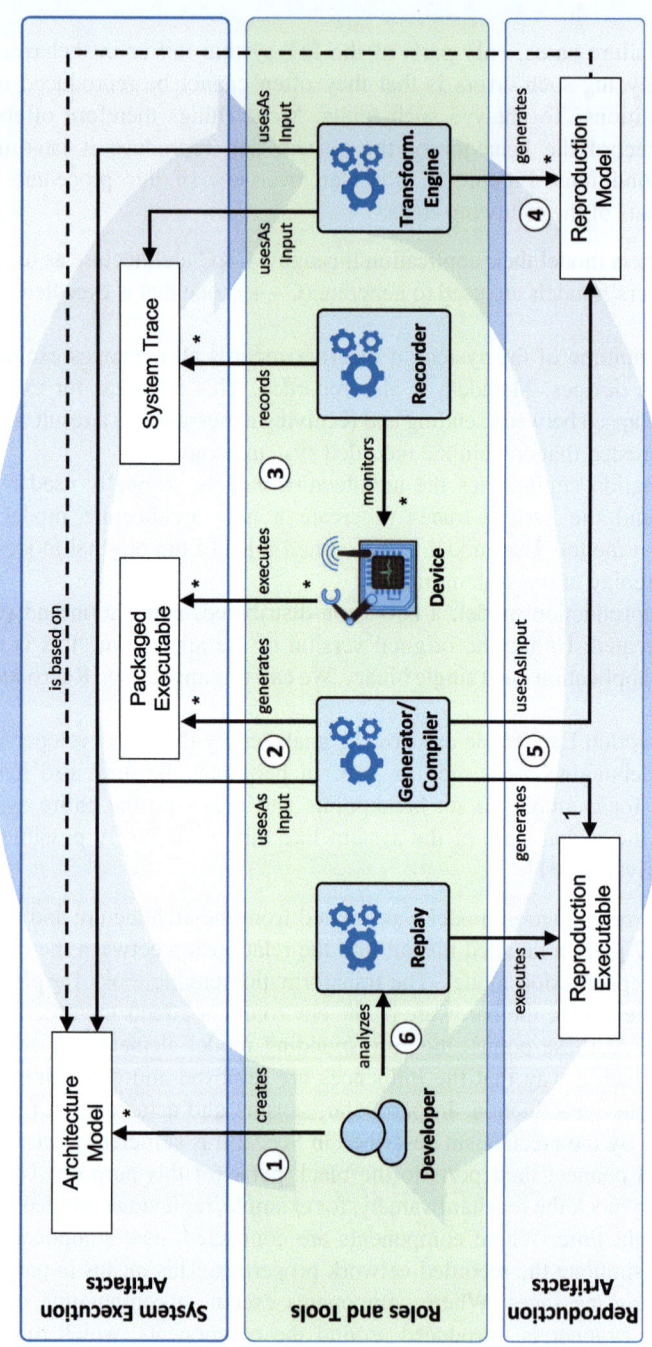

Fig. 16 Developers can recreate recorded errors in a reproduction. During runtime, exchanged data and metadata are recorded. These are used to create a reproduction model. This reproduction model can be analyzed by the developer. Figure taken from [18]

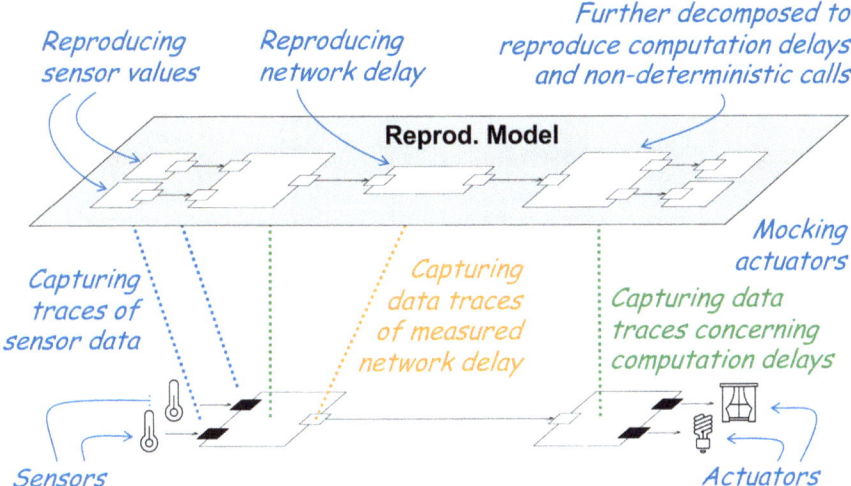

Fig. 17 The reproduction model (top) replaces hardware- or environment-dependent model elements in the original model (bottom) with elements that replay the recorded data. Figure adapted from [18]

delay by the computations of the processor. Further details like the handling of non-deterministic computations can be read in [18].

6.3 Web-Based Failure Tracing

The method presented in the previous section analyzes faults in an environment separated from the real system. Another popular option for debugging is the analysis of logs. The difficulty with IoT devices is that they are distributed applications. The logs of the individual IoT devices are therefore not necessarily available in a coherent form. If errors occur, such as clocks not being perfectly synchronized, the logs can be misleading. In order to analyze errors, a large amount of additional information must be logged that may not be relevant to the analysis of the problem at hand. These log messages further complicate troubleshooting by distracting from the relevant messages.

In practice, error analysis often takes the form of noticing misbehavior at a certain point. In the best case, this misbehavior can be detected in the logs. From this point, the developers perform a reverse search and try to identify how the error occurred. If the application is modeled in the form of a C&C application, the modeled data flow yields additional information that can narrow down the error search: by knowing which component exchanges data with which other components, log messages can be filtered.

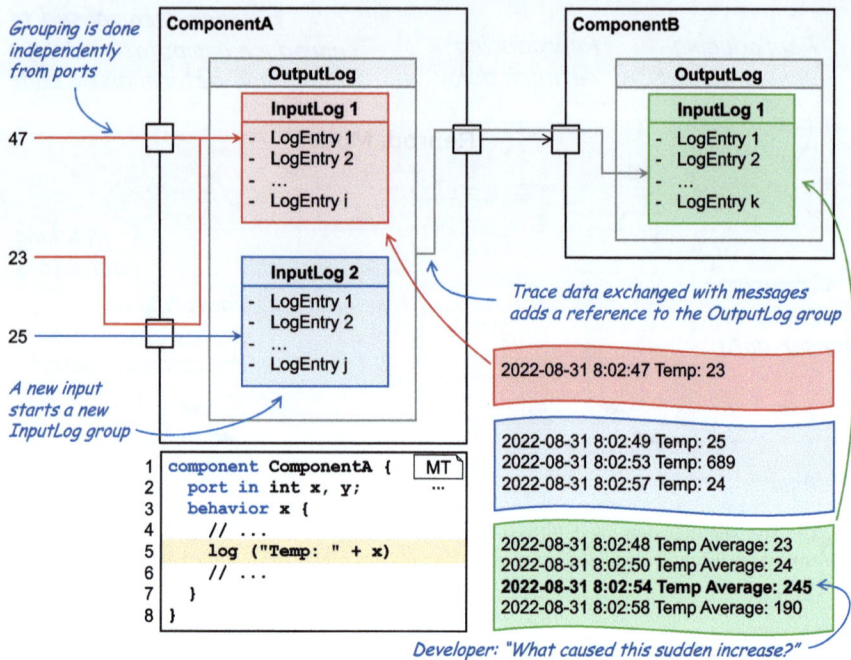

Fig. 18 MontiThings correlates log messages from interacting components. Thus, in large logs, it is possible to trace which logs have led to the generation of a log message. Figure taken from [21] and based on [23]

MontiThings offers a tool for this that lets developers interact with the real system at runtime. The logs of each individual component are displayed. If a developer clicks on a log message, it is displayed which other log messages are related to this log message. For this purpose, a graph is built that graphically represents the architecture, reducing it to the relevant communication paths.

Technically, this works as shown in Fig. 18. When a message arrives at a port, MontiThings starts to bundle log messages. A unique ID is assigned for each bundle. If the component now sends a message on a port in response to the incoming message, the ID of the current bundle of log messages is also sent. In this way, a graph structure of bundles of log messages can be created. When a developer asks for the origin of a particular log message, the log system communicates with the components to get the log messages associated with the IDs. Details about this process can be found in [21].

7 Conclusion

Developing distributed IoT applications based on heterogeneous, error-prone IoT devices is complex. GPLs are not designed for this task. Model-driven approaches promise to make this problem manageable through abstraction. In this chapter, we presented *MontiThings*, a model-driven ecosystem for developing, deploying, and analyzing IoT applications. MontiThings also outlines an app store concept that decouples hardware and software development. Overall, MontiThings' deployment algorithm and app store concept help give device owners more control over their devices. By negotiating deployment with device owners, the deployment algorithm increases the flexibility of IoT systems. Possible future work includes more automated exploitation of cloud services, integration of user-defined behavior (including, e.g., through Large Language Models), and generation of user-understandable explanations for system behavior.

Source Code

MontiThings is available on GitHub: https://github.com/MontiCore/montithings.

Acronyms

C&C	Component and connector	45
CD	Continuous deployment	61
CD4A	Class diagrams for analysis	50
CI	Continuous integration	170
DTIS	Digital twin information system	57
GPL	General-purpose programming language	46
IoT	Internet of Things	45
OCL	Object constraint language	50
SI	International System of Units	50

Acknowledgments Funded by the Deutsche Forschungsgemeinschaft (DFG, German Research Foundation) under Germany's Excellence Strategy—EXC 2023 Internet of Production—390621612. Website: https://www.iop.rwth-aachen.de.

References

1. Adam, K., Michael, J., Netz, L., Rumpe, B., Varga, S.: Enterprise Information Systems in Academia and Practice: Lessons learned from a MBSE Project. In: 40 Years EMISA: Digital Ecosystems of the Future: Methodology, Techniques and Applications (EMISA'19). Lecture Notes in Informatics, vol. P-304, pp. 59–66. Gesellschaft für Informatik e.V., Bonn (2020)

2. Ahmad, S., Mehmood, F., Mehmood, A., Kim, D.H.: Design and Implementation of Decoupled IoT Application Store: A Novel Prototype for Virtual Objects Sharing and Discovery. Electronics **8**(3) (2019)
3. Angelsmark, O., Persson, P.: Requirement-Based Deployment of Applications in Calvin. In: Žarko, I.P., Broering, A., Soursos, S., Serrano, M., (eds.) Interoperability and Open-Source Solutions for the Internet of Things, pp. 72–87. Springer International Publishing, Cham (2017)
4. Brooks, C., Jerad, C., Kim, H., Lee, E.A., Lohstroh, M., Nouvelletz, V., Osyk, B., Weber, M.: A Component Architecture for the Internet of Things. Proc. IEEE **106**(9), 1527–1542 (2018)
5. Bröring, A., Schmid, S., Schindhelm, C.K., Khelil, A., Käbisch, S., Kramer, D., Le Phuoc, D., Mitic, J., Anicic, D., Teniente, E.: Enabling IoT Ecosystems through Platform Interoperability. IEEE Softw. **34**(1), 54–61 (2017)
6. Butting, A., Kirchhof, J.C., Kleiss, A., Michael, J., Orlov, R., Rumpe, B.: Model-Driven IoT App Stores: Deploying Customizable Software Products to Heterogeneous Devices. In: Proceedings of the 21th ACM SIGPLAN International Conference on Generative Programming: Concepts and Experiences (GPCE 22), pp. 108–121. ACM, New York (2022)
7. Corno, F., De Russis, L., Sáenz, J.P.: How is Open Source Software Development Different in Popular IoT Projects? IEEE Access **8**, 28337–28348 (2020)
8. Dalibor, M., Jansen, N., Rumpe, B., Schmalzing, D., Wachtmeister, L., Wimmer, M., Wortmann, A.: A cross-domain systematic mapping study on software engineering for Digital Twins. J. Syst. Softw. **193** (2022)
9. Dias, J.P., Restivo, A., Ferreira, H.S.: Designing and constructing internet-of-Things systems: An overview of the ecosystem. Internet of Things **19**, 100529 (2022)
10. Eclipse Foundation: IoT Developer Survey 2020. [Online]. Available: https://outreach.eclipse.foundation/eclipse-iot-developer-survey-2020 (2020). Last accessed 20 June 2021
11. Eclipse Mita Project Website: [Online]. Available: https://www.eclipse.org/mita/. Last accessed: 13 April 2023
12. Gerasimov, A., Heuser, P., Ketteniß, H., Letmathe, P., Michael, J., Netz, L., Rumpe, B., Varga, S.: Generated Enterprise Information Systems: MDSE for Maintainable Co-Development of Frontend and Backend. In: Michael, J., Bork, D., (eds.) Companion Proceedings of Modellierung 2020 Short, Workshop and Tools & Demo Papers, pp. 22–30. CEUR Workshop Proceedings (2020)
13. Harrand, N., Fleurey, F., Morin, B., Husa, K.E.: ThingML: A Language and Code Generation Framework for Heterogeneous Targets. In: Proceedings of the ACM/IEEE 19th International Conference on Model Driven Engineering Languages and Systems, MODELS '16, pp. 125–135. ACM, New York (2016)
14. Hermerschmidt, L., Perez, A.N., Rumpe, B.: A Model-based Software Development Kit for the SensorCloud Platform. In: Workshop Wissenschaftliche Ergebnisse der Trusted Cloud Initiative, pp. 125–140. Springer, Schweiz (2013)
15. Hölldobler, K., Kautz, O., Rumpe, B.: MontiCore Language Workbench and Library Handbook: Edition 2021. Aachener Informatik-Berichte, Software Engineering, Band 48. Shaker Verlag, Herzogenrath (2021)
16. Kirchhof, J.C.: Model-Driven Development, Deployment, and Analysis of Internet of Things Applications. Aachener Informatik-Berichte, Software Engineering, Band 54. Shaker Verlag, Herzogenrath (2023)
17. Kirchhof, J.C., Michael, J., Rumpe, B., Varga, S., Wortmann, A.: Model-driven Digital Twin Construction: Synthesizing the Integration of Cyber-Physical Systems with Their Information Systems. In: Proceedings of the 23rd ACM/IEEE International Conference on Model Driven Engineering Languages and Systems, pp. 90–101. ACM, New York (2020)
18. Kirchhof, J.C., Malcher, L., Rumpe, B.: Understanding and Improving Model-Driven IoT Systems through Accompanying Digital Twins. In Tilevich, E., De Roover, C. (eds.) Proceedings of the 20th ACM SIGPLAN International Conference on Generative Programming: Concepts and Experiences (GPCE '21), pp. 197–209. ACM SIGPLAN, New York (2021)
19. Kirchhof, J.C., Kleiss, A., Michael, J., Rumpe, B., Wortmann, A.: Efficiently Engineering IoT Architecture Languages—An Experience Report (Poster). STAF 2022 Workshop Proceedings:

10th International Workshop on Bidirectional Transformations (BX 2022), 2nd International Workshop on Foundations and Practice of Visual Modeling (FPVM 2022) and 2nd International Workshop on MDE for Smart IoT Systems (MeSS 2022) (co-located with Software Technologies: Applications and Foundations federation of conferences (STAF 2022)) (2022)
20. Kirchhof, J.C., Kleiss, A., Rumpe, B., Schmalzing, D., Schneider, P., Wortmann, A.: Model-driven Self-adaptive Deployment of Internet of Things Applications with Automated Modification Proposals. ACM Trans. Internet of Things **3**(4) (2022)
21. Kirchhof, J.C., Malcher, L., Michael, J., Rumpe, B., Wortmann, A.: Web-Based Tracing for Model-Driven Applications. In: Proceedings of the 48th Euromicro Conference Series on Software Engineering and Advanced Applications (SEAA'22). In Press (2022)
22. Kirchhof, J.C., Rumpe, B., Schmalzing, D., Wortmann, A.: MontiThings: Model-driven Development and Deployment of Reliable IoT Applications. J. Syst. Softw. **183**, 111087 (2022)
23. Malcher, L.: Reconstructing the Behavior of Cyber-Physical Systems through Digital Shadows and Deterministic Replay in Component & Connector Architectures. Master Thesis. RWTH Aachen University. Software Engineering Group (2021)
24. Morin, B., Harrand, N., Fleurey, F.: Model-Based Software Engineering to Tame the IoT Jungle. IEEE Softw. **34**(1), 30–36 (2017)
25. Munjin, D., Morin, J.-H.: Toward Internet of Things Application Markets. In: IEEE International Conference on Green Computing and Communications, pp. 156–162 (2012)
26. Nguyen, X.T., Tran, H.T., Baraki, H., Geihs, K.: FRASAD: A framework for model-driven IoT Application Development. In: IEEE 2nd World Forum on Internet of Things (WF-IoT), pp. 387–392 (2015)
27. Node-RED—Low-code programming for event-driven applications: [Online]. Available: https://nodered.org. Last accessed 13 April 2023
28. Persson, P., Angelsmark, O.: Calvin – Merging Cloud and IoT. Procedia Comput. Sci. **52**, 210–217 (2015). 6th International Conference on Ambient Systems, Networks and Technologies (ANT 2015)
29. Persson, P., Angelsmark, O.: Kappa: Serverless IoT deployment. In: Proceedings of the 2nd International Workshop on Serverless Computing, WoSC '17, pp. 16–21. Association for Computing Machinery, New York (2017)
30. Rumpe, B., Michael, J.: Digital Twins 2.1. [Online]. Available: https://www.se-rwth.de/essay/Digital-Twin-Definition/. Last accessed 05 April 2023
31. Serror, M., Kirchhof, J.C., Stoffers, M., Wehrle, K., Gross J.: Code-Transparent Discrete Event Simulation for Time-Accurate Wireless Prototyping. In: Proceedings of the 2017 ACM SIGSIM Conference on Principles of Advanced Discrete Simulation, SIGSIM-PADS '17, pp. 161–172. Association for Computing Machinery, New York (2017)
32. Taivalsaari, A., Mikkonen, T.: A Roadmap to the Programmable World: Software Challenges in the IoT Era. IEEE Softw. **34**(1), 72–80 (2017)

Open Access This chapter is licensed under the terms of the Creative Commons Attribution 4.0 International License (http://creativecommons.org/licenses/by/4.0/), which permits use, sharing, adaptation, distribution and reproduction in any medium or format, as long as you give appropriate credit to the original author(s) and the source, provide a link to the Creative Commons licence and indicate if changes were made.

The images or other third party material in this chapter are included in the chapter's Creative Commons licence, unless indicated otherwise in a credit line to the material. If material is not included in the chapter's Creative Commons licence and your intended use is not permitted by statutory regulation or exceeds the permitted use, you will need to obtain permission directly from the copyright holder.

Security Compliance in Model-Driven Software Development

Sven Peldszus

Abstract To ensure the security of a software system, it is vital to keep up with changing security precautions, attacks, and mitigations. Although model-based development enables addressing security already at design-time, design models are often inconsistent with the implementation or among themselves. Such inconsistencies hinder the effective realization and verification of secure software systems. In addition, variants of software systems are another burden to developing secure systems. Vulnerabilities must be identified and fixed on all variants or else attackers could be well-guided in attacking unfixed variants. To ensure security in this context, in the thesis (Peldszus, Security Compliance in Model-driven Development of Software Systems in Presence of Long-Term Evolution and Variants. Springer, Berlin; 2022), we present GRaViTY, an approach that allows security experts to specify security requirements on the most suitable system representation. To preserve security, based on continuous automated change propagation, GRaViTY automatically checks all system representations against these security requirements. To systematically improve the object-oriented design of a software-intensive system, GRaViTY provides security-preserving refactorings. For both continuous security compliance checks and refactorings, we show the application to variant-rich software systems. To support legacy systems, GRaV-iTY allows to automatically reverse-engineer variability-aware UML models and semi-automatically map existing design models to the implementation. Besides evaluations of the individual contributions, we demonstrate applicability of the approach in two real-world case studies, the iTrust electronics health records system and the Eclipse Secure Storage. This book chapter provides a summary of the thesis, focusing on the addressed problems, identified and answered research questions, the general solution, and its application of it to two case studies. For details on the

---

The author obtained his Doctorate from the University of Koblenz-Landau.

S. Peldszus (✉)
Ruhr University Bochum, Bochum, Germany
e-mail: sven.peldszus@rub.de

individual solutions, please refer to the thesis and the corresponding publications referenced in this book chapter.

1 Introduction

Software has become a considerable part of today's life, and we rely on it to be safe and secure and respect our privacy. Even in critical domains like healthcare, modern medical imaging devices are exposed to the Internet. Furthermore, software systems tend to be used on a long-term basis in environments prone to changes, and at the same time successors of a software system are developed rapidly. A successor is often a variant of the previous system as significant parts are reused. Besides, multiple variants of a software system can exist at the same time. In all cases, to ensure the security of a software-intensive system, all changes, e.g., due to maintenance or extension, have to be continuously reflected in the whole software system, including all variants. These circumstances result in significant challenges regarding the security of evolving software systems and their variants.

Traditionally, manufacturers ensure security by implementing security standards such as the *Common Criteria*. Currently, such security standards focus more on the processes of how the software is developed than the concrete artifacts. Concerning today's short product cycles and the vast amount of product versions, certifying each product manually is impossible. One missing key to improve security is integrated tool support covering all software development phases. Furthermore, it can already support avoiding security violations during implementation.

A widely accepted development approach is *Model-Driven Development* (MDD) [3, 10] that allows planning well-structured software systems. To support evolution, MDD can include systematic variation points for future extensions or variants. Furthermore, it enables us to address security in the early phases of the software design using approaches such as UMLsec [14] or SecDFD [43]. Design models are annotated with security requirements, and the approaches provide reasoning about their consistency. In many domains, establishing appropriately documented design-time artifacts is mandatory due to legal requirements, e.g., according to the ISO/IEC 62304 for medical device software. Unfortunately, these artifacts are often inconsistent with the implementation [11], eventually causing security issues and a significant effort for harmonizing all artifacts before a certification.

One reason for this inconsistency is the way software is developed. Programming practices involve successive steps of edits, updates, and refinements to improve the implementation and incrementally meet ever-changing requirements [36]. Unfortunately, these changes are often not reflected in the design-time models. In addition, this continuous evolution causes internal decay that can lead software systems to end up in incomprehensible or even inconsistent states [23]. This continuous evolution increases the effort required to extend and maintain a software system and paves the way for security problems. Ultimately, this leads to certification issues as the implementation does not comply with the security design.

In practice, software systems need frequent restructuring to keep them maintainable [9]. To support the efficient restructuring of a software system, refactorings have been proposed and documented in a human-readable form. Despite intense studies and widespread application, a verifiable specification of refactoring operations and the execution of this specification is still an open problem. The same applies to the interaction of refactorings with nonfunctional properties of the software system, such as security.

In summary, the increasing amount of security-critical data and the faster-changing environments are a burden to develop secure software systems. However, there are already some approaches to address the individual sub-problems. However, there is a lack of holistic security engineering support throughout the development life cycle, especially with respect to tracing security requirements and verifying the compliance of all artifacts produced with them.

2 Background and Problem Identification

Software security has been addressed in various ways, but the systematic development of secure software-intensive systems is still not fully addressed when it comes to supporting the entire software development life cycle, as evidenced by frequent news of security incidents. Considering existing solutions, we identify four main reasons that hinder the effective development of secure software systems.

2.1 Non-integrated Solutions

Several approaches have been developed to support the development of secure software systems. MDD-based approaches allow planning of the software system and allow developers to incorporate security considerations from the beginning, but only abstractly [14, 43]. Similarly, common threat modeling approaches, such as STRIDE [40], abstractly model the system to identify security threats. In contrast, implementation-level approaches support the verification of concrete aspects, such as the correct use of cryptographic APIs [15], but not whether these are used where needed. In the best case, design-time security considerations should be reused until the final product is certified, but in practice, there are many non-integrated solutions. Security-related information collected in design or threat models must be manually transferred to the implementation in order to use appropriate security tools or perform manual code reviews.

2.2 Inconsistency and Missing Traceability

Often, the initial security requirements of a software-intensive system and the documentation of the system are inconsistent with the implementation, making it difficult to reason about security at the system level. Checking whether an object in a medical management system contains personal or medical information, and the resulting security requirements, can become a nontrivial task. To enable traceability, the continuous changes in security assumptions and design must be reflected in both the design-time models and the implementation. Currently, developers must manually trace between the various artifacts to identify and apply the necessary changes in the right places. In practice, this often leads to models not being used at all, despite their obvious benefits, such as systematic threat modeling planning for secure system designs. Therefore, we need to maintain correspondences between artifacts used in all development phases and automate the underlying mapping process.

2.3 Security-Aware Restructuring

As software systems are continuously subject to changes, we have to continuously check their security compliance, e.g., with design-time security requirements. In the best case, we can evaluate the desired change before applying it. Current refactoring approaches do not consider nonfunctional properties such as security. We can only evaluate the impact of a refactoring on security aspects after executing the refactoring, e.g., to notice that medical information has been moved to an object that is sent over a non-encrypted connection. This entails the risk of not being able to undo the change entirely. In summary, security-preserving restructurings are required to support the restructuring of security-critical systems without requiring a complete re-certification. If changes cannot be checked upfront, we need means to efficiently check only security properties that might be affected.

2.4 Variant-Rich Software Systems

While existing security approaches can be applied to each product or variant of a software product line, due to the vast amount of possible product configurations, this is not feasible within a reasonable time. We need means for applying security compliance checks and security-preserving refactorings to software product lines without enumerating every single variant. Consequently, the intended measures discussed above must also support software systems with many variants.

3 Research Questions

Based on the problems identified, we formulate five research questions that are answered in the thesis [26]. Figure 1 maps the research questions to the development artifacts considered by GRaViTY. We introduce the research questions discussed in the thesis in detail in what follows.

3.1 RQ1: How Can Security Requirements Be Traced Among System Representations Throughout the Development Process?

During the development of a software system, various artifacts are produced, such as models or source code. Following security by design [14, 38], security requirements are already planned and validated on the early design artifacts. These security requirements specified on model elements have to be addressed on later models by planning concrete security measures or their concrete realization in the implementation. To ensure the security of a software system, we need to trace the specified security requirements through all artifacts created. In doing so, we have to take into account continuous changes to the software system, e.g., due to ongoing development activities or maintenance, under which we have to preserve the validity of the created trace links. Furthermore, we need to identify an appropriate granularity of trace links to support security requirements on design-time models and code. Early design-time models are at a different level of abstraction than

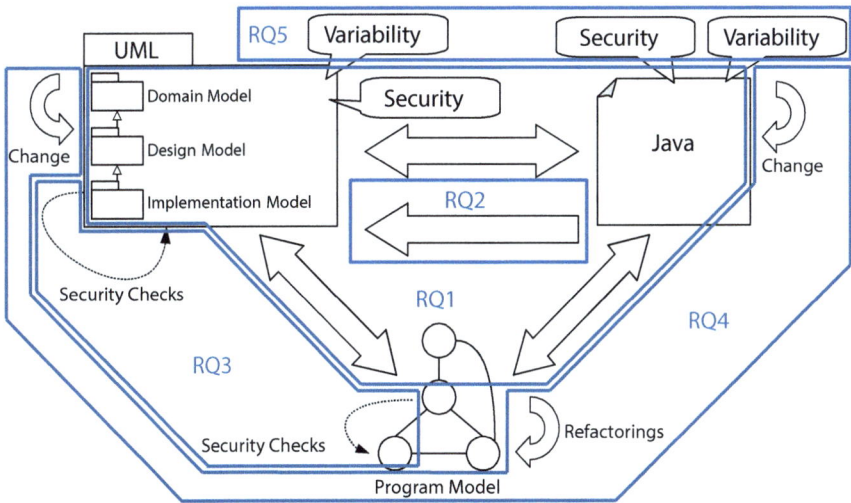

Fig. 1 Concept of GRaViTY with RQs

the final implementation of the software system, where individual methods or statements may be security critical, e.g., a security requirement on a communication link in a deployment diagram that is reflected by a call to a cryptographic API.

3.2 RQ2: How Can We Apply Model-Based Security Engineering to Legacy Projects That Have No or Disconnected Design Models?

Many software systems that were developed decades ago are still in use and are more or less actively maintained. For such legacy systems, often, no models are available, or the existing models have been created in the early phases of system development and are disconnected from the implementation. As most legacy software systems have not been developed using the approach presented in the thesis, the question is how these legacy systems can switch to using the introduced model-based security engineering approach for further development and maintenance. Since tracing between design-time models and implementation is essential, we need efficient and effective means, automated as much as possible, to reverse-engineer these trace links for legacy projects. Thereby, we distinguish between two kinds of legacy projects: projects that do not have design-time models and projects for which early models were initially created but no traces have been maintained.

3.3 RQ3: How Can Developers Be Supported in Realizing, Preserving, and Enforcing Design-Time Security Requirements?

Various approaches have been developed to plan the required security mechanisms in the early stages of software design. However, when it comes to verifying the implementation of security requirements in a software system, most checks have to be performed in manual code reviews. This is due to the local scope of individual security analyses and the lack of automated reuse. To effectively support developers in implementing and verifying design-time security, automated reuse of security specifications and appropriate checks for verifying security properties on other system representations are required. The most relevant question is what we need to check and where we have to check it to show that the specified security requirements are met. For example, a fundamental security requirement for a medical system is that no personal or medical data is accessible to unauthorized entities. In the design models, we can identify what we consider to be such sensitive data and plan appropriate measures at an abstract level, e.g., that only certain parts in a security core of the application are allowed to access this information and that it must be encrypted when it leaves that core. Verification of compliance involves a variety of checks, including dependency and taint analysis, which must be configured according to the specific requirements, as well as verification that the information is actually encrypted when required. In addition, it may not be sufficient to only statically check the code, as a exchanged library at deployment or a newly discovered attack vector may cause security violations in a software system that has passed all static security checks.

3.4 RQ4: How Do Changes Affect a System's Security Compliance, and How Can These Effects Be Handled?

The development of a software system consists not only of adding new elements but also of modifying existing elements. Both changes require the continuous update of the traces studied in RQ1. However, as part of RQ1, we do not look at how such changes might affect security requirements. Suppose we want to guide developers. In that case, we have to inform them if some changes, which have automatically been performed by our tool support or manually by them, affect security requirements. For example, this is of particular interest in the certified software scenario [27, 31], where it has to be ensured that a change violates no security requirement.

3.5 RQ5: How Can We Verify and Preserve Security Compliance in Variant-Rich Software Systems?

Often, software systems come in many variants that share huge parts in common. Thereby, the number of possible variants can quickly reach an astronomical scale, making the security analysis of every single product infeasible [22]. Nevertheless, for every single variant or product, we have to ensure that it does not contain any security violation. Furthermore, we have to preserve security compliance also in case of changes, e.g., in case of applied restructuring operations. Here, the goal is to find means to apply the developed security engineering approach also to variant-rich software systems.

4 Research Methodology

To answer the presented research questions and provide a solution to the outlined problems, we followed the design science research methodology [6, 13, 24]. The goal of this research approach is to develop artifacts that overcome current boundaries. Thereby, new knowledge is achieved by building and investigating the application of the developed artifact. Accordingly, this approach requires that, initially, a general solution concept is developed, which is afterward implemented and evaluated. If necessary, the developed solution concept is adapted based on the observations during application and evaluation until the desired goals are met. We divided the topics of the thesis into small sub-problems with individual research questions that can be investigated separately for solving the identified problems and incorporated them into one approach afterward.

5 Approach

To overcome the outlined challenges in developing and maintaining secure software systems, we identified five research questions, focusing on aspects required for improving the model-based development and maintenance of secure variant-rich software systems. To allow continuous model-based security engineering, we mainly focus on the automated tracing of security requirements throughout the whole development process and their continuous verification. In general, the idea of the presented GRaViTY development approach is to automatically create and maintain detailed low-level trace links between design and code artifacts. These trace links are intended to be processed by the tool and not for direct manual use. Developers benefit from the trace links through tool support that uses them for automated navigation between different artifacts. In addition, trace links are used to propagate security-related information between models and the implementation of a software system. Also, the trace links allow to automatically reflect changes on any artifact to all other artifacts. Due to this continuous automated synchronization, which allows changing all artifacts of a software system at any time, the GRaViTY development approach supports both sequential and agile development processes.

In this section, we discuss from a developer's perspective how a secure software system can be developed with GRaViTY to overcome the identified problems. First, we discuss our assumptions on how to allow developers to work efficiently at the development of secure software systems. By doing this, we derive key ideas on which we will build our solution. Afterward, we show the development process for developing secure software systems using GRaViTY. Also, we show the provided tool support and how it is integrated into this process. Finally, we demonstrate the development using our approach from the perspective of a developer.

5.1 Key Ideas of the GRaViTY Approach

Developers play an essential role in the success of a software project. The more developers can focus on their tasks, the more efficient they can be in solving these tasks. The primary goal of GRaViTY is to enable the successful development and maintenance of secure software systems. To achieve this goal, we identified four key ideas to be realized in GRaViTY.

5.1.1 Suitable Views

The first key idea is that developers should work on the most suitable view for their task. For every task, there is a view in which this task can be carried out most effectively. For example, when a security expert is planning or updating the general security requirements of a software system, an abstract view of the software system, such as a thread model or an architectural model, is more likely to be appropriate than the source code with all its details. However, due to circumstances from the used development process or tooling, all the required information might not be available in this view, or the view cannot easily be created. For example, while a software system has initially been designed using means to specify security requirements and measures on abstract design-time models, such as UMLsec [14] or SecDFD [43], due to missing trace links, changes in the security requirements have to be specified on the implementation level. Such situations should be avoided by the design of our approach and proper tool support. Tool support must ensure that software developers and experts, such as security experts or software architects, can always work in the view of the system best suited to their task.

5.1.2 Side Effects

When working on their task, developers should only focus on their tasks and should not have to care about potential side effects. Nearly every task a developer performs comes with side effects she has to think about. Accordingly, these side effects draw attention from the main task and hinder the development. In the thesis, we explicitly consider two kinds of side effects.

Local side effects: First, side effects within the artifact that a developer is changing, e.g., replacing a cryptographic library to better fit the needs at a particular location in the source code, requires also updating the other locations where the previous library was used. Handling such side effects is essential for maintaining the correct behavior of a software system. Automated tool support as part of a development approach can help identify such side effects. For example, compilers can detect calls to non-existent APIs, and UMLsec checks can detect side effects of model-level changes that affect design-time security requirements.

Global side effects: Second, in addition to local side effects, there might be side effects on other artifacts. If these artifacts do not immediately relate to the correct function of the software system, developers should not have to care about side effects on these. For example, consider a developer optimizing a software system's implementation-level design quality. Most changes might not affect the architecture of the software system, since they are too fine-grained and do not affect the borders of components. In this case, the developer should not have to care about the effects on the architecture during his or her task.

However, coming back to the suitability of views, an architect should also not have to review the local restructurings at the implementation level of the software system. Side effects that occurred and changed the architectural level should be propagated to the architectural level.

Furthermore, refactorings might have side effects regarding a software system's security requirements, e.g., by making sensitive information accessible. Here, the developer should still be able to focus on the code quality, and tool support should take care of preventing changes with such side effects.

To this end, with GRaViTY, we want to get one step closer to the point where developers do not have to think about such side effects. The ultimate goal is to automatically propagate all changes made by a developer to all other artifacts and then present the propagated changes to an appropriate expert for review. In addition, tool support should reduce the risk of changes leading to violations in other artifacts.

5.1.3 Synchronization

To avoid the individual artifacts of a software system, such as design-time models and code, to diverge, a continuous synchronization in the sense of reflecting every change on all artifacts is necessary. Keeping all artifacts synchronized in case of changes usually requires a significant manual effort, even when tool support is used, and is likely to give rise to inconsistencies. Using GRaViTY, developers should be able to change artifacts in arbitrary order, and their changes will be automatically propagated by GRaViTY for keeping all artifacts synchronized. Furthermore, this step is a prerequisite for allowing developers, architects, and security experts to work on the most suitable view of the software system as depicted in the previous two ideas. Accordingly, the synchronization of the artifacts should happen as far as possible in the background with as few user interactions as possible.

5.1.4 Continuous Security

To ensure the security of a software system under development, it is essential to check every change for its security implications at some point of time. This can be either aggregated before a release, when a commit is pushed to a repository, or, in the best case, continuously during the development as part of the live checks provided in an IDE. Similar to bugs, the earlier a security violation is discovered, the easier and cheaper it is to fix. For this reason, in GRaViTY, developers are continuously assisted by automated security compliance checks helping to preserve the security of the software system. Due to the needed runtime, which can vary depending on the size of the system and the properties selected to be checked from a few seconds to multiple hours, security compliance checks of the entire system are provided as batch checks but should be also integrated into continuous integration pipelines in the future. For live support in an IDE, we discuss how checks can be executed incrementally to only consider the changed parts.

Such continuous automated security checks are also an essential concept in other approaches, e.g., SecDevOps [20]. We consider these in GRaViTY, but the goal is to go even one step further. Usually, when talking about continuous automated security checks, low-level security checks with a limited scopes are meant. In our approach, we target the security compliance of the implementation with the specification in design-time models. Nevertheless, security checks with limited scopes, such as UMLsec that only targets the model-level, are essential to ensure the consistency of the security specifications with which we check the compliance. However, these automated security checks should not replace manual reviews but support these. Also, continuous automated security checks allow to review changes quicker and study their effects. This eases incremental reviews.

To summarize, we need a development process that allows developers to focus on their tasks and allows them to perform the tasks on the most suitable view on the software system. In addition, such an approach might also assist in performing the tasks themselves. The consideration of tool support can be a fundamental part of such an approach. However, in the intended GRaViTY approach, tool support is not meant to replace developers, security experts, or software architects but to assist them. While the desired tool support might not be easy to implement from a technical perspective, the main challenges lie in the design of a development approach supporting the outlined key ideas and in the underlying challenges that have to be solved for realizing the approach.

5.2 The GRaViTY Development Approach

Next, we show the general development process using the GRaViTY approach and the automatically executed tasks within this sequence. Figure 2 shows a conceptual overview of the development using the GRaViTY development approach.

The artifacts that will be created are shown on the left side of Fig. 2. We assume that three levels of design models are used in addition to the concrete implementation of the software system. At the most abstract level, a domain model captures the essential elements and relationships of a domain, usually in the form of a UML class diagram. These elements are then detailed according to the planned system and related to the coarse-grained element of the planned system, e.g., in an early class model or threat model. In the implementation model, the coarse-grained elements such as components, classes, or processes from the system model are detailed to the point where they can be implemented in source code.

As soon as a model is created, it is denoted by a circle representing an instance of the model or the software system's source code. Following the figure, we assume, that all models are created in the order of their abstraction level, and none is temporarily skipped. However, we do not assume that any of these models is

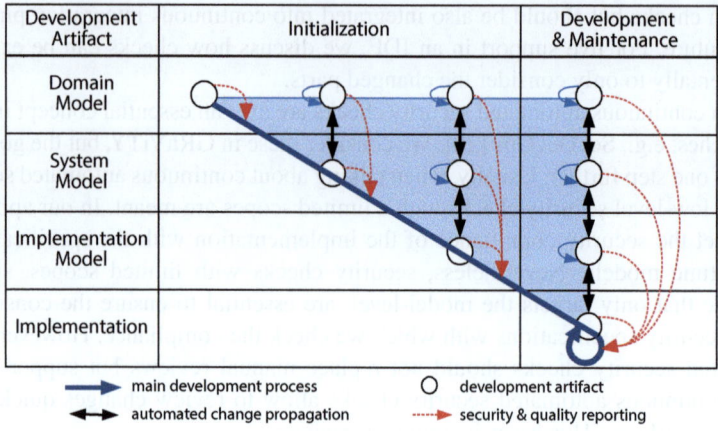

Fig. 2 Development process of the GRaViTY development approach

completed before the next one is created. Incrementally, developing the models in iterations is explicitly possible and allows the usage of GRaViTY in agile development processes.

In agile development, the main development process has three initialization steps in which initial versions of all models are created. In the fourth step, the development and maintenance phase is reached, in which we iterate until the software system has been developed. If we want to consider the maintenance of the software system, we stay in this step and iterate until the software system's end of life.

The blue area above the main development process arrow contains all artifacts available in the current step of the main development process. Whenever a change is applied to any of the artifacts, this change is propagated to all other artifacts that have been developed automatically. The corresponding development activities are denoted in the figure by blue arrows.

A software system's development is supported by security and quality reports covering all artifacts that have been developed. While working in the way as presented above, trace links are created and maintained continuously that will be leveraged for selecting and executing security compliance checks. The security and quality aspects derived this way are centrally reported into the main development process, which is denoted by red, dotted arrows.

5.3 Developer Perspective on Using GRaViTY

In Fig. 3, we show the interaction of a developer with the software system under development while using GRaViTY. The software system under development is depicted in the center of the figure. Thereby, the software system consists out of

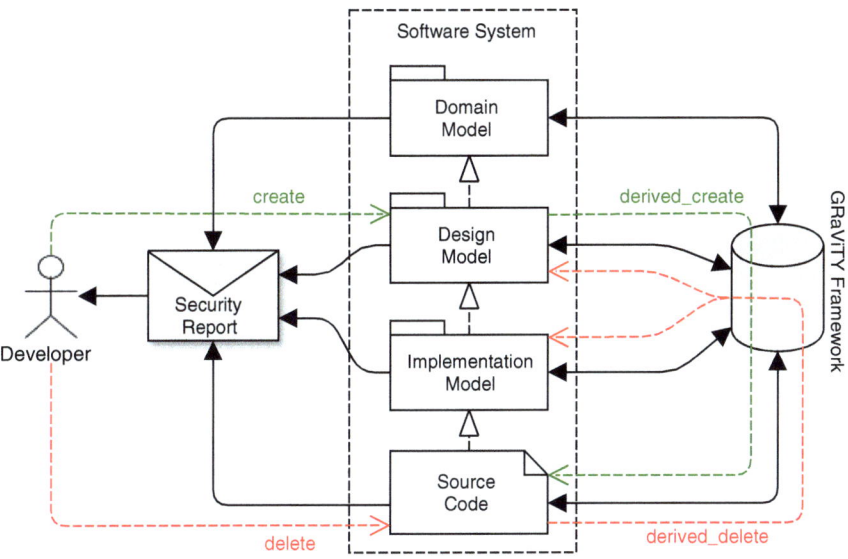

Fig. 3 A developer performing changes using GRaViTY

the discussed development artifacts, namely, different design models and the source code of the software system. These artifacts as well as their relations are shown in the center of the figure.

The GRaViTY framework is indicated by a cylindrical shape on the figure's right side. This shape connects all development artifacts and operates invisibly for a developer in the background. It takes care of synchronizing all artifacts in case of changes, the propagation of security requirements, and security checks.

On the left of the figure, a developer is shown that can directly interact with the development artifacts of the software system. In our case, interaction means that the single artifacts of the software system can directly be edited by the developer, using an IDE into which GRaViTY is integrated. This integration comprises user interfaces allowing developers to make use of the GRaViTY tool support, e.g., by using refactorings for restructuring the implementation. Currently, only Java in the Eclipse IDE in combination with the Papyrus model editor [16, 42] for UML models and data flow diagrams is supported.

Within this IDE, GRaViTY continuously provides reports to developers. For example, this reporting comprises details on security violations currently present in the software system in the form of error markers on the models and code but also more detailed reports via an integration with the UMLsec tooling. For other cases, such as details on the effects of planned refactoring operations, the information is immediately provided as part of the refactoring UI. Based on the reports, developers and experts can plan improvements to the software system. For the generation of reports, GRaViTY considers all artifacts present in the software system.

Whenever a developer edits a development artifact, e.g., by deleting and adding elements in models or source code, these changes are propagated to all other artifacts by GRaViTY. For example, the developer's addition to the design model leads to a derived addition in the source code, and a deletion of elements in the source code leads to deletions in the implementation model and design model. After every change, an updated report is created and presented to the developer. This report can then be used for estimating the impact of the change but also be shared with experts, e.g., software architects or security experts.

While working with GRaViTY, there should be no difference between working on a single product or a variant-rich software system. A developer can still change the software product line in his or her preferred way. Also, security and quality reports are continuously provided but now consider the whole software product line.

6 Research Outcomes

In the thesis, we present GRaViTY, an integrated approach for continuous security compliance checks at model-driven development. While answering the research questions, the approach addresses the challenges identified at problem discussion.

6.1 Inconsistency and Missing Traceability

While we use standard UML technologies for tracing among UML models with different levels of abstraction, we employ Triple Graph Grammars (TGG) [39], a bidirectional graph transformation technology, for tracing between models and code. Based on transformation rules, TGGs build a correspondence model and allow changes to be synchronized between models and code. While the TGG rules allow us to abstract details from the statement level, we still end up with very detailed models that need to be connected to more abstract, manually created instances, for which we provide tool support. However, in combination, this approach allows us to automatically prevent inconsistencies throughout software development (RQ1) and allows developers to work on the more abstract instances [25, 28, 29]. We also discuss semi-automated traceability recovery and reverse engineering of UML models (RQ2) [33, 44].

6.1.1 Continuous Tracing

In the thesis, we have shown that we can propagate arbitrary security requirements within UML models of different abstraction but also between UML models and the implementation and an implementation-level program model. For this purpose, we investigated two different mechanisms for tracing security requirements. First, we extended the TGG transformation to create corresponding security requirements in the implementation as Java annotations. Second, we looked at dynamic tracing using the correspondence model. In both variants, the TGGs allow to automatically propagate changes to keep all artifacts synchronized.

The dynamic tracing avoids enriching the implementation with additional annotations, but it can have the disadvantage of being inefficient. Since the metamodels of the considered models are given, the trace links contained in the correspondence model can point to elements from the different models, but are not directly accessible from them, resulting in a search for all trace links pointing to an element of interest. If only a few traces are required across the correspondence model or an efficient cache has been created, dynamic tracing should be used to avoid distracting developers. However, if many annotations are required for analysis, the propagation is more likely to be efficient. Also, the created annotations are available at runtime. Altogether, small local lookups should be realized using dynamic tracing, while for full compliance checks or at deployment, the UMLsec security requirements should be propagated into the implementation using additional TGG rules.

To conclude, we provide an automated mechanism to preserve consistency between different program representations for managing evolving Java programs. As a result, we obtain a model-based framework for arbitrarily interleaving program evolution and maintenance steps while ensuring consistency. Furthermore, we can use this approach to also translate and synchronize security requirements of model elements between different system representations, thereby providing traceability of security requirements. Our evaluation on real-world software projects up to 200k LOC shows that our approach allows efficient synchronization between code and models after changes with a speedup of 95% compared to extracting the models after the change.

6.1.2 Restoring Traceability

For legacy projects, we discussed the application of GRaViTY considering two different scenarios. First, we considered software projects in which no design-time models exist. Here, we discussed how the required models and correspondence models between the design-time models and the implementation can be reverse-engineered using GRaViTY's synchronization mechanism [25]. Second, we considered legacy projects in which early design models are available but are disconnected from the implementation. To restore this connection in terms of a correspondence model, we introduced a semi-automated mapping approach [33, 44] that provides the user with suggestions for correspondences and learns from its decisions.

The two approaches can be used complementary in projects containing early design models. First, developers can reverse-engineer UML class diagrams using the TGGs and, afterward, reconstruct the correspondence model between early data flow diagrams (DFD) and the implementation. These correspondence models can then be used to create trace links between the DFDs and reverse-engineered UML class diagrams, which is again supported by suggestions that are provided by tooling. This allows to transfer security requirements from security annotations on the DFDs (using the SecDFD notation [43]) into the class diagrams and avoids specifying these again, preventing potential errors.

To conclude on the application of GRaViTY on legacy projects, the proposed reverse-engineering approaches allow reconstructing models and correspondence models that allow the application of GRaViTY. The reverse-engineered UML class diagrams can continuously be synchronized with the implementation using GRaViTY's synchronization mechanism without any adaptions. We evaluated the scalability of the reverse engineering on real-world Java projects up to a size of 200k LOC. The correspondence model created between early design models and the implementation is a snapshot of the current state and cannot be automatically synchronized. However, as outlined, they build a basis for propagating security requirements and reconstructing the model hierarchy used by GRaViTY. For the semi-automated approach, we have shown in our evaluation on five open-source projects that we already reach a precision of 50.5% and recall of 69.8% in the first iteration, reaching 87.2% and 92% after a few iterations. Thereby, the user has on average an impact on the recall of 7.9% and provides new input for the automatization. Notice that on average, 75% of all correct correspondences are suggested to the user and do not have to be manually defined. All in all, the user is not only guided through the implementation by our tool but also assisted in creating the correspondence model between SecDFDs and their implementations.

6.2 Non-integrated Solutions

To overcome non-integrated solutions, for ensuring security compliance, we connect design-time security with implementation-level security. The presented automation allows us to effectively check security at low cost by allowing security experts to only specify security requirements once in combination with an automated propagation based on our tracing mechanism (RQ3) [1, 25, 34, 44]. We leverage design-time security requirements for static and dynamic implementation-level security checks. Besides newly developed checks, specifically tailored for verifying considered design-time security requirements, we also discussed how state-of-the-art taint analysis can be improved by connecting design-time security with a data flow analyzer [2]. Finally, we present a runtime monitor for detecting and mitigating violations of design-time security requirements. Furthermore, we support an adaption of the design models to allow an inspection of observed security violations.

6.2.1 Static Security Checks

We introduce a novel approach for tackling the problem of automating the code-level verification of planned security mechanisms. In particular, we have developed a solution with tool support for executing security compliance checks between an abstract design model and its implementation (in Java). Once defined, the correspondence model is leveraged for an automated security analysis of the implementation against the security design. Two types of security compliance checks are executed: a check whether cryptographic operations are used at the expected locations and a local data flow check for data processing contracts specified in the model. The results of the compliance checks (convergence, absence, and divergence) are lifted to the attention of the user via the user interface of our tool. Similarly, the mapped design is also leveraged to initialize and execute a state-of-the-art data flow analyzer over the entire Java project. We can optimize and automate taint analysis by automatically identifying sources of sensitive information while improving precision by identifying allowed sinks in the design.

Our approach was evaluated with two studies on open-source Java projects, focused on assessing the performance from different angles. The rule-based security compliance checks are very precise (100%) and rarely overlook implemented cryptographic operations (recall is 94.5%). In addition, the local data flow checks are fairly precise (79.6%) but may overlook some implemented flows (recall is 65.6%), due to the large gap between the design-time SecDFD models and the implementation. Further, our approach enables a project-specific data flow analysis with up to 62% fewer false alarms.

6.2.2 Dynamic Security Checks

To ensure security compliance at runtime, we introduce an approach for coupling model-based security analyses with the code level at runtime and supporting round-trip engineering by providing feedback into the models [35]. We realized support for checking secure call dependencies at runtime, by extending the realization of UMLsec *Secure Dependency*, which could only be checked statically (and thus partly) by now. We provide a runtime monitor that leverages the implementation-level security annotations discussed above for enforcing the design-time secure dependency security property. Reaction to detected security issues is supported by passive reactions like call trace logging or actively by providing modified return values to protect real application data. Round-trip engineering is supported both by feeding additional associations monitored during execution back into the model and automatically generating sequence diagrams of attacks to support developers in investigating attacks with graphical support and related to the model. Thus, software system evolution detection is also tackled.

We evaluated the effectiveness and applicability of the security monitoring against real CWEs and DaCapo benchmark. Results show that we support realistic application scenarios and real-world software systems. Further, a user survey shows that the generated sequence diagrams are useful for investigation security violations that were observed or mitigated.

6.3 Security-Aware Restructuring

To detect security violations after changes, we introduce security violation patterns that encode implementation-level security checks against design-time security requirements as graph patterns (RQ4) [34]. Especially, we discuss their incremental execution for efficiently verifying security compliance instead of full-security compliance checks. In addition, we provide security-preserving refactorings for ensuring security compliance at restructuring (RQ3 & 4). The security-preserving refactorings allow checking security compliance before modifying the implementation [28, 29, 37].

While the refactoring of a software system is already challenging, this challenge even gets greater on security-critical software systems. We have shown how refactorings can be formalized using graph transformation languages [28, 29]. Existing works show that such formalizations allow reasoning about the correctness of the refactorings regarding them not changing a software system's behavior [19]. Also, such formalization allows checking the applicability of the refactorings upfront. However, the correctness of the refactored implementation could not be guaranteed as the refactorings had to be performed manually on the implementation. Here, we show how to overcome this gap using the program model and synchronization mechanism introduced in the thesis. Finally, we have shown how the formalized refactorings can be extended with security constraints, leveraging design-time security requirements.

In summary, the presented solutions allow the restructuring of security-critical software systems as part of the GRaViTY development approach. In our evaluation, we show that the incremental execution of the security violation patterns provides a significant speedup against security compliance checks of the entire system (which did not terminate within a reasonable time). During refactoring, the discussed security extensions allow to automatically prevent security-violating refactorings. Further, we have shown that our refactoring approach also prevents behavior-changing refactorings that are executed by the Eclipse IDE.

6.4 Variant-Rich Systems

Finally, we investigated the application of GRaViTY to variant-rich software systems (RQ5). To verify UMLsec security requirements in model product lines, we have encoded the checks as OCL constraints and applied a template interpretation approach [32]. Developers verifying their product lines can use the our OCL constraints as a black box and do not have to look into the complicated logic. Detected violations are automatically presented on a concrete variant containing the violation, and other affected variants are listed. To apply arbitrary pattern-based checks, such as security violation patterns or security-preserving refactorings, we have extended the Henshin graph transformation engine to support variability within transformation rules and models at the same time [41].

6.4.1 Design Time Variability

We provide a comprehensive methodology for the model-based security analysis of software product lines. We extended our UMLsec to also support variability within the security requirements by adding presence conditions to the security annotations [32]. Users specify security requirements as well as variability information as part of the design-time system models. Furthermore, we investigated how we can detect security violations on the UML product lines without iterating all products. For this purpose, we specified UMLsec checks as OCL constraints and evaluated these using a state-of-the-art template interpretation technique [7]. This way, our analysis addresses the scalability issues encountered in this setting by lifting the analysis to the level of the entire product line rather than individual products. In our evaluation, this solution enables the analysis of realistic product lines where the naive approach terminated without a result; a user study indicates the usefulness of our methodology.

6.4.2 Variability on the Implementation Level

To allow the application of refactorings and security violation patterns to SPLs, we introduce a multivariant model transformation approach allowing applying variability-based transformation rules to software product lines. To be more precise, we propose a methodology for software product line transformations in which not only the input product line but also the transformation system contains variability. At the heart of our methodology, a staged rule application technique exploits reuse potential concerning shared portions of the involved products and rules. We present a formalization of our technique, including an optimization that supports an efficient checking of negative application conditions (an advanced transformation feature). We demonstrated practical benefit by applying our technique to two scenarios from a software evolution context. We observed speedups in all considered cases, in some of them by one order of magnitude. As part of this evaluation, we have shown how our methodology can be used for refactoring software product lines using security-preserving refactorings. The application of security violation patterns to SPLs works analogously. The proposed multivariant transformation approach is not only applicable to our two scenarios but to every variability-based transformation rule and product line. For example, the variability-supporting UMLsec checks, currently expressed by us using OCL constraints, could also be implemented using this technique.

7 Case Studies

In addition to the individual evaluations, we applied GRaViTY in two case studies to demonstrate that the approach works as a whole. The first case study is the Electronics Health Management System *iTrust*, and the second case study is the

Eclipse Secure Storage of the Eclipse IDE. As the developers of iTrust provide complete documentation and models are available in existing research, we used iTrust to demonstrate the feasibility of the GRaViTY approach for developing a new software system taking security into account. While the Eclipse IDE also provides good documentation of the implementation, there are no requirements or models available. For this reason, we applied the GRaViTY approach to Eclipse Secure Storage to demonstrate its feasibility on legacy projects.

7.1 Case Study 1: iTrust

The iTrust case study comprises a realistic and working *electronic health records* system that has been developed and maintained in university classes over 25 semesters and is compliant with the HIPAA Security and Privacy Rules [12, 18]. The main documentation is provided as requirements describing use cases of the iTrust system. The software system itself has been implemented in Java using Java Server Pages (JSP). This project has been used as a subject in various research projects, resulting in the creation of design-time models in addition to the original source code [4, 5, 12].

In this case study, we simulate the implementation of the iTrust system using GRaViTY from the very beginning, starting with requirements engineering. After the initial development of the software system, we focus on the restructuring of iTrust as part of the maintenance. Finally, we showcase the conversion of iTrust into an SPL. In all steps, we reuse the existing iTrust artifacts and create all required artifacts following the GRaViTY development approach.

7.1.1 Requirements Engineering

Usually, the development of a software system starts with an analysis of the domain as part of the requirements engineering. The knowledge about entities and relations within the software system's domain is captured in a domain model. The domain model elements are then used to specify their realization in the software system. Here, the specification of the software system's intended functionality is one of the first steps of requirements engineering. For this purpose, the UML provides the notation of use case diagrams. To simulate the requirements engineering, we manually recreated iTrust's use case diagram based on iTrust's requirements by redrawing a diagram in less than an hour. Thereby, we took a domain model as given and refined it by specifying the use case diagram. The used domain model shows basic concepts in a hospital such as doctors treating patients. Whenever there was a refinement relation between the use case diagram and the domain model, we explicitly modeled this relation. In the next step, the domain model and use case diagrams are refined further to specify an architecture that allows the implementation of the specified use cases.

7.1.2 Software Architecture and Security Modeling

After requirements engineering, based on the requirements models and the textual requirements, the software system's architecture is specified. Following the principle of security by design, we have to consider security requirements explicitly in this step. Accordingly, we discuss the simulation of the architecture specification for the iTrust system. To this end, we focus on the feasibility of refinements for specifying software architecture and security engineering. Starting from the models developed at requirements engineering, we iteratively refine these models until we reach a detailed specification of the iTrust system.

After every extension step, comprising the addition of a coherent set of model elements, a security engineering step takes place. Here, we considered the security engineering using UMLsec and SecDFDs. As the SecDFD and UMLsec specifications and checks are known from the literature, we do not focus on their usage but the *Secure Realization* security-refinement mechanism introduced in the thesis.

As part of our case study, we simulated these steps by selecting parts of the design and implementation models and iteratively rebuilding the models. Whenever we added a new part to the models, we also created the corresponding refinement relations. We started our simulation with a domain model already containing fundamental security requirements, such as that personal data has to be classified at the security level of secrecy. Based on this model, we simulated three evolution steps:

1. In the first step, we defined classes in the design model refining persons and actors of the domain model and use case diagram.
2. Afterward, we added the data classes for storing medical information about patients to the design model.
3. Finally, we added classes and operations for implementing the functionality of the use cases.

Figure 4 shows on the right-hand side of the figure a corresponding excerpt of the domain model of the healthcare domain in which sensitive information such as the home address of a person is classified using UMLsec. On the left-hand side, the figure shows the design of iTrust and using realization edges how it realizes to the elements from the domain model.

7.1.3 Implementation

After reaching a state in which the design-time models are detailed enough, we have to start implementing the software system. Thereby, tracing is required from the first written line of code for applying the GRaViTY approach. For this reason, we focus on the integration of GRaViTY's tracing approach into software development.

Using the synchronization mechanism of GRaViTY, we generated an early Java class layout from the implementation model. Afterward, we filled this layout manually with functionality. During this step, the implementation model has been

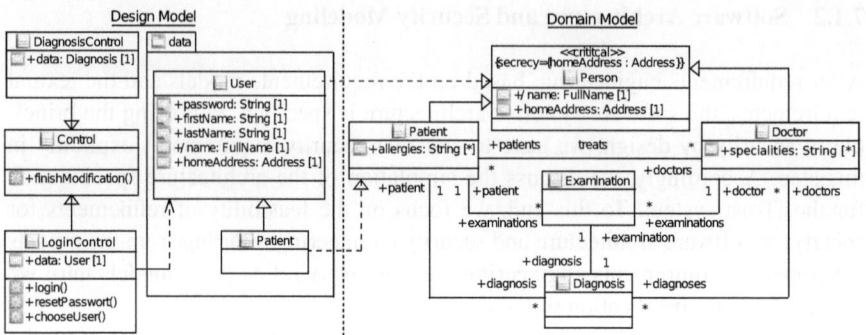

Fig. 4 Refinement relations between the design model of iTrust and a domain model of the healthcare domain

kept synchronized by GRaViTY with the manual changes. We performed this manual extension by copying and pasting implementation fragments of the iTrust implementation into the generated class layout. However, as the MoDisco parser is not incremental, in addition, we had to simulate these changes on the MoDisco model by manually copying the corresponding changes into this model. After every set of source code changes, we generated a MoDisco model and copied the changes into the MoDisco model previously used by GRaViTY, making the changes processable for the used TGG this way.

7.1.4 Security Compliance

The continuous verification of the planned and implemented security is an essential contribution of GRaViTY. As part of this case study, we investigate how these verification steps integrate into the software development process.

Comparable to the incremental specification of the software system's architecture, we also interleaved security verification steps with the implementation steps. These implementation steps have been discussed as the subject of the previous part of this case study. After synchronizing every change made on the implementation with the design models, we manually executed all security compliance checks.

As in the generated class design and the first pasted code fragments, no security mechanisms have been contained, and all have been reported as absent. For this reason, initially, we faced a long list of absences regarding the planned security design. However, as we incrementally added more functionality from iTrust's implementation, the size of the lists of absences reduced until we got rid of all absences. Thereby, the absences functioned as a kind of to-do lists for security-related tasks and as selection criteria for the next code fragments to paste. For example, Fig. 5 shows a screenshot of the corresponding tooling with detected issues at the bottom. In the example, the security-critical change password process considered in the design represented as data flow diagram has not been implemented

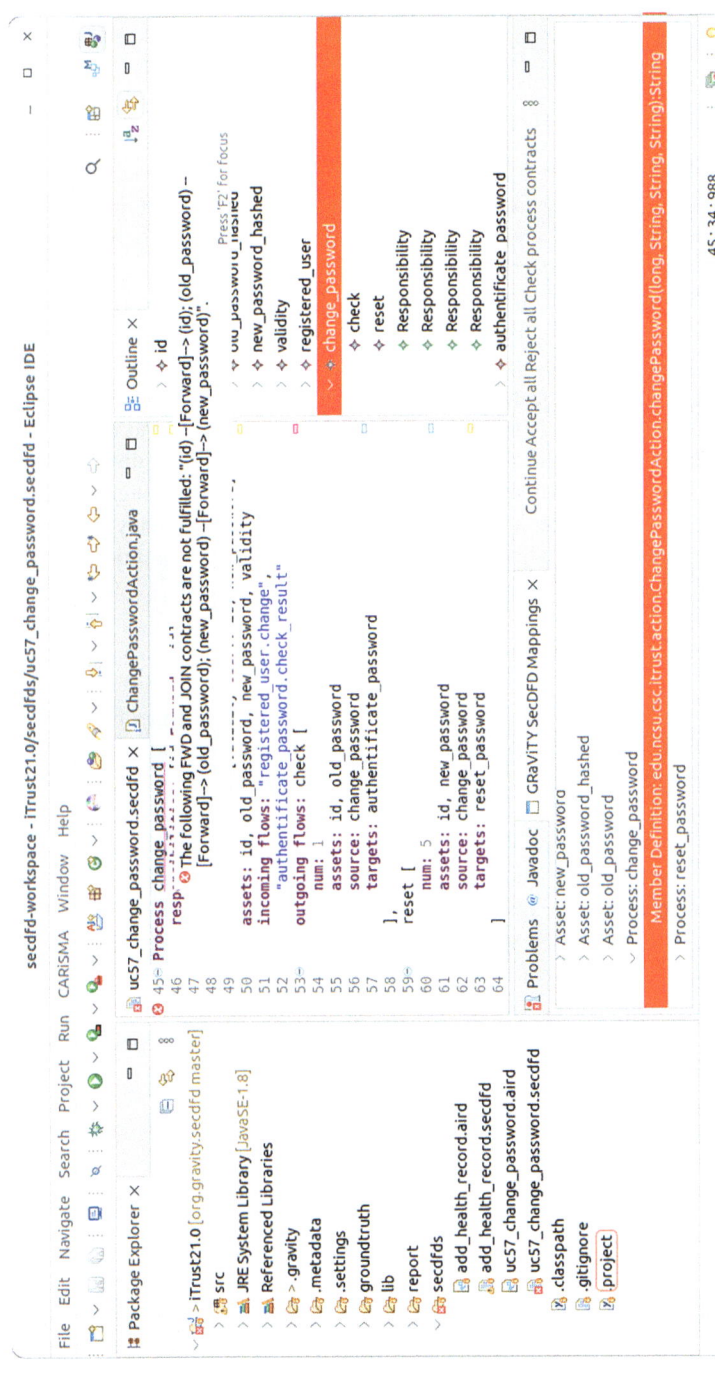

Fig. 5 Security compliance check between a data flow diagram describing an iTrust use case and the implementation

in the implementation yet. As the source code inserted this way was always security compliant, no other violations have been reported.

7.1.5 Restructuring

After reaching the state in which our case study system's implementation was identical to the original iTrust implementation, we investigated this implementation regarding possibilities for restructuring the software system. Thereby, we only focused on restructuring in terms of refactorings.

To find additional refactoring opportunities, we executed the search-based optimization tool GOBLIN [37]. Thereby, we added all three refactorings introduced in the thesis (*Create Superclass*, *Pull-Up Method*, and *Move Method*) to GOBLIN. Besides, the optimization criteria considered in the summarized experiment of Ruland et al. (design-flaws [31], coupling/cohesion, visibilities, and the number of changes), we also added the *Critical Design Proportion* metric discussed in the thesis as an optimization criterion. Due to iTrust's architecture along with the Java server pages, most times, the implemented functionality was already well located, and we only rarely found additional beneficial refactoring opportunities.

7.1.6 Variability Engineering

As the last part of this case study, we considered the re-engineering of iTrust into an SPL. In this case study, we mainly focus on the specification of an SPL in terms of the variability within all artifacts of the software system. However, we also consider the security checks for SPLs.

We started on the use case diagrams with the identification of possible features and ended in assigning individual use cases to features. Afterward, we investigated two different approaches for realizing the identified features in the software system: first, a top-down approach by specifying variability on the models and propagating it to code and, second, a bottom-up approach in which we specified variability on the source code and propagated it into the design-time models. After realizing the variability in the iTrust system, we executed the SecPL checks to verify the security of the iTrust SPL.

7.2 Case Study 2: Eclipse Secure Storage

Our second case study focuses on applying GRaViTY to relatively small (2,900 LLOC) but security-critical part of the Eclipse IDE. *Eclipse Secure Storage* [8] is used by Eclipse plugins such as the Eclipse git client to store confidential data like passwords. The Eclipse Secure Storage is implemented as an Eclipse plugin itself using Java. How exactly the secure storage works is described in the help document of Eclipse [8]. However, this description is rather high level and complemented by the low-level API documentation. We consider Eclipse Secure Storage due to its security criticality, good documentation, and wide usage in practice.

In this case study, we focused on migrating legacy projects to GRaViTY. In what follows, we first discuss the reverse engineering of the Eclipse Secure Storage to create a state in which the application of the GRaViTY approach is possible. Next, we discuss security engineering, aiming at making security requirements explicit and checking the software system regarding compliance with them. Finally, we discuss the runtime monitoring of the Eclipse Secure Storage based on a fictive malicious Eclipse plugin and the adaption of the reverse-engineered models.

7.2.1 Reverse Engineering of Models

As there are no models available for Eclipse Secure Storage, the first step of this case study was the reverse engineering of models. For the reverse engineering of models, we followed a three-step approach. First, based on the documentation of Eclipse Secure Storage, we manually created data flow diagrams and UML activity diagrams, which are similar to the DFDs but include control flow, for two use cases, accessing a value from the secure storage and resetting a password. As usual in threat modeling, these diagrams are at a high level of abstraction and are limited to the essential elements; in our case, they include only 7 assets per diagram and 7 or 10 nodes, respectively. Afterward, we automatically reverse-engineered a detailed UML class diagram from the source code of Eclipse Secure Storage using GRaViTY. Finally, we used the semi-automated mapping approach to establish refinements between the manually created diagrams, the automatically reverse-engineered class diagram, and the software system's implementation.

7.2.2 Static Security Specification and Checks

One of the two main goals of applying GRaViTY to legacy projects is to create artifacts that allow an easier specification of security requirements, compared to their specification on the implementation, and the security compliance checks with these security requirements. The other main goal is to continue with the continuous verification of the software system's security after the initial state has been proven to be secure. In this part of the case study, we focus on creating such an initial secure state using GRaViTY.

After reverse engineering, we started to annotate the models with security requirements. Here, we started by specifying essential security requirements on the DFDs, which were automatically propagated to the detailed reverse-engineered class diagram. These propagated security requirements served as starting points for the specification of detailed security requirements with annotations according to UMLsec *Secure Dependency*, which was guided by the UMLsec tooling.

Unlike the iTrust case study, there is only one level of inheritance, which still simplified this step, but required us to look into the very detailed UML model more often than it was necessary in the iTrust case, where almost all detailed security requirements were propagated from more abstract models. After this specification, the propagation to the source code worked without problems, and as expected, the compliance checks showed no issues. Technically, we demonstrated the feasibility of the tools for annotating the models and, in particular, of GRaViTY's synchronization mechanism for propagating the security requirements to the implementation. An extension of the tooling with clustering approaches to generate additional more abstract models could be helpful.

7.2.3 Runtime Monitoring

In the last part of this case study, we focused on leveraging the specified security requirements to enforce these at runtime. In the implementation of a software system specified by a UML model, the dependencies stereotyped with «call» are usually implemented as method calls and field accesses. Even if a model does not contain violations, at runtime, it has to be guaranteed that the security requirements specified at design time are not violated. Furthermore, detecting all dependencies which can occur at runtime is statically undecidable, e.g., due to the use of Java reflection [17, 21]. What can also not be foreseen from a static perspective are violations caused by an exchanged library or malicious code.

In Eclipse, for example, every installed plugin can access the password store. Which plugins a developer installs into his or her Eclipse IDE is not predictable. However, considering the discussed security annotations, only plugins that comply with the *secrecy* security level should be allowed to access the password store.

To conduct this part of the case study, we implemented a malicious plugin that attempts to illegally access passwords stored in Eclipse Secure Storage. In addition to the security requirements annotated to the design models discussed above, we extended the Eclipse Secure Storage implementation with countermeasures to actively prevent illegal accesses that violate these security requirements. Based on this, we monitored Eclipse for security violations with respect to UMLsec secure dependency and executed the malicious plugin. The runtime monitoring successfully detected and mitigated the security violations caused by the malicious Eclipse plugin we prepared. In addition, the models were modified as expected, providing details about the operation of our malicious plugin and allowing a detailed investigation of the security violation.

7.3 Observations

In the two case studies, we demonstrated the technical suitability of the developed approach to work as a whole and being technically applicable for developing secure software systems. Although some parts of the case studies required manual simulations of parts of the approach, our case studies revealed that the current implementation of GRaViTY already provides much support for effectively and efficiently aiding the development of secure software systems. As for most research prototypes, especially the user interface should be improved for practical application and there is room for automation to more seamlessly integrate into the workflow, currently, most tooling that could run automatically has to be triggered manually. Altogether, the case studies demonstrated the technical feasibility of GRaViTY.

Considering the key assumptions on users of the GRaViTY approach, we made the following observations.

Suitable Views: As part of the case studies, we were able to specify security requirements mainly on design models, as we suggest security experts do. While it was necessary to specify some security requirements on a fairly detailed version of these models, it was often possible to specify security requirements on abstract models and propagate them to more detailed models and the implementation. It may be that we have enforced working on the model rather than the code, but this still shows technical feasibility. However, we agree that the usability should be improved, but this is only partly related to our own tools, but mainly to the Papyrus UML editor used.

Side effects: While conducting the case studies, we explicitly tried not to let our actions be influenced by their potential side effects, to inspect if we would be notified about them. As expected due to this behavior, there were some situations where we had to resolve conflicts caused by side effects, but they were always prominently presented to us by the tool support. For example, a dependency added due to an implementation-level change caused a security problem on the design models but was detected by the continuous security checks and displayed as an error marker. Therefore, we believe that this approach allows us to focus more on security engineering or implementation, but it remains to be verified with external developers.

Synchronization: In the case study, we were always able to synchronize our changes without any technical problems. This is not surprising, as our case studies mainly contained changes that resided at the detailed source code level, and TGGs can propagate all changes from a more detailed to a more abstract model. The opposite direction is more challenging, as changes cannot be reflected one to one and sometimes ended up with the change being applied to the source code but requiring manual post-processing. For example, when we deleted a dependency in a design model to fix a security issue due to an illegal access, the source code was adjusted accordingly by deleting a method call, but the variable to which the method's return value was assigned was now unassigned. We considered this to be intentional and not a significant problem, since the method had to be changed as a result of a design decision. Instead of accepting this compilation error, the entire body of the method could be automatically commented out and a to-do added as a more elegant solution. In practice, there may be cases where large changes to the UML models that need to be propagated to the implementation, or parallel changes, may cause synchronization problems. However, what such cases are is explicitly discussed in the thesis.

Continuous Security: Throughout the case studies, the primary goal of being able to continuously check for compliance with security requirements was possible. After the initial specification of security requirements, we were able to continuously check the software system for security violations and were notified of violations. However, this only demonstrates the technical feasibility of the approach and the ability to tailor implementation-level security checks based on design-time security requirements in all situations we faced. Based on the case study, we can only state that we did not receive any false positives for security violations, but we cannot judge whether the results were always correct or whether security issues were missed.

8 Outlook

In the thesis, we mainly looked at individual software systems that are located in critical domains. In these domains, standards such as ISO/IEC 62304 for medical device software, which was relevant to our first case study, require developers to deliver all of the artifacts that are created when following MDD and are also considered in GRaViTY. However, there are still many domains with individual challenges that need to be addressed. Also, the approach is designed in principle not to be limited to the Java world but any object-oriented language, which remains to be confirmed.

One particularly relevant domain that requires extremely complex software-intensive systems and is utmost security and safety critical toward which we are currently expanding GRaViTY is autonomous driving. While autonomous driving systems are in principle located in a strongly regulated domain that would guarantee the perfect applicability of GRaViTY due to standards such as the IEEE 26262 on functional safety management, most autonomous driving projects, especially the open-source projects such as Autoware.auto or Baidu Apollo, do not seem to follow strict model-based development processes. The same also applies to many other domains such as mobile apps, and we have to identify more lightweight tracing approaches to allow an easy application of GRaViTY to these domains.

Further, autonomous vehicles are extremely distributed systems as well on the individual vehicle as on external systems that are communicating with the autonomous vehicle. Popular robotic middlewares, such as the Robotic Operation System (ROS), which is the basis for Autoware.auto, foster the realization of such systems as a multitude of individually running nodes that are deployed on the vehicle itself or on external servers and communicate through a message API of the middleware with each other. In the thesis, we have already seen that we can extract much information about the borders of the system, e.g., to optimize security checks with information that is not contained in the source code. Leveraging such information becomes even more important for effective security checks in such massively distributed systems. Also, we have to integrated different kinds of checks on different nodes. Especially in autonomous driving, there is a significant use of machine learning approaches for tasks such as perception of the environment and prediction of behavior. Here, we have to work with assumptions on the machine learning-based nodes when checking other nodes that interact with these. For checking these nodes themselves, we have to create more dynamic verification approaches. However, as already shown in the thesis even for handwritten code, many aspects cannot be verified statically. We have to develop approaches to trace nonfunctional requirements throughout the entire development process to the runtime and to verify them in all phases to provide developers with a holistic picture.

Finally, we are currently extending our approaches to consider not only security but also other nonfunctional requirements such as safety. In most software-intensive systems, the various nonfunctional requirements do not stand alone, but there is significant interaction. For example, in autonomous driving, a successful attack will potentially lead to a malfunction of the car's behavior, e.g., because some nodes of the system do not provide required data. Such a malfunction is obviously also safety critical, and we cannot consider these two aspects completely separately. Our ultimate goal is to provide an approach that allows the selection of relevant domain-specific profiles of nonfunctional requirements, such as safety and security, and provides a holistic verification of whether the system satisfies all these requirements. In combination with the demonstrated change handling and incremental verification, this will form the basis for an incremental certification framework.

9 Summary

In the thesis, we present the GRaViTY approach for continuously supporting developers with automated propagation of changes to avoid security-critical inconsistencies. Based on this synchronization, security experts can specify security requirements on the most suitable system representation. We can verify and enforce these security requirements on all system representations using automated security checks, allowing us to check the implementation's security compliance, as needed in certifications. To preserve this compliance when restructuring the system, we provide semantics-preserving refactorings that are enriched with security-preserving constraints. For both security checks and refactorings, we show their application to variant-rich software systems. To support legacy systems, we show how UML models can be reverse-engineered also for systems with variants and how existing early SecDFD design models can be semi-automatically mapped to the implementation. In addition to an evaluation of the single parts of the approach, the overall approach is demonstrated in two real-world case studies, the iTrust electronics health records system and the Eclipse Secure Storage.

References

1. Ahmadian, A.S., Peldszus, S., Ramadan, Q., Jürjens, J.: Model-based privacy and security analysis with CARiSMA. In: Proceedings of the 11th Joint Meeting on Foundations of Software Engineering (2017)
2. Arzt, S., Rasthofer, S., Fritz, C., Bodden, E., Bartel, A., Klein, J., Le Traon, Y., Octeau, D., McDaniel, P.: FlowDroid: precise context, Flow, field, object-sensitive and lifecycle-aware taint analysis for android apps. In: Proceedings of the 35th Conference on Programming Language Design and Implementation (2014)
3. Brambilla, M., Cabot, J., Wimmer, M.: Model-driven software engineering in practice. Synth. Lect. Softw. Eng. **1**(1) (2012)
4. Bürger, J.: Recovering Security in Model-Based Software Engineering by Context-Driven Co-Evolution. PhD thesis, University of Koblenz-Landau (2019)
5. Bürger, J., Gärtner, S., Ruhroth, T., Zweihoff, J., Jürjens, J., Schneider, K.: Restoring security of long-living systems by co-evolution. In: Proceedings of the 39th Annual Computer Software and Applications Conference (COMPSAC) (2015)
6. Crnkovic, G.D.: Constructive research and info-computational knowledge generation. In: Proceedings of the International Conference on Model-based Reasoning in Science and Technology (MBR) (2010)
7. Czarnecki, K., Pietroszek, K.: Verifying feature-based model templates against well-formedness OCL constraints. In: Proceedings of the 5th International Conference on Generative Programming and Component Engineering (GPCE) (2006)
8. Eclipse contributors: Workbench User Guide – Secure Storage – How secure storage works. Technical report. The Eclipse Foundation (2013). https://help.eclipse.org/
9. Fowler, M.: Refactoring: Improving the Design of Existing Code. Object Technology Series (1999)
10. France, R., Rumpe, B.: Model-driven development of complex software: a research roadmap. In: Proceedings of the Conference on the Future of Software Engineering (FOSE) (2007)
11. Gorschek, T., Tempero, E., Angelis, L.: On the use of software design models in software development practice: an empirical investigation. J. Syst. Softw. (JSS) **95**, 176–193 (2014)
12. Heckman, S., Stolee, K.T., Parnin, C.: 10+ years of teaching software engineering with iTrust: the good, the bad, and the ugly. In: Proceedings of the 40th International Conference on Software Engineering: Software Engineering Education and Training (2018)
13. Hevner, A.R., March, S.T., Park, J., Ram, S.: Design science in information systems research. MIS Quaterly **28**(1), 75–105 (2004)
14. Jürjens, J.: Secure Systems Development with UML, Springer (2005)
15. Krüger, S., Nadi, S., Reif, M., Ali, K., Mezini, M., Bodden, E., Göpfert, F., Günther, F., Weinert, C., Demmler, D., Kamath, R.: CogniCrypt: supporting developers in using cryptography. In: Proceedings of the 32nd International Conference of Automated Software Engineering (ASE), pp. 931–936 (2017)
16. Lanusse, A., Tanguy, Y., Espinoza, H., Mraidha, C., Gerard, S., Tessier, P., Schnekenburger, R., Dubois, H., Terrier, F.: Papyrus UML: an open source toolset for MDA. In: Proceedings of the 5th European Conference on Model-driven Architecture Foundations and Applications (ECMDA-FA), pp. 1–4 (2009)
17. Livshits, B., Whaley, J., Lam, M.S.: Reflection analysis for Java. In: Proceedings of the 3rd Asian Symposium on Programming Languages and Systems (APLAS), pp. 139–160 (2005)
18. Meneely, A., Smith, B., Williams, L.: iTrust Electronic Health Care System Case Study. (2021) https://github.com/ncsu-csc326/iTrust2
19. Mens, T., Taentzer, G., Müller, D.: Model-driven software refactoring. In: Model-driven Software Development: Integrating Quality Assurance, pp. 170–203 (2008)
20. Mohan, V., Othmane, L.B.: SecDevOps: is it a marketing buzzword? - mapping research on security in DevOps. In: Proceedings of the 11th International Conference on Availability, Reliability and Security (ARES), pp. 542–547 (2016)

21. Murphy, G.C., Notkin, D., Griswold, W.G., Lan, E.S.: An empirical study of static call graph extractors. Trans. Softw. Eng. Methodol. **7**(2), 158–191 (1998)
22. Oster, S., Markert, F., Ritter, P: Automated incremental pairwise testing of software product lines. In: Proceedings of the 14th International Conference on Software Product Lines (SPLC), pp. 196–210 (2010)
23. Parnas, D.L.: Software aging. In: Proceedings of the 16th International Conference on Software Engineering (ICSE), pp. 279–287 (1994)
24. Peffers, K., Tuunanen, T., Gengler, C.E., Rossi, M., Hui, W., Virtanen, V., Bragge, J.: The design science research process: a model for producing and presenting information systems research. In: Design Science Research in Information Systems and Technology, pp. 83–106 (2006)
25. Peldszus, S.: Model-driven development of evolving secure software systems. In: Collaborative Workshop on Evolution and Maintenance of Long-Living Software Systems (EMLS) (2020)
26. Peldszus, S.: Security Compliance in Model-driven Development of Software Systems in Presence of Long-Term Evolution and Variants. Springer, Berlin (2022)
27. Peldszus, S., Jürjens, J.: Werkzeuggestützte Sicherheitszertifizierung – Anwendung auf den Industrial Data Space. In: Proceedings of the Software Quality Days, Software Quality Lab GmbH, pp. 10–14 (2017)
28. Peldszus, S., Kulcsár, G., Lochau, M.: A Solution to the Java refactoring case study using eMoflon. In: Proceedings of the Transformation Tool Contest (TTC), pp. 118–122 (2015)
29. Peldszus, S., Kulcsár, G., Lochau, M., Schulze, S.: Incremental co-evolution of Java programs based on bidirectional graph transformation. In: Proceedings of the Principles and Practices of Programming on The Java Platform (PPPJ), pp. 138–151 (2015)
30. Peldszus, S., Kulcsár, G., Lochau, M., Schulze, S.: Continuous detection of design flaws in evolving object-oriented programs using incremental multi-pattern matching. In: Proceedings of the 31st International Conference on Automated Software Engineering (ASE) (2016)
31. Peldszus, S., Cirullies, J., Jürjens, J.: Sicherheitszertifizierung für die Digitale Transformation – Anwendung auf den Industrial Data Space. In: Software-QS-Tag (2017)
32. Peldszus, S., Strüber, D., Jürjens, J.: Model-based security analysis of feature-oriented software product lines. In: ACM SIGPLAN International Conference on Generative Programming (GPCE), pp. 93–106 (2018)
33. Peldszus, S., Tuma, K., Strüber, D., Jürjens, J., Scandariato, R.: Secure data-flow compliance checks between models and code based on automated mappings. In: MODELS, pp. 23–33 (2019)
34. Peldszus, S., Bürger, J., Kehrer, T., Jürjens, J. Ontology-driven evolution of software security. Domain Knowl. Eng. **134**, 1–31 (2021)
35. Peldszus, S., Bürger, J., Jürjens, J.: UMLsecRT: reactive security monitoring of java applications with round-trip engineering. IEEE Trans. Softw. Eng. https://doi.org/10.1109/TSE.2023.3326366
36. Rajlich, V., Gosavi, P.: Incremental change in object-oriented programming. IEEE Softw. **21**(4), 62–69 (2004)
37. Ruland, S., Kulcsár, G., Leblebici, E., Peldszus, S., Lochau, M.: Controlling the attack surface of object-oriented refactorings. In: International Conference on Fundamental Approaches to Software Engineering (FASE), pp. 38–55 (2018)
38. Santos, J.C.S., Tarrit, K., Mirakhorli, M.: A catalog of security architecture weaknesses. In: Proceedings of the International Conference on Software Architecture Workshops (ICSAW), pp. 220–223 (2017)
39. Schürr, A.: Specification of graph translators with triple graph grammars. In: Proceedings of the International Workshop on Graph-theoretic Concepts in Computer Science (WG), pp. 151–163 (1995)
40. Shostack, A.: Threat Modeling: Designing for Security. John Wiley & Sons, New York (2014)
41. Strüber, D., Peldszus, S., Jürjens, J.: Taming multi-variability of software product line transformations. In: International Conference on Fundamental Approaches to Software Engineering (FASE), pp. 337–355 (2018)

42. The Eclipse Foundation: Papyrus Modeling Environment. (2019) https://www.eclipse.org/papyrus/
43. Tuma, K., Scandariato, R., Balliu, M.: Flaws in flows: unveiling design flaws via information flow analysis. In: Proceedings of the International Conference on Software Architecture (ICSA), pp. 191–200 (2019)
44. Tuma, K., Peldszus, S., Strüber, D., Scandariato, R., Jürjens, J.: Checking security compliance between models and code. Softw. Syst. Model. **22**, 273–296 (2022)

Open Access This chapter is licensed under the terms of the Creative Commons Attribution 4.0 International License (http://creativecommons.org/licenses/by/4.0/), which permits use, sharing, adaptation, distribution and reproduction in any medium or format, as long as you give appropriate credit to the original author(s) and the source, provide a link to the Creative Commons licence and indicate if changes were made.

The images or other third party material in this chapter are included in the chapter's Creative Commons licence, unless indicated otherwise in a credit line to the material. If material is not included in the chapter's Creative Commons licence and your intended use is not permitted by statutory regulation or exceeds the permitted use, you will need to obtain permission directly from the copyright holder.

Model-Driven Engineering of Microservice Architectures—The LEMMA Approach

Florian Rademacher, Philip Wizenty, Jonas Sorgalla, Sabine Sachweh, and Albert Zündorf

Abstract This chapter presents LEMMA (Language Ecosystem for Modeling Microservice Architecture). LEMMA enables the application of Model-Driven Engineering (MDE) to Microservice Architecture (MSA). LEMMA mitigates the complexity of MSA by decomposing it along four viewpoints on microservice architectures, each capturing the concerns of different MSA stakeholders in dedicated architecture models. LEMMA formalizes the syntax and semantics of these models with specialized modeling languages that are integrated based on an import mechanism, thus enabling holistic MSA modeling. LEMMA also bundles its own model processing framework (MPF) to facilitate model processor implementation for technology-savvy MSA stakeholders without a background in MDE.

We describe the design and development of LEMMA and exemplify the usage of its modeling languages and MPF for a case study microservice architecture. In addition, we present practical applications of LEMMA for microservice code generation, architecture reconstruction, quality analysis, defect resolution, and establishing a common architecture understanding. A comparison of LEMMA with related approaches reveals that LEMMA has particular strengths in (i) language-level extensibility, allowing model-based reification of architectural patterns; (ii) model processing, by bundling sophisticated code generators and static quality analyzers; and (iii) versatility, making LEMMA applicable in microservice development, operation, architecture reconstruction, and quality assessment.

F. Rademacher (✉)
Software Engineering, RWTH Aachen University, Aachen, Germany
e-mail: rademacher@se-rwth.de

P. Wizenty · J. Sorgalla · S. Sachweh
IDiAL Institute, University of Applied Sciences and Arts Dortmund, Dortmund, Germany
e-mail: philip.wizenty@fh-dortmund.de; jonas.sorgalla@fh-dortmund.de; sabine.sachweh@fh-dortmund.de

A. Zündorf
Software Engineering Research Group, University of Kassel, Kassel, Germany
e-mail: zuendorf@uni-kassel.de

1 Introduction

Microservice Architecture (MSA) [65] is an approach to architecting distributed software systems that promotes system decomposition into *microservices*. The notion of microservice comprises all characteristics of a *service*, i.e., it is a functional software component that (i) minimizes dependencies to other components; (ii) clusters coherent business logic; (iii) agrees on *contracts* that specify communication relationships with other components by means of *interfaces*; and (iv) interacts with other components to realize coarse-grained tasks [23]. While MSA emerged from Service-Oriented Architecture (SOA) [17, 23], other than an SOA service, a microservice aims to maximize *service-specific independence*. From the aspects that are concerned by this maximization, the notion of microservice can be defined as follows [6, 13, 14, 17, 44, 64, 65, 93, 101]:

Definition 1 (Microservice) A microservice is a service with the following characteristics:

- It provides a distinct capability to other components, and all of its functionalities address a single concern of either functional or infrastructure nature.
- It is as independent as possible from other components in terms of implementation, data management, testing, deployment, and operation.
- It is fully accountable for its interaction with other components including, e.g., the actual decision for interaction, communication protocol determination, data format conversion, and failure handling. Without a sound technical reason, a microservice supports at most two communication protocols—one for synchronous one-to-one and one for asynchronous one-to-many interactions.
- It is owned by exactly one team. The team is fully responsible for all aspects related to the microservice's design, implementation, and operation.

Starting from these characteristics, MSA is expected to benefit the architectures of distributed software systems in several ways. First, microservices can improve performance efficiency, and especially *scalability* [42], making it possible to scale heavily frequented functionalities independently and horizontally [19]. Second, microservices may have a positive impact on maintainability and, more precisely, *modifiability* [42], because they facilitate isolated replacement of functionality as long as interfaces remain stable [65]. Third, MSA can increase the *testability* [42] of software systems by demanding stand-alone component executability.

While performance efficiency and maintainability are the most important quality attributes of MSA and key drivers for its adoption [17, 119], microservices can benefit further quality attributes [42] such as (i) *reliability*, due to each microservice being expected to include its own failure handling mechanisms for preventing failure cascades across service boundaries [13, 65]; (ii) *portability*, by deploying microservices using lightweight virtualization technologies like containers [9, 18, 111]; and (iii) *compatibility*, as independent executability and standardized communication protocols foster interoperability and gradual migration of legacy systems toward MSA [13, 119].

However, these benefits come at the cost of an increased complexity that affects architecture design, implementation, and operation [109]. For example, granularity determination is a major challenge in MSA design as too fine-grained microservices induce frequent interactions and thus network overhead [119]. Concerning implementation, MSA aggravates technology management by supporting dedicated technology choices per service and delegation of decisions for technology stacks to microservice teams [52]. The resulting increase of *technology heterogeneity* [65] also concerns operation because the corresponding infrastructure of a microservice architecture usually consists of loosely coupled components for diverse tasks like service discovery, API provisioning, load balancing, and monitoring [7].

Model-Driven Engineering (MDE) [15] is an approach to software engineering that leverages *models* as a means to abstract from selected details of a software system to mitigate complexity. More precisely, MDE focuses on the systematic construction, evolution, and maintenance of software models, and making them actionable within one or more phases of the software engineering process. For a certain set of purposes, models can then act as substitutes of more complex artifacts. For instance, models may abstract from implementation details of the conversion between data-format-specific network messages and data-format-agnostic in-memory objects. Yet they can enable the automated derivation of source code for this purpose [94]. On another note, models are well suited to reify structures of software systems and facilitate reasoning about them, e.g., for quality assessment and improvement [16].

As an orthogonal approach to software architecting that strives for purposeful complexity mitigation, MDE is a predestined means for the description, development, and analysis of complex software systems [28, 104]. Indeed, it has successfully been applied in different domains of software architectures such as cyber-physical systems [62], Industry 4.0 [127], Internet of Things [51], and SOA [2]. Hence, it is evident to investigate the applicability of *MDE-for-MSA* [31].

This chapter presents recent findings of this investigation by (i) summarizing the main results of a corresponding dissertation [93], which manifested in the Language Ecosystem for Modeling Microservice Architecture (LEMMA) [108]; and (ii) showing how LEMMA stimulates ongoing research on MDE-for-MSA beyond the dissertation.

The remainder of the chapter is structured as follows. Section 2 presents background information on MDE-for-MSA. Section 3 describes LEMMA's design and implementation. Section 4 focuses on its applications, e.g., for microservice code generation, architecture reconstruction, and defect resolution. Sections 5 and 6 compare LEMMA with related works and conclude the chapter.

2 Preliminaries

This section describes challenges in MSA engineering (Sect. 2.1), the MDE paradigm (Sect. 2.2), and the adoption of MDE to tackle MSA engineering challenges (Sect. 2.3).

2.1 Challenges in Microservice Architecture Engineering

Following the *taxonomy for pains of microservices* by Soldani et al. [109], we summarize challenges in MSA engineering along the dimensions Design (Sect. 2.1.1), Implementation (Sect. 2.1.2), and Operation (Sect. 2.1.3). Given MSA's impact on development organizations [64], we also consider the Organization dimension (Sect. 2.1.4).

2.1.1 Design Challenges

The *identification of microservices* is pivotal in MSA design [29, 109, 119]. It entails the decomposition of functionality and is closely related to granularity determination (see below). Domain-Driven Design (DDD) is a popular methodology for microservice identification [24, 30, 56, 57, 64, 65]. It provides model-based techniques and patterns to identify coherent parts in an application domain and eventually derive *bounded contexts* from them. A bounded context clusters coherent domain concepts, their structures, and relationships in a *domain model* [24]. Similar to microservices, bounded contexts gather coherent functionality, belong to one team, and require interactions via well-defined interfaces. Despite the perceived closeness of DDD and MSA [65], the adoption of the former in the context of the latter is often considered complex [13, 29] and additional effort when domain models act as mere documentation artifacts [24].

Determining the optimal granularity of a microservice is a major challenge in MSA design [109, 119]. Besides the vague suggestion to align a microservice to a distinct capability (Definition 1), there exist no broadly accepted guidelines on how to tailor a microservice's responsibilities. Additionally, the independence of microservice teams fosters divergent intuitions of microservice granularity and, in the worst case, may result in a centralized architecture team that balances varying granularities by frequent refactoring [13]. On the other hand, certain microservices may intentionally be more coarse-grained than others to decrease network load, eliminate interaction dependencies, or reduce the number of microservices [13, 18].

By contrast to SOA, MSA considers *APIs as contracts* [128], thereby rendering the formal specification of interactions and *explicit contract negotiation* [66] redundant. Instead, the interaction relationship between two microservices concludes an *implicit service contract*, which reduces design complexity. As a drawback, microservices are confronted with API versioning and assuring consumer compliance [109]. Moreover, the waiver of explicit contracts fosters ad hoc communication and thus the accidental occurrence of cyclic service dependencies [118].

2.1.2 Implementation Challenges

As already mentioned (Sect. 1), MSA can increase the technology heterogeneity of a software system. While it may be beneficial that each microservice can rely on those implementation technologies that are the most suitable for its capability [65], this level of freedom in technology choices incurs risks for increased technical debt, additional maintainability costs, and steeper learning curves for new team members [13, 52, 118].

Moreover, MSA's emphasis on loose coupling also leads to a decoupling of technical concerns [38]. Hence, technology management is additionally aggravated due to an increased number of *technology variation points* [95] like the following:

- **Programming languages:** The programming language of a microservice is opaque to clients. Java, JavaScript, and C# are among the most popular service programming languages [106]. However, certain specifics of a service's capability can motivate the adoption of an alternative programming language. For instance, the built-in support for data collection handling and the availability of sophisticated frameworks for scientific computing or time series processing make Python a viable choice for corresponding microservices [46, 54, 95].
- **Database management systems (DBMSs):** To decrease coupling, each microservice should have its own database [63, 102]. A service's capability may also favor DBMS mechanisms like NoSQL or graphs over the relational paradigm [52].
- **Communication protocols:** A microservice architecture should employ at most two communication protocols (Sect. 1). However, some situations may require more than two protocols, e.g., when gradually modernizing legacy systems [58].
- **Data formats:** The interaction scenario or choice of a communication protocol may impact the selection of a format for data encoding and decoding.

2.1.3 Operation Challenges

Microservices are usually packaged, deployed, and executed in virtualized *containers* [111]. Containers enable the combined deployment of software components and pre-configured runtime environments while being more resource-efficient than virtual machines due to kernel and library sharing with the host operating system. Containers benefit microservices' scalability and portability [18] but typically require additional orchestration platforms, e.g., to fulfill elasticity requirements [40, 52]. These platforms expose microservice architectures to continuous service partitioning and relocation with additional effort to keep track of [109].

Next to container orchestration platforms, MSA requires additional infrastructure components, e.g., for service discovery, API provisioning, load balancing, and monitoring [7]. The loose coupling of these components increases technology heterogeneity on the operation level. Furthermore, each component may have its own requirements w.r.t. configuration and life cycle management [109].

2.1.4 Organizational Challenges

MSA assumes an alignment of the development organization with the software architecture to be effective [4]. A common practice is to decompose homogeneous development organizations into teams, possibly assembled from members with heterogeneous skill sets, of which each is responsible for one or more microservices. Consequently, MSA fosters DevOps [64] and thus faces challenges like establishing and maintaining a *collaborative culture*, *automation*, and *knowledge sharing* [55].

2.2 Model-Driven Engineering

To unfold its potential for complexity mitigation, MDE anticipates systematic model construction, evolution, and maintenance. *Modeling languages* specify models' *syntaxes* and *semantics* [15]. The syntax consists of an *abstract syntax* and one or more *concrete syntaxes*. The former defines modeling concepts' structures, relationships, and tool-internal representation. The latter determine user-facing notations of modeling concepts, e.g., as graphical constituents of box-and-line diagrams or grammar-based textual strings. Modeling language syntaxes may impose constraints on model well-formedness, thus contributing to the definition of language-specific model validity. The semantics of a modeling language assigns meaning to modeling concepts and their instantiation as model elements; and can restrict the set of valid models even further [37].

Model processors turn models into actionable software engineering artifacts [15]. *Code generation* is often perceived to drive MDE adoption because of an expected increase of development productivity [123]. However, there exists a plethora of other model processing approaches with relevance to software architecting, e.g., *reverse engineering* [117] and *static model analysis* [15]. Most of these approaches resort to *model transformation* [15], i.e., the (semi-) automated conversion of one or more source models into one or more target models based on *transformation rules* [59]. The syntaxes of source and target models may differ, e.g., when model elements are transformed into programming language constructs (code generation) or implementation artifacts are transformed into models (reverse engineering).

2.3 Employing Model-Driven Engineering to Cope with Challenges in Microservice Architecture Engineering

Table 1 maps MDE means (Sect. 2.2) to MSA engineering challenges (Sect. 2.1) and substantiates our hypothesis that MDE-for-MSA can cope with MSA's complexity. Sections 2.3.1 to 2.3.4 describe the mapping per MSA engineering dimension.

Table 1 Mapping of supportive MDE means to MSA engineering challenges [93]

Dimension	Challenge	Summary	MDE means
Design	C.1	Manage[a] services' granularities	Modeling languages
	C.2	Facilitate domain-driven service identification	Modeling languages
	C.3	Increase the value of domain models	Model processing
	C.4	Manage services' APIs	Modeling languages
	C.5	Cope with cyclic service dependencies	Context conditions, static analysis
Implementation	C.6	Manage technology heterogeneity	Abstraction, code generation
Operation	C.7	Cope with complexity in service partitioning and location	Abstraction
	C.8	Manage architecture components for service deployment and infrastructure provisioning	Modeling languages
Organizational	C.9	Automate as much manual tasks as possible	Model processing
	C.10	Provide formats and guidelines for knowledge sharing	Modeling languages

[a] In the context of the table, the term "manage" covers the actions elicitation, adaptation, and consistent documentation of managed entities

2.3.1 Design

Modeling languages have proven suitable for granularity and API specification in other approaches to service-based architecting [2, 94]. Hence, they can tackle Challenges C.1 and C.4. Modeling languages are also a natural choice for Challenge C.2 because DDD (Sect. 2.1) constructs domain models with modeling languages [24]. Model processing then increases domain models' value (Challenge C.3) by elevating them from documentation artifacts to first-class citizens in software engineering. When resorting to MDE-based microservice design, the detection of cyclic service dependencies (Challenge C.5) is possible at design time using (i) context conditions that constrain model validity to non-cyclic service dependencies; and (ii) static analysis to detect cycles across models.

2.3.2 Implementation

MDE's abstraction from technology [70] predestines it for coping with technology heterogeneity (Challenge C.6). Nonetheless, model-based technology abstraction can be tailored per stakeholder group [95, 110]. Code generation then produces technology-specific code from technology-agnostic models [15, 96]. For MSA, code generation can even increase maintainability (Sect. 1) by automating steps in migrating microservice implementations to other technology stacks.

2.3.3 Operation

For Challenge C.7, we rely on abstraction as it allows capturing of service partitioning and location agnostic to deployment and orchestration technologies. For Challenge C.8, the existence of model-based approaches to operation environment specification [25, 67] proves modeling languages well suited for infrastructure management in MSA.

2.3.4 Organizational

Model processing supports task automation and is therefore inherently suited to deal with Challenge C.9. Modeling languages facilitate sharing of architecture knowledge (Challenge C.10) by formalizing its model-based expression [123], especially in combination with stakeholder-oriented viewpoints for knowledge decomposition [28].

3 LEMMA—A Language Ecosystem for Modeling Microservice Architecture

Here, we present LEMMA [93] in detail. Section 3.1 specifies *architecture viewpoints* [43] for MSA to which LEMMA's modeling languages (Sect. 3.2) and model processing facilities (Sect. 3.3) align. Section 3.4 illustrates LEMMA's usage.

3.1 Microservice Architecture Viewpoints

We leverage the notion of architecture viewpoint ("viewpoint" henceforth) from ISO 42010 [43] to decompose MSA's complexity (Sect. 2.1). A viewpoint frames stakeholder concerns toward a software system. It prescribes languages and techniques to construct *architecture models* as well as operations to process them [43].

For LEMMA, we focused on the following stakeholder groups and their concerns in MSA engineering [13, 29, 36, 38, 102]:

- **Domain experts:** Domain experts demand a software that covers the relevant domain-specific requirements in a cost-effective manner in the expected quality.

- **Microservice developers:** Microservice developers implement and test owned microservices w.r.t. specifications, e.g., of requirements or the architecture.
- **Microservice operators:** Microservice operators are concerned with microservice and operation infrastructure deployment and configuration.
- **Software architects:** Software architects deal with architecture specification and examination to assess quality attribute satisfaction. In addition, they communicate with and across development teams.

From these stakeholders and their concerns, we derived viewpoints for the model-based description of microservice architectures:

- **Domain viewpoint:** This viewpoint supports the construction of *domain models* for microservice architectures. Following DDD, domain model construction may be a collaborative activity by domain experts and microservice developers [24].
- **Technology viewpoint:** This viewpoint reifies the technology heterogeneity of microservice architectures. It captures the concerns of microservice developers and operators toward technology management within *technology models*.
- **Service viewpoint:** The viewpoint addresses the concerns of microservice developers by the construction of *service models* for microservices, their interfaces, and operations. Service models may refer to technology models to reify technology decisions. To enable model reuse and facilitate technology exchange, the viewpoint also considers the construction of *service technology mapping models*, which externalize technology decisions from service models.
- **Operation viewpoint:** This viewpoint allows microservice operators the capturing of microservice deployment and operation in *operation models*.

To increase information content and reusability, MSA models are composable by element references. For example, operation parameters in service models may refer to domain concepts in domain models as types. Figure 1 shows LEMMA's viewpoints and composition relationships between model kinds of different viewpoints. Model composition inherently addresses the concerns of software architects by fostering architecture specification and examination with a coherent architecture representation.

3.2 Modeling Languages

Following ISO 42010, we devised modeling languages (Sect. 2.2) for the construction of MSA viewpoint models (Fig. 1). Figure 2 shows the language development process.

Sections 3.2.1 to 3.2.5 describe the activities of the development process.

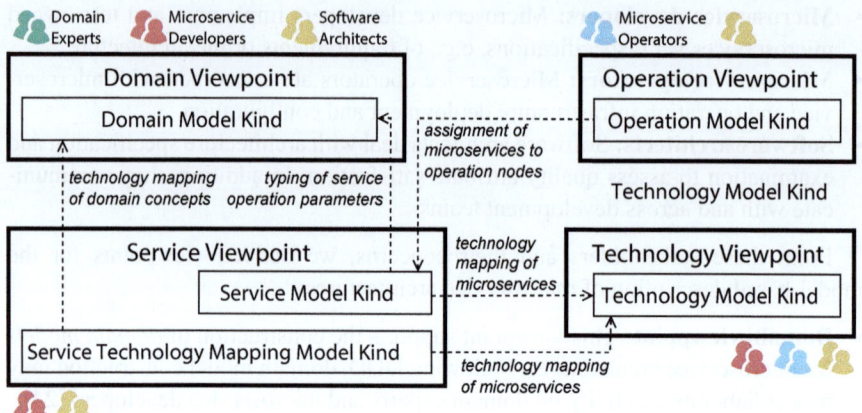

Fig. 1 LEMMA's MSA viewpoints and reference-based composition relationships between model kinds of different viewpoints. The relationships are depicted as dashed arrows from referencing to referred model kinds. Colored icons on a viewpoint box identify the stakeholder groups whose concerns are framed by the viewpoint [43]

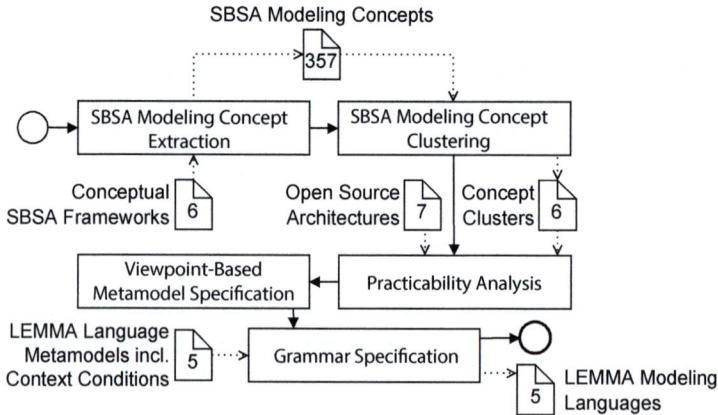

Fig. 2 BPMN diagram [69] of LEMMA's language development process

3.2.1 SBSA Modeling Concept Extraction

We identified and extracted an initial set of potential modeling concepts for LEMMA's modeling languages from six conceptual frameworks [10, 60, 66–68, 121] for the model-based description of service-based software architectures (SBSAs) [23]. We selected these frameworks because they explicitly consider various stakeholder groups, viewpoints, and engineering phases, without prescribing a certain solution architecture. In total, we extracted 357 SBSA modeling concepts and their definitions [92].

Table 2 Count of SBSA modeling concepts per Essential SOA Elements category

Essential SOA Elements category	Concept count
Contract	53
Governance	19
Implementation	31
Infrastructure & Management	77
Interface	177
SLA	19
Not classifiable	58
Sum	**434**

3.2.2 SBSA Modeling Concept Clustering

We clustered the SBSA modeling concepts into the categories of the Essential SOA Elements taxonomy [2], i.e., "Contract," "Governance," "Implementation," "Infrastructure & Management," "Interface," and "Service Level Agreement (SLA)." For the clustering, we relied on concepts' definitions extracted in the previous activity. The clustering enabled us to relate a concept to one or more of the MSA model kinds described in Sect. 3.1. Table 2 summarizes the clustering results.

The mismatch between the sums of clustered modeling concepts (434) and extracted modeling concepts (357) stems from ambiguous concept definitions. For example, based on its definition, SoaML's Capability concept [68] was clustered into the Implementation and Interface categories. On the other hand, some concept definitions were too narrow to permit classification, e.g., the Clipped Structural Modeling Connector concept from the Service-Oriented Modeling Framework [60]. Section 4.3.1 and Appendix B of the dissertation that conceived LEMMA [93] provide more details on the clustering activity.

3.2.3 Practicability Analysis

The previous activities established a conceptual baseline for LEMMA's model languages on the basis of SBSA modeling concepts. This focus on SBSA was necessary as no conceptual frameworks for MSA modeling existed. To assess the applicability of the extracted SBSA modeling concepts for MSA engineering and balance conceptual rigor with practice orientation, we analyzed concepts' manifestation and actual usage in seven open-source microservice architectures. We derived the set of these architectures by joining two subsets of microservice architectures that (i) provide their source code on GitHub;[1] and (ii) have already been academically investigated to gain insights about MSA implementation concepts and patterns [63, 100]. Table 3 lists the considered architectures. They account for 51.35% of the overall lines of code of all architectures in the unified set. For further

---
[1] https://www.github.com.

Table 3 Open-source microservice architectures selected for practicability analysis of SBSA modeling concepts. Table entries are arranged in descending order by the value in the "Lines of Code" column as of February 1st, 2020

Architecture name	Academic reference	GitHub path[a]	Programming languages	Lines of code
eShopOnContainers	[100]	/dotnet-architecture/eShopOnContainers/tree/20238d53	C#, JavaScript	94,660
Micro company	[63]	/idugalic/micro-company/tree/5a4ee50	Java, JavaScript	83,685
Lakeside Mutual Insurance company	[100]	/Microservice-API-Patterns/LakesideMutual/tree/35a67ac	Java, JavaScript	83,181
Pitstop - garage management system	[63, 100]	/EdwinVW/pitstop/tree/e3afc74	C#, JavaScript	53,591
Microservices reference	[63]	/mspnp/microservices-reference-implementation/tree/69a8f63	C#, Java, JavaScript	18,751
WeText	[63]	/daxnet/we-text/tree/6bab01c	C#, JavaScript	18,523
FTGO - restaurant management	[100]	/microservices-patterns/ftgo-application/tree/9f85c77	Cucumber, Java, JavaScript	15,069

[a] Relative to host https://www.github.com

details, we refer to Sect. 4.3.2 and Appendix C of the dissertation that conceived LEMMA [93].

3.2.4 Viewpoint-Based Metamodel Specification

For each of the viewpoint-specific model kinds in Fig. 1, we defined the abstract syntax of a LEMMA modeling language (Sect. 2.2) as *metamodel* [15]. Consequently, LEMMA comprises five modeling languages, each targeting a different MSA viewpoint. Table 4 provides an overview of these languages.

LEMMA's modeling languages support MSA stakeholders as follows:

- **Domain Data Modeling Language (DDML):** The DDML enables the collaborative construction of domain models by domain experts and microservice developers (Sect. 2.1). It integrates constructs for the model-based expression of domain concepts and their augmentation with DDD patterns.
- **Technology Modeling Language (TML):** The TML addresses microservice developer and operator concerns (Sect. 3.1) in capturing technology decisions.

Model-Driven Engineering of Microservice Architectures—The LEMMA Approach   117

Table 4 LEMMA's languages per stakeholder group, viewpoint, and model kind

Stakeholder group	Viewpoint	Modeling languages (# Modeling concepts/ context conditions)	Model kind
Domain experts	Domain	Domain Data Modeling Language (28/36)	Domain Model Kind
Microservice developers	Domain	Domain Data Modeling Language	Domain Model Kind
	Service	Service Modeling Language (24/39)	Service Model Kind
	Service	Service Technology Mapping Modeling Language (20/39)	Service Technology Mapping Model Kind
	Technology	Technology Modeling Language (24/37)	Technology Model Kind
Microservice operators	Operation	Operation Modeling Language (12/36)	Operation Model Kind
	Technology	Technology Modeling Language	Technology Model Kind
Software architects	All	All	All

- **Service Modeling Language (SML):** The SML targets microservice developer concerns. Service models constructed with the SML thus specify microservice APIs including operation signatures and physical or logical endpoints.
- **Service Technology Mapping Modeling Language (STMML):** The STMML enables the construction of service technology mapping models to augment service model elements with technology information, thereby keeping service models technology-agnostic and reusable across technologies.
- **Operation Modeling Language (OML):** The OML supports operators in specifying microservice deployment, infrastructure configuration and usage.

We base the composition relationships between model kinds (Fig. 1) on imports, i.e., specific elements in a model can refer to specific elements in imported models.

For each LEMMA modeling language, Table 4 also shows the number of modeling concepts and *context conditions* [15] that prescribe model well-formedness.

Figure 3 shows an excerpt of the SML's metamodel and thus illustrates the influence of the practicability analysis on the eventual definition of metamodel concepts.

An SML ServiceModel comprises an arbitrary number of Microservices, each having a name, type, visibility, and, optionally, a version. A microservice can require other microservices to express service dependencies. Required microservices may originate from the same or an imported service model (Import and PossiblyImportedMicroservice concepts). A non-imported microservice has one or more Interfaces. The notImplemented flag specifies whether an interface lacks an implementation, which is useful for iterative API refinement prior to API exposure. An interface has one or more Operations that model the respective microservice's behavioral signatures. An

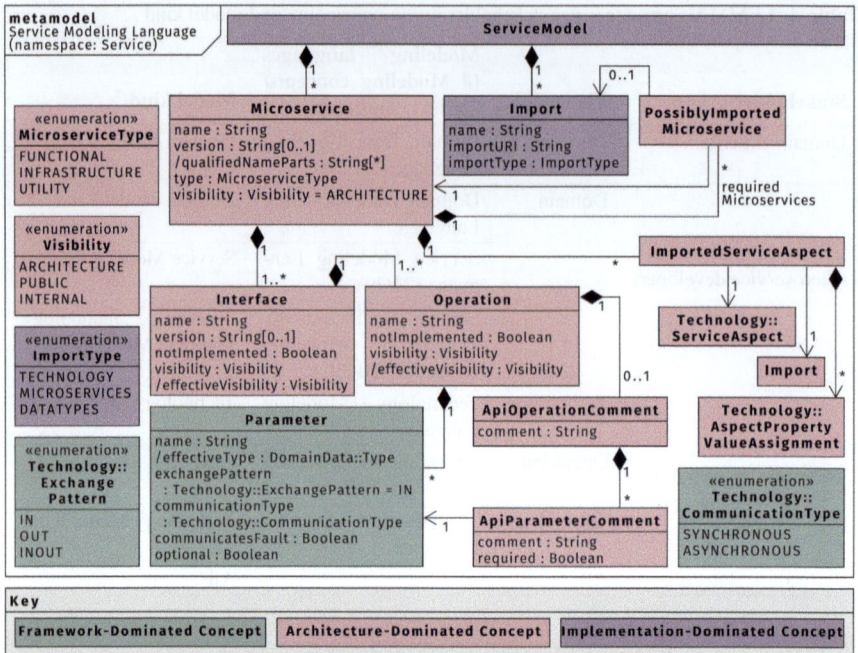

Fig. 3 Excerpt of the SML's metamodel with concepts' structures and relationships in a UML class diagram [73]. The term "dominated" identifies the driving source for a concept's eventual metamodel reification

operation consists of incoming or outgoing `Parameters`. Each parameter has a `CommunicationType` that allows, e.g., modeling of synchronously activated operations that yet exhibit asynchronous behavior. With its `ApiOperationComment` and `ApiParameterComment` concepts, the SML supports API documentation. Since LEMMA relies on *aspects* [105] to augment model elements with metadata, the SML associates microservices with `ImportedServiceAspects`. While originally intended for capturing technology decisions, aspects can also incorporate architectural patterns into LEMMA models [93].

Listing 1 illustrates our usage of OCL [71] to specify metamodel constraints that exceed class diagram expressivity.

Listing 1 Excerpt of the OCL-based [71] context conditions for the SML's metamodel

```
 1  -- Imports in a service model must be unique
 2  context ServiceModel inv uniqueImports:
 3    self.imports->forAll(i1, i2 | i1 <> i2 implies
 4      i1.name <> i2.name and i1.importURI <> i2.importURI)
 5  -- Aspects on microservices must have the correct join point
 6  context Microservice inv validJoinPointTypes:
 7    self.aspects->forAll(a | a.importedAspect.joinPoints
 8      ->includes(technology::JoinPointType::MICROSERVICES))
 9  -- Interfaces must define at least one operation
10  context Interface inv notEmpty: self.operations->size() > 0
```

We used the Eclipse Modeling Framework (EMF) [116] and, more precisely, Xcore[2] and Xbase[3] for metamodel implementation. All LEMMA metamodel implementations can be found on Software Heritage [86–90].

3.2.5 Grammar Specification

We specified *concrete syntaxes* [15] for LEMMA's metamodels to make the resulting modeling language practically usable. Based on our experiences with the development and application of a graphical MSA modeling language [98, 114], we decided for textual concrete syntaxes. Since microservice architectures usually involve many services and infrastructure components, graphical models quickly become unclear.

We employed the Xtext framework [11] for grammar specification. Listing 2 shows an excerpt of the Xtext grammar for LEMMA's SML.

Listing 2 Excerpt of the Xtext grammar for LEMMA's SML

```
enum Visibility returns Visibility:
  INTERNAL='internal' | ARCHITECTURE='architecture' | PUBLIC='public';
enum MicroserviceType returns MicroserviceType:
  FUNCTIONAL='functional' | UTILITY='utility' |
  INFRASTRUCTURE = 'infrastructure';
Microservice returns Microservice:
  visibility=Visibility? type=MicroserviceType
  'microservice' name=QualifiedNameWithAtLeastOneLevel
  ('version' version=ID)? '{' interfaces+=Interface+ '}';
```

First, the grammar determines keywords for the literals of the metamodel enumerations `Visibility` and `MicroserviceType` (Fig. 3). Next, it specifies the grammar for the `Microservice` metamodel concept. A microservice is introduced by a visibility modifier and type, followed by the `microservice` keyword and the service's name, which must exhibit at least one qualifying level to support service clustering. The `version` keyword sets the service's version. The `interface` keyword introduces an interface definition of the service within curly brackets. Listing 3 illustrates the SML's usage for modeling the `OrderService` of the microservice architecture used by Richardson to exemplify MSA [102] (Sect. 3.4).

Listing 3 Example of a microservice definition based on the metamodel (Fig. 3) and concrete syntax (Listing 2) of LEMMA's SML

```
public functional microservice org.example.OrderService {
  interface Orders { ... }
}
```

The grammar specifications of LEMMA's modeling languages and the SML code for the `OrderService` can be found on Software Heritage [76–80, 91].

---

[2] https://wiki.eclipse.org/Xcore.
[3] https://wiki.eclipse.org/Xbase.

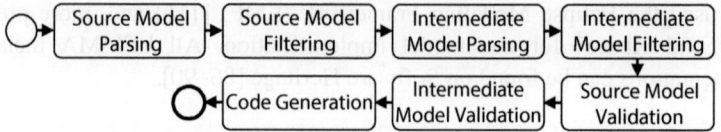

Fig. 4 Built-in phases of LEMMA's MPF

3.3 Model Processing Framework

We devised a modeling processing framework (MPF) to make LEMMA models actionable as envisioned by MDE (Sect. 2.2). The MPF targets technology-savvy MSA stakeholders, e.g., Microservice Developers and Operators (Sect. 3.1), who not necessarily have an MDE background. Therefore, the MPF (i) structures model processing into phases w.r.t. the Phased Construction pattern [53]; (ii) focuses on Java as the most popular service programming language [13, 106]; (iii) supports programming approaches common in Java-based microservice development, e.g., annotation-based Inversion of Control (IoC) [47] in combination with the Abstract Class pattern [107]; (iv) abstracts from MDE technologies used by LEMMA; and (v) yields stand-alone executable model processors for continuous integration [48].

Figure 4 shows the MPF's model processing phases. It is possible to add custom phases for other model processing purposes like simulation [15].

The phases' responsibilities are as follows:

- **Source/Intermediate Model Parsing:** These phases parse LEMMA models (*source models*; Sect. 3.2) and their intermediate representations (*intermediate models*). LEMMA intermediate models incorporate preprocessed data such as explicit configuration values resulting from implicit default values. Model processors thus need not calculate this data, which also imposes consistency in model processing. Moreover, intermediate models expressed in the generic XML Metadata Interchange format [72] decouple model processors from EMF.
- **Source/Intermediate Model Filtering:** These phases allow the selection of model elements for subsequent processing phases. Each phase expects an OCL file whose queries [71] are evaluated against the source or intermediate model. The MPF then applies follow-up phases only on elements matching the queries.
- **Source/Intermediate Model Validation:** These phases support the provisioning of model validity checks with specific severities. Source model validation may also happen interactively via the Language Server Protocol (LSP).[4] That is, MPF-based model processors leverage the LSP to connect with the Eclipse editor of the respective LEMMA modeling language to display validation results during model construction. Hence, modelers need not invoke a processor separately from the IDE and trace validation results to erroneous model elements manually.

---

[4] https://microsoft.github.io/language-server-protocol/specifications/lsp/3.17/specification.

- **Code Generation:** The MPF incorporates this phase as code generation is one of the key drivers for MDE adoption [5, 61, 123].

The Kotlin[5]-based MPF can be found on Software Heritage [83].

3.4 Illustrative Example

We illustrate the construction of a microservice with LEMMA's modeling languages (Sect. 3.2) and the processing of the resulting models with LEMMA's MPF (Sect. 3.3).

Listing 4 shows four coherent LEMMA model excerpts in the DDML, TML, and SML (Sect. 3.2). The complete models can be found on Software Heritage [81]. They cover the Order and Restaurant microservices of Richardson's MSA case study [102].

Listing 4a contains the domain model of the Order microservice in LEMMA's DDML. The model consists of the two bounded contexts (Sect. 2.1), Order and API.

The Order context comprises two domain concepts. Order is a structured domain concept that consists of five fields of which four have the built-in primitive type long, while the state field is typed by the enumeration domain concept OrderState (Lines 11–16). LEMMA's DDML also integrates keywords for *DDD patterns* [24], e.g., Aggregate and Entity. The Order structure combines both these patterns. As an aggregate, its instances cluster instances of other domain concepts, which are only accessible from the Order instance. As an entity, two Order instances are distinguishable by a domain-specific identifier (see the id field in Line 4).

The API context comprises three domain concepts for the Order microservice's interactions. The CreateOrderRequest concept is a DDD valueObject [24], i.e., its instances transport information between architecture components. Therefore, all of its fields are immutable and receive a value once during instance initialization.

Listing 4b shows a technology model for Java and Spring[6] in the TML (Sect. 3.2). The types section defines technology-specific *type synonyms* for LEMMA's built-in primitive types. During model processing, these synonyms replace all instances of LEMMA primitive types in models that apply the technology model. Since LEMMA's type system is based on Java [33], the mapping of built-in types to technology-specific synonyms Listing 4b is straightforward. For example, the boolean type has the synonym Boolean (Lines 4–5). The technology model also specifies the PostMapping aspect (Lines 20–21). It maps to the

---

[5] https://www.kotlinlang.org.
[6] https://www.spring.io.

```
// File: Order.data
context Order {
  structure Order<aggregate, entity> {
    long id<identifier>,
    immutable long ^version,
    immutable OrderState state,
    immutable long consumerId = -1,
    immutable long restaurantId = -1
  }

  enum OrderState {
    APPROVED,
    APPROVAL_PENDING,
    REJECTED,
    REVISION_PENDING
  }
}

context API {
  structure CreateOrderRequest
    <valueObject> {
    immutable long consumerId,
    immutable long restaurantId,
    immutable LineItems lineItems
  }

  structure LineItem {
    immutable string menuItemId,
    immutable int quantity
  }

  collection LineItems { LineItem i }
}
```
(a)

```
// File: JavaSpring.technology
technology JavaSpring {
  types {
    primitive type Boolean
      based on boolean default;
    primitive type Byte
      based on byte default;
    primitive type Character
      based on char default;
    primitive type Date
      based on date default;
    primitive type Double
      based on double default;
    primitive type Float
      based on float default;
    ...
  }

  service aspects {
    aspect PostMapping<singleval>
      for operations;
  }
}
```
(b)

```
// File: Protocols.technology
technology Protocols {
  protocols {
    sync rest data formats "json"
      default with format "json";
  }
}
```
(c)

```
// File: Order.services
import datatypes from "Order.data" as OrderDomain
import technology from "JavaSpring.technology" as JavaSpring
import technology from "Protocols.technology" as Protocols

@technology(JavaSpring)
@technology(Protocols)
public functional microservice org.example.OrderService {
  @endpoints(Protocols::_protocols.rest: "/orders";)
  interface Orders {
    ---
    Create order
    @required request Request
    ---
    @JavaSpring::_aspects.PostMapping
    create(
      sync in request : OrderDomain::API.CreateOrderRequest,
      sync out response : OrderDomain::API.CreateOrderResponse
    );
  }
}
```
(d)

Listing 4 Example models in LEMMA's (a) DDML, (b, c) TML, and (d) SML. The models are excerpts from the models for the order and restaurant microservices of Richardson's MSA case study [102] used to illustrate LEMMA's model processing capabilities [81] eponymous Spring annotation[7] and is applicable to microservice operations (`for operations`) exactly once (`singleval`).

Listing 4c constructs a technology model with the `rest` protocol for the REST architectural style [26]. REST is often applied in synchronous microservice interactions [13]. The `rest` protocol uses the JSON data format [21] and is the `default` synchronous protocol when a microservice applies the technology model.

Listing 4d shows a service model in the SML. It exemplifies the imported-based composition of LEMMA models (Sect. 3.2) as it imports the domain model in Listing 4a under the alias `OrderDomain`, and the two technology models in Listing 4b and c under the aliases `JavaSpring` and `Protocols` (Lines 2–4). The two technology models are applied to the `OrderService` microservice (Line 8) by the built-in `@technology` annotation. These applications lead to implicit replacement of types with synonyms (Listing 4b) and the assumption of default protocols (Listing 4c).

The `OrderService` has a `public` visibility, which allows its exposure to external clients, and a `functional` type, which identifies the service's capability to stem from the application domain. The `OrderService` consists the `Orders` interface (Lines 10–20) with a `rest` endpoint (Line 9). In LEMMA, an endpoint is a combination of a protocol from a technology model being applied to a microservice (Line 7 and Listing 4c) and one or more addresses, i.e., "/orders" (Line 9).

The `Orders` interface consists of the `create` operation (Lines 16–19). The API comment (Lines 11–14) informs about the operation's function. `create` defines the synchronous input parameter `request` and the synchronous output parameter `response`. The type of the former is the structured domain concept `CreateOrderRequest` imported from the domain model in Listing 4a. The type of the latter is the response-specific counterpart of `CreateOrderRequest`, i.e., `CreateOrderResponse` [81]. `create` applies the `PostMapping` aspect from the technology model in Listing 4b to specify that the operation is invokable by HTTP POST requests [27].

Listing 5 shows excerpts from an MPF-based model processor (Sect. 3.3), whose complete Java sources are available on Software Heritage [81]. The processor yields the number of microservices' interfaces in a LEMMA service model and also distinguishes between interfaces with only asynchronous or synchronous operations. Such classifications of interfaces are crucial to MSA-specific quality metrics [22].

Listing 5a shows the Java class of the processor's source model validator (Sect. 3.3). The annotation `@SourceModelValidator` allows LEMMA's MPF to find source model validators on the classpath. A source model validator must extend `AbstractXtextModelValidator` and override its `getSupportedFileExtensions` method to inform the MPF about the validator's supported

---

[7] https://docs.spring.io/spring-framework/docs/current/javadoc-api/org/springframework/web/bind/annotation/PostMapping.html.

```
 1  @SourceModelValidator
 2  public class ServiceModelValidator extends AbstractXtextModelValidator {
 3    @Override
 4    public Set<String> getSupportedFileExtensions() {
 5      return new HashSet<>() {{ add("services"); }};
 6    }
 7
 8    @Check
 9    private void checkMicroservice(Microservice microservice) {
10      info("Model contains a microservice named " + microservice.getName(),
11        ServicePackage.Literals.MICROSERVICE__NAME);
12    }
13  }
```

(a)

```
 1  @CodeGenerationModule(name = "main")
 2  public class CodeGenerationModule extends AbstractCodeGenerationModule {
 3    @Override
 4    public String getLanguageNamespace() {
 5      return IntermediatePackage.eNS_URI;
 6    }
 7
 8    @Override
 9    public Map<String, Pair<String, Charset>> execute(String[] phaseArguments,
10      String[] moduleArguments) {
11      var resultFileContents = new StringBuilder();
12      var serviceModel = (IntermediateServiceModel) getResource()
13        .getContents().get(0);
14      for (IntermediateMicroservice m : serviceModel.getMicroservices()) {
15        var syncCount = 0;
16        var asyncCount = 0;
17        for (IntermediateInterface i : m.getInterfaces()) {
18          var paramTypes = i.getOperations().stream()
19            .map(IntermediateOperation::getParameters)
20            .flatMap(Collection::stream)
21            .map(IntermediateParameter::getCommunicationType)
22            .collect(Collectors.toList());
23          if (paramTypes.isEmpty() ||
24            paramTypes.stream().noneMatch(t -> t.equals("ASYNCHRONOUS")))
25            syncCount++;
26          else if (paramTypes.stream()
27            .noneMatch(t -> t.equals("SYNCHRONOUS")))
28            asyncCount++;
29        }
30        resultFileContents.append(String.format(
31          "Interface count for microservice %s: %d\n" +
32          "\tSynchronous interface count: %d\n" +
33          "\tAsynchronous interface count: %d\n",
34          m.getQualifiedName(), m.getInterfaces().size(), syncCount,
35          asyncCount
36        ));
37      }
38      var resultFilePath = getTargetFolder() + File.separator + "results.txt";
39      var resultMap = new HashMap<>()
40        {{ put(resultFilePath , resultFileContents.toString()); }};
41      return withCharset(resultMap, StandardCharsets.UTF_8.name());
42    }
43  }
```

(b)

```
 1  public class ModelProcessor extends AbstractModelProcessor {
 2    public static void main(String[] args) {
 3      new ExampleModelProcessor().run(args);
 4    }
 5
 6    public ExampleModelProcessor() {
 7      super("de.fhdo.lemma.examples.model_processing");
 8    }
 9  }
```

(c)

Listing 5 Example model processor written in Java based on LEMMA's MPF. For each microservice in the input service model, the processor (a) prints an information message; and (b) generates a file with the overall interface count as well as with the share of asynchronous and synchronous interfaces. The code in (c) shows the processor's entry point model file types. Methods with the @Check annotation are validation methods. The types of their first parameters must correspond to the metamodel concepts for whose instances in a model the validation methods shall be invoked by the MPF. Thus, the checkMicroservice method in Lines 9–12 validates Microservice instances in LEMMA service models (Fig. 3).

Listing 5b contains a code generation module of the example model processor. The MPF modularizes the Code Generation phase (Sect. 3.3) to enable separation of concerns in complex model processors [49]. A code generation module is a Java class that (i) exhibits the @CodeGenerationModule annotation; (ii) extends AbstractCodeGenerationModule; and (iii) overrides the getLanguage-Namespace method to signal the MPF the namespace of the metamodel targeted by code generation. In case of the module in Listing 5b, this namespace identifies the intermediate representation of LEMMA service models (Sects. 3.2 and 3.3). The execute method (Lines 9–42) implements the module's logic. The for-loop in Lines 17–29 iterates over all microservices and interfaces in the given intermediate service model and counts the number of interfaces whose operations have only asynchronous or synchronous parameters. Lines 30–36 map this information to a string and buffer it in the resultFileContents variable. Finally, Lines 38–41 inform the MPF about the generated file content for its eventual serialization.

Listing 5c comprises the processor's entrypoint, i.e., a Java class that inherits from AbstractModelProcessor and has a main method that delegates execution to the MPF. This delegation informs the MPF about the processor's Java package that shall be scanned for phase implementations like those in Listing 5a and b.

4 Applications of LEMMA

This section presents applications of LEMMA for microservice code generation (Sect. 4.1), model-based architecture reconstruction (Sect. 4.2), static quality analysis (Sect. 4.3), defect resolution by model refactoring (Sect. 4.4), and establishing a common architecture understanding (Sect. 4.5).

4.1 Plugin-Based Generation of Technology-Specific Microservice Code

MSA's technology heterogeneity (Sect. 1) not only concerns architecture models (Sect. 3.1) but also microservice implementations [95]. Therefore, we devised a code generator for Java-based microservice programming that maps LEMMA models in their intermediate representations (Sect. 3.3) to basic Java abstract syntax trees (ASTs). Besides Java, these basic ASTs are technology-agnostic in that they do not leverage a specific microservice implementation technology. For the specification of the mapping between intermediate LEMMA model element types and Java AST node types, we refer to Appendix K of the dissertation that conceived LEMMA [93].

Our Java Base Generator (JBG) [82] draws on LEMMA's MPF and is also a framework for the development of technology-specific code generation plugins, called Genlets. The JBG may load an arbitrary number of pre-compiled Genlets and execute them in a specific order after the creation of basic Java AST nodes from traversed intermediate model elements. Genlets consist of a set of code generation handlers, which are Java classes that exhibit the @CodeGenerationHandler annotation and implement the GenletCodeGenerationHandlerI interface.

A Genlet requests the JBG to invoke it for a combination of model element type and AST node type and pass to it both the element and the mapped node. The JBG then passes the element and node to the Genlet for technology-specific adaptation after which the JBG integrates the adapted node in the Java AST. After the execution of all given Genlets, the JBG serializes the adapted Java ASTs, which may involve a reordering of the ASTs to comply with patterns that preserve manual changes to generated code upon re-generation [35].

Figure 5 exemplifies the interaction between the JBG and its Genlets in the context of the Orders interface from Listing 4d.

The JBG maps an interface modeled in LEMMA's SML to an eponymous Java class (NormalClassDeclaration instance [33] in Compartment 1 of Fig. 5). Modeled operations become Java methods (MethodDeclaration instance [33] in Compartment 1). The Spring Genlet adapts the generated class to behave as a REST controller that invokes the create operation when receiving an HTTP POST request (Compartment 2 in Fig. 5). This adaptation follows from the modeled rest endpoint of the Orders interface (Listing 4d) and the application of the PostMapping aspect to the create operation. In the serialization phase (Compartment 3 in Fig. 5), the JBG adapts the AST to be compatible with the Generation Gap to preserve manual changes to generated code. Next to this pattern, the JBG also supports its extended variant [35], which reduces the amount of pattern-specific boilerplate code.

LEMMA currently bundles Genlets for Spring, the Kafka message broker,[8] DDD, and the Domain Event and CQRS patterns [75, 102]. Since a Genlet is inherently a LEMMA model processor, it can leverage functionality provided by the MPF including stand-alone execution for interactive model validation (Sect. 3.3). We applied the JBG in a research project from the Electromobility domain and were able to generate the implementations of all domain concepts, microservice interfaces, and extensible infrastructure for asynchronous interaction. The generation efficiency ranged between 5.90 and 6.26, i.e., from one line of LEMMA model, roughly six lines of Java microservice code were producible, making generative microservice development with LEMMA basically efficient. For details, we refer to

---

[8] https://kafka.apache.org.

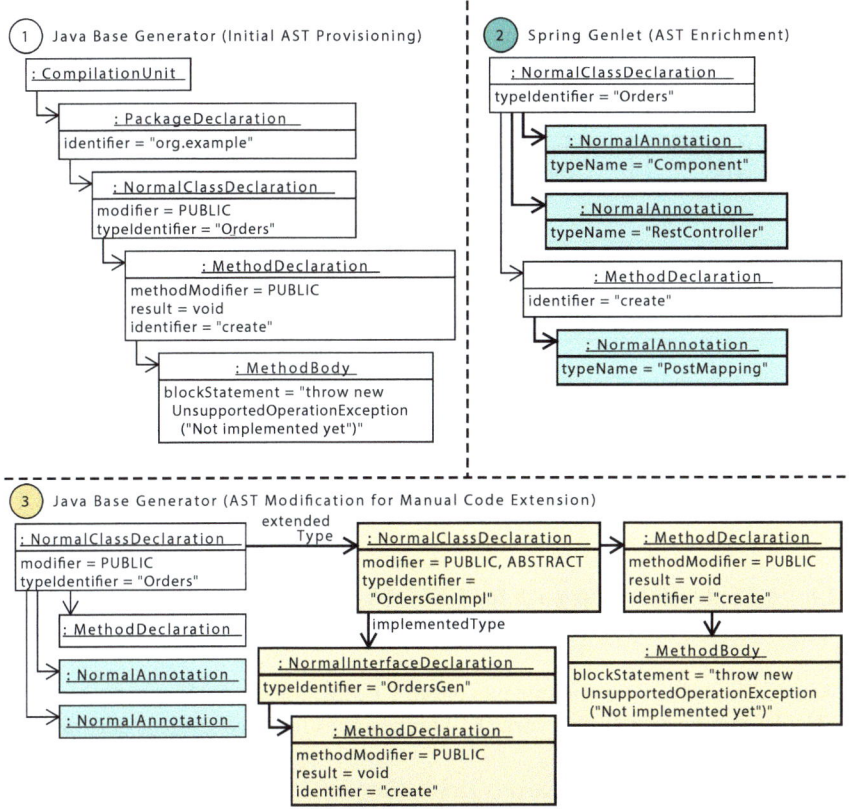

Fig. 5 Sample Java AST enrichment with the JBG and the Spring Genlet [99]

Sect. 8.7 of the dissertation that conceived LEMMA [93]. Recent works leveraged the JBG and its Genlets to derive microservice code from underspecified domain models [96], integrate blockchain technology into microservice architectures [122], and realize asynchronous microservice interactions [99].

4.2 Model-Based Reconstruction of Microservice Architectures

MSA's emphasis on service-specific independence (Sect. 1) may lead to service proliferation and the subsequent erosion of the anticipated architecture design because teams can autonomously advance different architecture parts [13]. Software Architecture Reconstruction (SAR) [8] is thus an important area in MSA research [1]. This section describes the design, development, and evaluation of an extensible LEMMA-based SAR approach that automates the translation of the source code of existing microservice architectures into LEMMA models, thereby

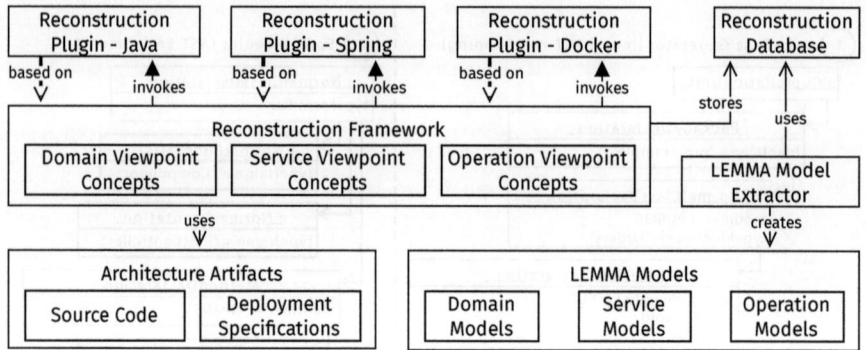

Fig. 6 Core components of our LEMMA-based SAR approach

facilitating the reasoning about the architecture and enabling the application of MDE techniques like quality assessment (Sect. 4.3) and defect resolution (Sect. 4.4).

4.2.1 An Extensible Approach for LEMMA-Based Microservice Architecture Reconstruction

Figure 6 depicts the core components of our LEMMA-based SAR approach.

The Reconstruction Framework (RF) orchestrates the SAR process according to Bass et al. [8].

In the first phase, the RF recovers architecture information from the artifacts of a microservice architecture including its source code and deployment specifications. To this end, the RF iterates over all artifacts of a given architecture and invokes reconstruction plugins on artifacts. These plugins cover different microservice technologies and LEMMA viewpoints. They are responsible for extracting architecture information from given artifacts, translate the information into the format expected by the RF, and return it to the RF. In the sense of Bass et al., the plugins perform a *raw view extraction* [8].

In the second phase, the RF stores all extracted architecture information in a reconstruction database. For this purpose, we specified data formats for each MSA viewpoint (Sect. 3.1). The database enables the RF's future extension by dynamic analyses where gathered architecture information originates from continuous monitoring. This phase corresponds to *database construction* and *view fusion* in the SAR process of Bass et al. [8] where heterogeneous architecture information are harmonized and stored in a common format.

In the third phase, the RF enables subsequent, LEMMA-based processing of reconstructed architecture information. In a first step, the RF invokes the LEMMA model extractor [97] to serialize information from the reconstruction database into LEMMA model files for the reconstructed viewpoints (Sect. 3.2). Starting from these reconstructed view models, software architects can perform efficient *architecture analyses*, e.g., for quality assessment (Sect. 4.3) or defect detection (Sect. 4.4), as suggested by Bass et al. [8].

4.2.2 Evaluation of the LEMMA-Based Reconstruction Approach

We evaluated our LEMMA-based SAR approach on Lakeside Mutual,[9] which is an MSA case study application for a fictitious insurance company. The architecture consists of a generic Customer Core microservice and four more specific microservices for customer, policy, and risk management as well as customer self-service. The Customer Self-Service and Policy Management microservices interact via asynchronous messaging. All remaining microservices rely on HTTP-based interaction. The services (i) use a registry to discover each other; (ii) are primarily implemented in Java and Spring (Sect. 3.4); (iii) produce logs for runtime monitoring; and (iv) store information in their own databases. We selected Lakeside Mutual for the evaluation of our SAR approach because its architecture is well documented [129, 130].

Table 5 shows the results of the evaluation of our SAR approach on Lakeside Mutual. The evaluation used reconstruction plugins for Java and Spring that cover LEMMA's Domain and Service viewpoints (Sect. 3.1 and Fig. 6). We use the Recall, Precision, and $F_{measure}$ metrics to assess the preciseness of the reconstruction process.

The evaluation showed that the current implementation of our SAR approach is able to reconstruct four of the five microservices of Lakeside Mutual in LEMMA service model. The RF did not recover the Risk Management microservice because it is based on Node.js[10] and our reconstruction plugins currently target Java. However, all expected interfaces and operations of the reconstructed microservices could be recovered with reconstructed data structures in LEMMA domain models originating from operations' parameter types (Sect. 3.4). The discrepancy between expected and recovered structures results from classes defined in external dependencies whose source code is currently not available to the RF.

4.3 *Assessment of Microservice Maintainability with Static Model Analysis*

Next to scalability, maintainability is the most crucial quality attribute in MSA [17, 119] (Sect. 1). There exist several metrics suites that define metrics for maintainability assessment of microservices [3, 22, 39, 41]. While the majority of these metrics does not target MSA, but SOA [3, 41] or REST [39], they are still known

---

[9] https://www.github.com/Microservice-API-Patterns/LakesideMutual/tree/bc79075.
[10] https://www.nodejs.org.

Table 5 Preliminary reconstruction results from the reconstruction process

Element	Expected	True positives	False positives	False negatives	Recall	Precision	F$_{measure}$
Microservices	5	4	0	1	80%	100%	88%
Interfaces	16	14	0	2	87%	100%	93%
Operations	61	50	3	8	86%	94%	90%
Data structures	161	117	29	14	89%	80%	84%

to be applicable to MSA [12]. We were interested in the assessment of these metrics by static LEMMA model analysis to provide fast feedback about modeled microservices' quality.

We investigated the LEMMA-based calculation of each of the 26 metrics from the aforementioned four metrics suites. They can be characterized as follows:

- **Hirzalla et al. [41]:** Hirzalla et al. define ten metrics for single SOA services and complete architectures. Among such metrics are (i) NOVS (Number of Versions per Service), which measures architecture complexity by calculating the ratio between service versions and services; and (ii) SRP (Service Realization Pattern), which measures the share of services exposed by intermediaries in the overall share of exposed services with a lower share hinting at lesser complexity. While NOVS is directly assessable from LEMMA service models, SRP requires operation models and a notion of intermediary like API gateway or edge server [7].
- **Athanasopoulos et al. [3]:** This suite consists of three metrics that measure service interface cohesion on the message, conversation, and domain level. Cohesion is important for microservices as it has a direct impact on maintainability [109, 119]. All metrics of the suite rely on *interface-level graphs* (ILG) which are undirected, labeled, and weighted graphs whose vertices represent interface operations and whose weighted edges inform about operations' similarity. The *ideal ILG* is a complete ILG with similarity weight 1, i.e., all interface operations are maximal similar. The *lack of interface-level cohesion* is then computable as the relative difference between the ILG and the ideal ILG.

  The metrics in the suite differ by their calculation rules for ILG similarity weights. For instance, the Message-Level Cohesion Lack metric considers the similarity of operations' message types, whereas the Domain-Level Cohesion Lack metric focuses on operation similarity based on domain terms. All metrics in the suite are directly computable from LEMMA service models.
- **Haupt et al. [39]:** Haupt et al. define seven metrics for structural REST API analysis. The metrics rely on *managed resources*, i.e., objects of information maintained via REST [26]. For their LEMMA-based computation, the majority of the metrics require a technology model that indicates REST application (Sect. 3.4) as well as domain and service models. For example, to assess the Number of Resources metric, it is mandatory to identify REST operations (technology and service model; cf. Listing 4) and managed resources as structural types of service operation parameters (domain model).
- **Engel et al. [22]:** This suite comprises six metrics for MSA core principles like loose coupling. Those metrics include Number of (A)Synchronous Interfaces and Average Size of Asynchronous Messages. While the former is computable from LEMMA service models (Listing 5b), the latter requires runtime monitoring and is only heuristically assessable. That is, parameter types of modeled asynchronous operations allow lower-bound assessment of message sizes.

From the 26 metrics defined in the presented suites, 20 were computable from LEMMA models. The remaining six metrics either require dynamic analysis or process modeling, which is currently out of LEMMA's scope. For details, we refer to Sects. 9.5.2 to 9.5.5 of the dissertation that conceived LEMMA [93].

We implemented a library for the computation of supported metrics [84] and an MPF-based static analyzer [85] (Sect. 3.3) allowing the library's usage. We evaluated the analyzer on the LEMMA reconstruction models of Lakeside Mutual (Sect. 4.2) and revealed weaknesses in service cohesion. In our ongoing works, we integrate the analyzer library with LEMMA's Eclipse plugins (Sect. 3.2) to provide MSA stakeholders with ad hoc visual feedback about microservice maintainability.

4.4 Defect Resolution by Model Refactoring

Defects of a software architecture refer to issues in its design that may cause unwanted behavior of the implemented system. They are often made unintentionally, and without the awareness of software architects and developers [74]. Furthermore, their manifestation and occurrence is impacted by the architectural style, e.g., MSA. For defect resolution, the architecture design and implementation usually need to undergo a refactoring process. In the following, we describe a preliminary approach for the LEMMA-based detection and resolution of security defects in microservice architectures [125].

We illustrate our approach for a common security defect in MSA, i.e., Publicly Accessible Microservices (PAM), where interfaces are not exposed in a restricted and controlled fashion by an intermediary but are instead freely accessible by architecture-external clients [74]. This public and complete exposure of service interfaces increases the risk for confidentiality violations and other security issues significantly. To resolve the defect, an intermediary for interface exposure, e.g., an API Gateway [7], should be integrated into the architecture.

Listing 6 shows LEMMA technology and operation models (Sect. 3.2) that allow detection of the PAM defect and eventually resolve it.

The technology model in Listing 6a defines aspects that allow the enrichment of `infrastructure` nodes in LEMMA operation models with functional semantics. For instance, the `isApiGateway` aspect can be used to communicate the intent that a certain infrastructure node represents an API Gateway independent of the actual technology used to realize this capability. Listing 6b is technology model for a concrete API Gateway technology, i.e., Zuul.[11] Listing 6c is a LEMMA operation model that applies the technology models in Listing 6a and b to specify a Zuul-based infrastructure node called `Gateway` and identify it as an API Gateway using the `isApiGateway` aspect. Listing 6d contains an operation model with a specification for container-based microservice deployment. More precisely, it models the Docker[12] deployment of the Lakeside Mutual's Customer Core

---

[11] https://github.com/Netflix/zuul.

[12] https://www.docker.com.

Model-Driven Engineering of Microservice Architectures—The LEMMA Approach

```
1  technology ComponentSemantics {
2    operation aspects {
3      aspect isApiGateway<singleval> for infrastructure;
4      ...
5  }}
```
(a)

```
1  technology Zuul {
2    infrastructure technologies {
3      Zuul {
4        operation environments =
5          "openjdk:11-jdk-slim";
6        service properties
7          { string hostname; }
8  }}}
```
(b)

```
1  @technology(ComponentSemantics)
2  @technology(Zuul)
3  Gateway is
4    Zuul::_infrastructure.Zuul {
5      aspects {
6        ComponentSemantics::
7          _aspects.isApiGateway;
8  }}
```
(c)

```
1  @technology(Docker)
2  container CustomercoreContainer
3    deployment technology Docker::_deployment.Docker
4    deploys customercore::com.lakesidemutual.CustomerCore
5    depends on nodes ServiceRegistry::Registry {
6  }
```
(d)

```
1  @technology(Docker)
2  container CustomercoreContainerContainer
3    deployment technology Docker::_deployment.Docker
4    deploys customercore::com.lakesidemutual.customercore.CustomerCore
5    depends on nodes ServiceRegistry::Registry, APIGateway::Gateway {
6  }
```
(e)

Listing 6 Example models for LEMMA-based defect resolution. We rely on aspects to assign semantics to infrastructure components (a). The technology model in (b) describes a concrete API Gateway technology used in the operation model in (c) by an infrastructure node denoting an API Gateway. The operation model in (d) captures the Docker-based deployment of a microservice that does not use the API Gateway, whereas (e) shows the refactored operation model resolving this defect

microservice (Sect. 4.2). The depends on directive (Line 5) shows that the Docker container only depends on a service registry from another imported operation model. Hence, it does not leverage the capabilities of an API Gateway, thereby introducing the PAM defect.

For the detection of defects in LEMMA models, we implemented a model processor using LEMMA's MPF (Sect. 3.3). The processor's validation phase identifies defects in given LEMMA models and reports them to the user by hinting at the defect-inducing model element. In order to facilitate defect resolution, we implemented an Eclipse plugin that enriches defect issues reported by the processor with quick fixes that are applicable to resolve the detected defect via automated model refactoring. For the PAM defect, the corresponding refactoring is the addition of an API Gateway and its usage by concerned microservices [74]. Listing 6d illustrates the defect resolution by adding the Gateway from Listing 6c to the nodes on which the container depends (Line 5).

We are currently working on integrating the defect resolution processor with LEMMA's JBG (Sect. 4.1) such that refactored models can directly be mapped to microservice code and configuration artifacts. As a result, we can eventually provide MSA stakeholders with means for defect detection, resolution, resolution reasoning, and evaluation, including the subsequent generation of code for the most suitable resolution.

4.5 Model Transformations for a Common Architecture Understanding

MSA poses challenges to organizations in restructuring their development processes to cope with service-specific independence and ownership (Definition 1). The division into different teams, each of which being holistically responsible for one or more microservices, can lead to a lack of architectural understanding across team boundaries. This lack of understanding can have a negative effect, e.g., when setting development priorities. We have observed this effect especially in small- and medium-sized enterprises, whose service landscapes evolve together with their development organizations [113].

Model-driven approaches such as LEMMA are particularly suitable for documenting and transferring knowledge [15]. Therefore, we argue that LEMMA constitutes an effective means to create and maintain a common and organization-wide architecture understanding by making (partial) MSA models available to teams and support their active exchange. For this purpose, due to microservices fostering technology heterogeneity (Sect. 2.1), the application of MDE technologies and techniques, e.g., code generation (Sect. 4.1) or model-based reconstruction (Sect. 4.2), cannot be assumed. However, LEMMA provides bidirectional model transformations [59] to derive LEMMA models from microservice API specifications based on OpenAPI[13] (synchronous APIs) or Apache Avro[14] (asynchronous APIs) and vice versa. Consequently, these transformations allow knowledge documentation and communication without requiring microservice teams to develop their services with MDE.

In the following, we (i) describe a development process for small- and medium-sized enterprises that supports both *code-first* and *model-first* microservice development in an integrated fashion; and (ii) how LEMMA's OpenAPI model transformation enables this process. For more details regarding the process, the transformation, and the corresponding artifacts, we refer to our previous work [115].

---

[13] https://www.openapis.org.

[14] https://avro.apache.org.

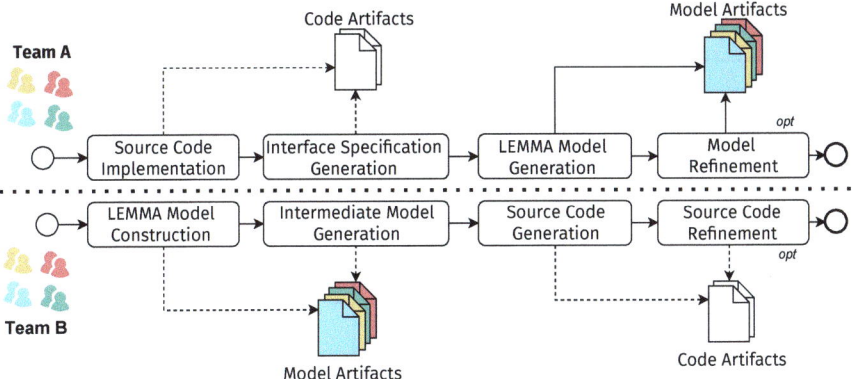

Fig. 7 Code-first vs. model-first microservice development in cross-functional teams

4.5.1 Code-First vs. Model-First Microservice Development

Figure 7 compares code-first with model-first microservice development in two *cross-functional* MSA teams [7].

Team A applies the code-first approach to microservice development in which source code is a first-class citizen and models are used, if at all, for mere documentation and communication. That is, Team A starts to implement a service by writing its source code, followed by the automated generation of interface specification. The latter step follows from insights of an exploratory study [113] in which we found that MSA teams in industry rarely and reluctantly create manual documentation of their interfaces but instead rely on automated approaches, e.g., Swagger[15] to generate OpenAPI specifications. With LEMMA, it is now possible to automatically transform generated interface specifications into corresponding LEMMA domain, service, and technology models (Sect. 3.2). Team A may then refine the derived LEMMA models, if desired, and eventually share them with other teams to stimulate the creation of a common architectural understanding by exploiting MDE's abstraction facilities (Sect. 2.2) and to support model-first development approaches. With the support of model generation in a code-first approach, thus enabling teams to communicate, share knowledge, and create a common understanding, LEMMA addresses a possible lack of expertise on the part of developers, which is a common challenge for the success of MDE tools in practice [124].

Team B in Fig. 7 practices model-first microservice development, which uses LEMMA models as first-class citizens, thereby directly following MDE's line of thought. From such models and their intermediate representations, a code generator

---

[15] https://www.swagger.io.

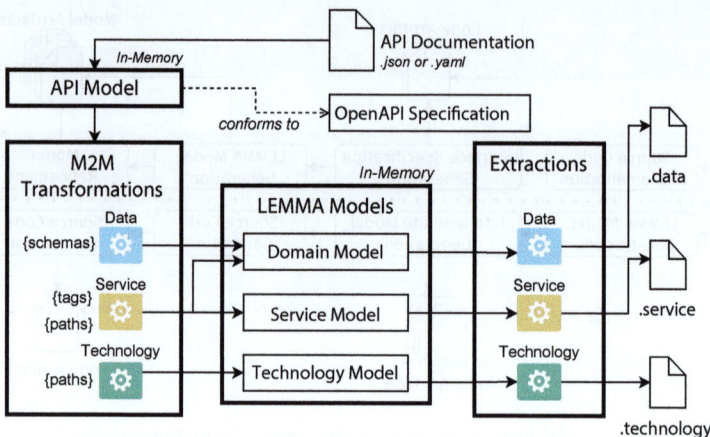

Fig. 8 M2M transformation process for deriving LEMMA domain, service, and technology models from OpenAPI specifications

like the JBG (cf. Sect. 4.1) can be used to produce refinable code. As for the code-first approach, both LEMMA model and source code artifacts exist in the end.

4.5.2 OpenAPI Model Transformation

LEMMA realizes the code-first approach (Fig. 7) through multiple model-to-model (M2M) transformations [15], which we detail on the example of the OpenAPI-to-LEMMA transformation in Fig. 8.

The M2M transformation process starts with an OpenAPI-conform interface specification in a file with the extension ".json" or ".yaml". This specification is parsed into an in-memory API Model fueling multiple M2M transformations. Since the intended use of OpenAPI is to describe HTTP resource APIs, corresponding specifications include utilizable information about data, interfaces, and transfer-specific technology information like media types. This information is translated into LEMMA domain, service, and technology models by means of dedicated M2M transformations.

In detail, the Data transformation operates on `schemas` objects in OpenAPI specifications and generates a data structure in a LEMMA domain model for each traversed schema. The Service transformation processes OpenAPI `tags` and `paths` objects. It creates a LEMMA service model that is populated with interfaces for each encountered `tag`. Paths corresponding to a tag result in interface operations with request and response parameters. Furthermore, the Service transformation generates matching LEMMA collection types for each OpenAPI array. The Technology transformation analyzes the OpenAPI `paths` object for specific media types and creates a corresponding LEMMA technology model. Subsequently, the resulting in-memory LEMMA models are serialized as files by specialized extractors and are thus immediately usable by MSA teams.

5 Related Work

Table 6 compares LEMMA with related MDE-for-MSA approaches. Additional details can be found in Sects. 4.6 and 5.6 of the dissertation that conceived LEMMA [93].

While related approaches cover some of the MSA viewpoints (Sect. 3.1), LEMMA is the only approach to support them all, including viewpoint-specific modeling languages and holistic MSA modeling by viewpoint integration (Sect. 3.2). A further strength of LEMMA is its extensibility on the language level, enabled by the aspect-oriented metadata mechanism of the TML. This extensibility allows, e.g., model-based reification of architecture patterns and selective technology-specificity, which is essential for *agile modeling* [103].

In comparison, LEMMA also facilitates model processing by bundling a specialized MPF (Sect. 3.3) and sophisticated model processors. Additionally, LEMMA has proven to be exceptionally versatile in a variety of MSA engineering scopes, ranging from development and operation over reconstruction to quality assessment (Sect. 4).

6 Conclusion and Future Work

This chapter presented LEMMA (Language Ecosystem for Modeling Microservice Architecture) [93]—an approach for the application of Model-Driven Engineering to Microservice Architecture (MSA) engineering. LEMMA mitigates the complexity of MSA (Sect. 2) by first decomposing it along four viewpoints on microservice architectures, each capturing the concerns of different MSA stakeholders in dedicated architecture models (Sect. 3.1). The Domain viewpoint supports the collaborative construction of domain models by domain experts and microservice developers. Domain models cluster all domain concepts relevant to a microservice architecture. The Technology viewpoint focuses on the concerns of microservice developers and operators and enables them to capture technologies for microservices and operation nodes within technology models. The Service viewpoint provides microservice developers with modeling facilities for microservices, their interfaces, operations, and endpoints. The Operation viewpoint addresses the concerns of microservice operators in deployment and infrastructure operation modeling. We accompanied each viewpoint with a specialized modeling language that formalizes the syntax and semantics of viewpoint-specific MSA models (Sect. 3.2). LEMMA's modeling languages are integrated by means of an import mechanism so that elements in one model can refer to elements in imported models, e.g., to configure the container-

Table 6 Comparison of LEMMA with related MDE-for-MSA approaches

Characteristic/approach	LEMMA [93]	CloudML [25]	Context Mapper [50]	DCSL [20]	JDL [45]	MDSL [50]	μART [34]	Micro Builder [120]	MiSAR [1]
MSA viewpoint (VP) support									
Domain VP	●	–	●	●	–	●	–	●	–
Service VP	●	–	–	–	–	●	●	●	●
Technology VP	●	●	◐	–	●	–	–	●	●
Operation VP	●	●	–	–	●	–	–	–	●
Specialized language per VP	●	–	–	●	●	●	N/A	–	–
VP Integration	●	●	●	N/A	●	●	N/A	●	●
Modeling languages									
Language-level extensibility	●	–	–	●	–	–	–	–	–
Selective technology-specificity	●	–	–	–	–	–	–	–	–
Technology-agnostic syntax	●	–	◐	●	–	●	–	–	–
Model processing									
Model processor creation	●	–	◐	–	–	–	–	–	–
Bundled code generators	●	●	●	●	●	●	N/A	–	–
Handwritten extension of generated code	●	–	–	●	–	–	–	–	N/A
Bundled static analyzers	●	–	–	–	–	–	–	–	–
MSA engineering scope									
Development	●	–	●	●	●	●	–	●	–
Operation	●	●	–	–	●	–	–	–	–
Reconstruction	●	–	–	–	–	–	●	–	●
Quality assessment	●	–	–	–	–	–	–	–	–

Symbol key: ● = Full support; ◐ = Partial support; – = No support based deployment of a modeled microservice within an operation model. The modeling languages are practically usable as plugins for the Eclipse IDE. LEMMA also bundles its own model processing framework (MPF; Sect. 3.3). The MPF facilitates model processor implementation for technology-savvy MSA stakeholders by decoupling model processing into phases and allow phase implementation by mechanisms that are popular in MSA engineering, e.g., Java and annotation-based Inversion of Control [47]. We exemplified the usage of LEMMA's modeling languages and MPF in the context of a case study microservice architecture (Sect. 3.4). Section 4 presented practical applications of LEMMA for microservice code generation (Sect. 4.1), architecture reconstruction (Sect. 4.2), quality analysis (Sect. 4.3), defect resolution (Sect. 4.4), and establishing a common architecture understanding (Sect. 4.5). Section 5 compared LEMMA to related approaches and concluded that LEMMA has particular strengths in (i) holistic MSA modeling based on viewpoint integration; (ii) language-level extensibility, enabling model-based reification of architecture patterns and selective technology-specificity; (iii) model processing, by bundling a specialized MPF together with sophisticated model processors for code generation and quality analysis; and (iv) versatility, making LEMMA applicable in microservice development, operation, architecture reconstruction, and quality assessment.

In our ongoing and future works, we combine LEMMA with formal techniques for correct microservice behavior specification [31, 32]. Moreover, while we have already empirically shown that LEMMA is effective for MSA modeling [112], we plan to evaluate it further in industry-related development processes of small- and medium-sized enterprises. In addition, two doctoral students currently improve LEMMA to (i) better integrate with distributed and non-modeling microservice teams [113, 115]; and (ii) increase the coverage and correctness of LEMMA-based reconstruction processes [126].

References

1. Alshuqayran, N., Ali, N., Evans, R.: Towards micro service architecture recovery: An empirical study. In: 2018 IEEE International Conference on Software Architecture (ICSA), pp. 47–56. IEEE, Piscataway (2018). https://doi.org/10.1109/ICSA.2018.00014
2. Ameller, D., Burgués, X., Collell, O., Costal, D., Franch, X., Papazoglou, M.P.: Development of service-oriented architectures using model-driven development: a mapping study. Informat. Softw. Technol. **62**, 42–66 (2015). Elsevier. https://doi.org/10.1016/j.infsof.2015.02.006
3. Athanasopoulos, D., Zarras, A.V., Miskos, G., Issarny, V., Vassiliadis, P.: Cohesion-driven decomposition of service interfaces without access to source code. IEEE Trans. Serv. Comput. **8**(4), 550–562 (2015). IEEE. https://doi.org/10.1109/TSC.2014.2310195
4. Ayas, H.M., Leitner, P., Hebig, R.: Facing the giant: A grounded theory study of decision-making in microservices migrations. In: Proceedings of the 15th ACM / IEEE International Symposium on Empirical Software Engineering and Measurement (ESEM), ESEM '21. Association for Computing Machinery, New York (2021). https://doi.org/10.1145/3475716.3475792

5. Baker, P., Loh, S., Weil, F.: Model-driven engineering in a large industrial context — Motorola case study. In: Briand, L., Williams, C. (eds.) Model Driven Engineering Languages and Systems, pp. 476–491. Springer, Berlin (2005). https://doi.org/10.1007/11557432_36
6. Balalaie, A., Heydarnoori, A., Jamshidi, P.: Microservices architecture enables DevOps: migration to a cloud-native architecture. IEEE Softw. **33**(3), 42–52 (2016). IEEE. https://doi.org/10.1109/MS.2016.64
7. Balalaie, A., Heydarnoori, A., Jamshidi, P.: Migrating to cloud-native architectures using microservices: An experience report. In: Celesti, A., Leitner, P. (eds.) Advances in Service-Oriented and Cloud Computing, pp. 201–215. Springer, Cham (2016). https://doi.org/10.1007/978-3-319-33313-7_15
8. Bass, L., Clements, P., Kazman, R.: Software Architecture in Practice, 3rd edn. Addison-Wesley, Boston (2013)
9. Bass, L., Klein, J.: Deployment and Operations for Software Engineers, 1st edn. Self-published (2019)
10. Benguria, G., Larrucea, X., Elvesæter, B., Neple, T., Beardsmore, A., Friess, M.: A platform independent model for service oriented architectures. In: Doumeingts, G., Müller, J., Morel, G., Vallespir, B. (eds.) Enterprise Interoperability, pp. 23–32. Springer, London (2007). https://doi.org/10.1007/978-1-84628-714-5_3
11. Bettini, L.: Implementing Domain-Specific Languages with Xtext and Xtend, 2nd edn. Packt Publishing, Birmingham (2016)
12. Bogner, J.: On the evolvability assurance of microservices: metrics, scenarios, and patterns. Ph.D. Thesis (2020). https://doi.org/10.18419/opus-10950
13. Bogner, J., Fritzsch, J., Wagner, S., Zimmermann, A.: Microservices in industry: Insights into technologies, characteristics, and software quality. In: 2019 IEEE International Conference on Software Architecture Companion (ICSA-C), pp. 187–195. IEEE, Piscataway (2019). https://doi.org/10.1109/ICSA-C.2019.00041
14. Cerny, T., Donahoo, M.J., Trnka, M.: Contextual understanding of microservice architecture: current and future directions. SIGAPP Appl. Comput. Rev. **17**(4), 29–45 (2018). ACM. https://doi.org/10.1145/3183628.3183631
15. Combemale, B., France, R.B., Jézéquel, J.M., Rumpe, B., Steel, J., Vojtisek, D.: Engineering Modeling Languages: Turning Domain Knowledge into Tools, 1st edn. CRC Press, Boca Raton (2017)
16. Cortellessa, V., Eramo, R., Tucci, M.: From software architecture to analysis models and back: model-driven refactoring aimed at availability improvement. Informat. Softw. Technol. **127** (2020). https://doi.org/10.1016/j.infsof.2020.106362
17. Di Francesco, P., Malavolta, I., Lago, P.: Research on architecting microservices: Trends, focus, and potential for industrial adoption. In: 2017 IEEE International Conference on Software Architecture (ICSA), pp. 21–30. IEEE, Piscataway (2017). https://doi.org/10.1109/ICSA.2017.24
18. Dragoni, N., Giallorenzo, S., Lafuente, A.L., Mazzara, M., Montesi, F., Mustafin, R., Safina, L.: Microservices: Yesterday, today, and tomorrow. In: Mazzara, M., Meyer, B. (eds.) Present and Ulterior Software Engineering, pp. 195–216. Springer, Berlin (2017). https://doi.org/10.1007/978-3-319-67425-4_12
19. Dragoni, N., Lanese, I., Larsen, S.T., Mazzara, M., Mustafin, R., Safina, L.: Microservices: How to make your application scale. In: Petrenko, A.K., Voronkov, A. (eds.) Perspectives of System Informatics, pp. 95–104. Springer, Cham (2018). https://doi.org/10.1007/978-3-319-74313-4_8
20. Le, D.M., Dang, D.-H., Nguyen, V.-H.: Domain-driven design using meta-attributes: A DSL-based approach. In: 2016 Eighth International Conference on Knowledge and Systems Engineering (KSE), pp. 67–72. IEEE, Piscataway (2016). https://doi.org/10.1109/KSE.2016.7758031
21. Ecma International: The JSON data interchange syntax. Standard ECMA-404, Ecma International (2017)

22. Engel, T., Langermeier, M., Bauer, B., Hofmann, A.: Evaluation of microservice architectures: A metric and tool-based approach. In: Mendling, J., Mouratidis, H. (eds.) Information Systems in the Big Data Era, pp. 74–89. Springer, Cham (2018). https://doi.org/10.1007/978-3-319-92901-9_8
23. Erl, T.: Service-Oriented Architecture (SOA): Concepts, Technology and Design, 1st edn. Prentice Hall, Hoboken (2005)
24. Evans, E.: Domain-Driven Design, 1st edn. Addison-Wesley, Boston (2004)
25. Ferry, N., Rossini, A., Chauvel, F., Morin, B., Solberg, A.: Towards model-driven provisioning, deployment, monitoring, and adaptation of multi-cloud systems. In: 2013 IEEE Sixth International Conference on Cloud Computing, pp. 887–894. IEEE, Piscataway (2013). https://doi.org/10.1109/CLOUD.2013.133
26. Fielding, R.T.: Architectural styles and the design of network-based software architectures. Ph.D. Thesis (2000)
27. Fielding, R.T., Reschke, J.F.: Hypertext Transfer Protocol (HTTP/1.1): Semantics and content. RFC 7231, RFC Editor (2014)
28. France, R., Rumpe, B.: Model-driven development of complex software: A research roadmap. In: 2007 Future of Software Engineering, FOSE '07, pp. 37–54. IEEE, Washington, (2007). https://doi.org/10.1109/FOSE.2007.14
29. Francesco, P.D., Lago, P., Malavolta, I.: Migrating towards microservice architectures: An industrial survey. In: 2018 IEEE International Conference on Software Architecture (ICSA), pp. 29–38. IEEE, Piscataway (2018). https://doi.org/10.1109/ICSA.2018.00012
30. Garriga, M.: Towards a taxonomy of microservices architectures. In: Cerone, A., Roveri, M. (eds.) Software Engineering and Formal Methods, pp. 203–218. Springer, Cham (2018). https://doi.org/10.1007/978-3-319-74781-1_15
31. Giallorenzo, S., Montesi, F., Peressotti, M., Rademacher, F.: Model-driven generation of microservice interfaces: From LEMMA domain models to Jolie APIs. In: ter Beek, M.H., Sirjani, M. (eds.) Coordination Models and Languages, pp. 223–240. Springer, Berlin (2022). https://doi.org/10.1007/978-3-031-08143-9_13
32. Giallorenzo, S., Montesi, F., Peressotti, M., Rademacher, F., Sachweh, S.: Jolie and LEMMA: Model-driven engineering and programming languages meet on microservices. In: Damiani, F., Dardha, O. (eds.) Coordination Models and Languages, pp. 276–284. Springer, Cham (2021). https://doi.org/10.1007/978-3-030-78142-2_17
33. Gosling, J., Joy, B., Steele, G., Bracha, G., Buckley, A., Smith, D., Bierman, G.: The Java language specification: Java se 17th edn. Specification JSR-392 Java SE 17, Oracle America, Inc. (2021)
34. Granchelli, G., Cardarelli, M., Francesco, P.D., Malavolta, I., Iovino, L., Salle, A.D.: Towards recovering the software architecture of microservice-based systems. In: 2017 IEEE International Conference on Software Architecture Workshops (ICSAW), pp. 46–53. IEEE, Piscataway (2017). https://doi.org/10.1109/ICSAW.2017.48
35. Greifenberg, T., Hölldobler, K., Kolassa, C., Look, M., Mir Seyed Nazari, P., Müller, K., Navarro Perez, A., Plotnikov, D., Reiss, D., Roth, A., Rumpe, B., Schindler, M., Wortmann, A.: Integration of handwritten and generated object-oriented code. In: Desfray, P., Filipe, J., Hammoudi, S., Pires, L.F. (eds.) Model-Driven Engineering and Software Development, pp. 112–132. Springer, Cham (2015). https://doi.org/10.1007/978-3-319-27869-8_7
36. Gu, Q., Parkin, M., Lago, P.: A taxonomy of service engineering stakeholder types. In: Abramowicz, W., Llorente, I.M., Surridge, M., Zisman, A., Vayssière, J. (eds.) Towards a Service-Based Internet, pp. 206–219. Springer, Berlin (2011). https://doi.org/10.1007/978-3-642-24755-2_20
37. Harel, D., Rumpe, B.: Meaningful modeling: what's the semantics of "semantics"? Computer **37**(10), 64–72 (2004). IEEE. https://doi.org/10.1109/MC.2004.172
38. Haselböck, S., Weinreich, R., Buchgeher, G.: Decision models for microservices: Design areas, stakeholders, use cases, and requirements. In: Lopes, A., de Lemos, R. (eds.) Software Architecture, pp. 155–170. Springer, Cham (2017). https://doi.org/10.1007/978-3-319-65831-5_11

39. Haupt, F., Leymann, F., Scherer, A., Vukojevic-Haupt, K.: A framework for the structural analysis of REST APIs. In: 2017 IEEE International Conference on Software Architecture (ICSA), pp. 55–58. Springer, Berlin (2017). https://doi.org/10.1109/ICSA.2017.40
40. Herbst, N.R., Kounev, S., Reussner, R.: Elasticity in cloud computing: What it is, and what it is not. In: Proceedings of the 10th International Conference on Autonomic Computing (ICAC 13), pp. 23–27. USENIX, San Jose (2013). https://www.usenix.org/conference/icac13/technical-sessions/presentation/herbst
41. Hirzalla, M., Cleland-Huang, J., Arsanjani, A.: A metrics suite for evaluating flexibility and complexity in service oriented architectures. In: Feuerlicht, G., Lamersdorf, W. (eds.) Service-Oriented Computing – ICSOC 2008 Workshops, pp. 41–52. Springer, Berlin (2009). https://doi.org/10.1007/978-3-642-01247-1_5
42. ISO/IEC: Systems and software engineering — Systems and software Quality Requirements and Evaluation (SQuaRE) — System and software quality models. Standard ISO/IEC 25010:2011(E), International Organization for Standardization/International Electrotechnical Commission (2011)
43. ISO/IEC/IEEE: Systems and software engineering — Architecture description. Standard ISO/IEC/IEEE 42010:2011(E), International Organization for Standardization/International Electrotechnical Commission/Institute of Electrical and Electronics Engineers (2011)
44. Jamshidi, P., Pahl, C., Mendonça, N.C., Lewis, J., Tilkov, S.: Microservices: The journey so far and challenges ahead. IEEE Softw. **35**(3), 24–35 (2018). IEEE. https://doi.org/10.1109/MS.2018.2141039
45. JHipster: JHipster Domain Language (JDL) (2023). https://www.jhipster.tech/jdl
46. Johanson, A., Flögel, S., Dullo, C., Hasselbring, W.: OceanTEA: Exploring ocean-derived climate data using microservices. In: Proceedings of the 6th International Workshop on Climate Informatics: CI 2016. National Center for Atmospheric Research (2016)
47. Johnson, R.E., Foote, B.: Designing reusable classes. J. Object-Oriented Programm. **1**(2), 22–35 (1988). SIGS Publications
48. Jongeling, R., Carlson, J., Cicchetti, A.: Impediments to introducing continuous integration for model-based development in industry. In: 2019 45th Euromicro Conference on Software Engineering and Advanced Applications (SEAA), pp. 434–441. IEEE, Piscataway (2019). https://doi.org/10.1109/SEAA.2019.00071
49. Kahani, N., Bagherzadeh, M., Cordy, J.R., Dingel, J., Varró, D.: Survey and classification of model transformation tools. Softw. Syst. Model. **18**(4), 2361–2397 (2019). Springer. https://doi.org/10.1007/s10270-018-0665-6
50. Kapferer, S., Zimmermann, O.: Domain-specific language and tools for strategic domain-driven design, context mapping and bounded context modeling. In: Proceedings of the 8th International Conference on Model-Driven Engineering and Software Development - Volume 1: MODELSWARD, pp. 299–306. INSTICC, SciTePress (2020). https://doi.org/10.5220/0008910502990306
51. Kirchhof, J.C., Rumpe, B., Schmalzing, D., Wortmann, A.: Montithings: Model-driven development and deployment of reliable IoT applications. J. Syst. Softw. **183**, 111087 (2022). https://doi.org/10.1016/j.jss.2021.111087
52. Knoche, H., Hasselbring, W.: Drivers and barriers for microservice adoption – a survey among professionals in Germany. Enterprise Modell. Informat. Syst. Architect. **14**(1), 1–35 (2019). German Informatics Society. https://doi.org/10.18417/emisa.14.1
53. Lano, K., Kolahdouz-Rahimi, S.: Model-transformation design patterns. IEEE Trans. Softw. Eng. **40**(12), 1224–1259 (2014).. IEEE https://doi.org/10.1109/TSE.2014.2354344
54. Le, V.D., Neff, M.M., Stewart, R.V., Kelley, R., Fritzinger, E., Dascalu, S.M., Harris, F.C.: Microservice-based architecture for the NRDC. In: 2015 IEEE 13th International Conference on Industrial Informatics (INDIN), pp. 1659–1664. IEEE, Piscataway (2015). https://doi.org/10.1109/INDIN.2015.7281983
55. Luz, W.P., Pinto, G., Bonifácio, R.: Building a collaborative culture: A grounded theory of well succeeded DevOps adoption in practice. In: Proceedings of the 12th ACM/IEEE International Symposium on Empirical Software Engineering and Measurement, ESEM '18,

pp. 6:1–6:10. ACM, New York (2018). https://doi.org/10.1145/3239235.3240299
56. Márquez, G., Villegas, M.M., Astudillo, H.: A pattern language for scalable microservices-based systems. In: Proceedings of the 12th European Conference on Software Architecture: Companion Proceedings, ECSA '18, pp. 24:1–24:7. ACM, New York (2018). https://doi.org/10.1145/3241403.3241429
57. Mazlami, G., Cito, J., Leitner, P.: Extraction of microservices from monolithic software architectures. In: 2017 IEEE International Conference on Web Services (ICWS), pp. 524–531. IEEE, Piscataway (2017). https://doi.org/10.1109/ICWS.2017.61
58. Mazzara, M., Dragoni, N., Bucchiarone, A., Giaretta, A., Larsen, S.T., Dustdar, S.: Microservices: migration of a mission critical system. IEEE Trans. Serv. Comput., 1–14 (2018). IEEE. https://doi.org/10.1109/TSC.2018.2889087
59. Mens, T., Gorp, P.V.: A taxonomy of model transformation. Electron. Notes Theoret. Comput. Sci. **152**, 125–142 (2006). Elsevier. https://doi.org/10.1016/j.entcs.2005.10.021
60. Methodologies Corporation: Service-oriented modeling framework (SOMF) version 2.1. (2011)
61. Mohagheghi, P., Dehlen, V.: Where is the proof? - A review of experiences from applying MDE in industry. In: Schieferdecker, I., Hartman, A. (eds.) Model Driven Architecture – Foundations and Applications, pp. 432–443. Springer, Berlin (2008). https://doi.org/10.1007/978-3-540-69100-6_31
62. Mohamed, M.A., Challenger, M., Kardas, G.: Applications of model-driven engineering in cyber-physical systems: a systematic mapping study. J. Comput. Lang. **59**, 1–54 (2020). https://doi.org/10.1016/j.cola.2020.100972
63. Márquez, G., Astudillo, H.: Actual use of architectural patterns in microservices-based open source projects. In: 2018 25th Asia-Pacific Software Engineering Conference (APSEC), pp. 31–40. IEEE, Piscataway (2018). https://doi.org/10.1109/APSEC.2018.00017
64. Nadareishvili, I., Mitra, R., McLarty, M., Amundsen, M.: Microservice Architecture: Aligning Principles, Practices, and Culture, 1st edn. O'Reilly, Sebastopol (2016)
65. Newman, S.: Building Microservices: Designing Fine-Grained Systems, 1st edn. O'Reilly, Sebastopol (2015)
66. OASIS: Reference architecture foundation for Service Oriented Architecture version 1.0. Standard OASIS Committee Specification 01, Organization for the Advancement of Structured Information Standards (2012)
67. OASIS: Topology and orchestration specification for cloud applications version 1.0. Standard, Organization for the Advancement of Structured Information Standards (2013)
68. OMG: Service oriented architecture Modeling Language (SoaML) specification version 1.0.1. Standard, Object Management Group (2012)
69. OMG: Business Process Model and Notation (BPMN) version 2.0.2. Standard formal/2013-12-09, Object Management Group (2013)
70. OMG: Model Driven Architecture (MDA) MDA Guide rev. 2.0. Standard ormsc/2014-06-01, Object Management Group (2014)
71. OMG: Object Constraint Language version 2.4. Standard formal/2014-02-03, Object Management Group (2014)
72. OMG: XML Metadata Interchange (XMI) specification. Standard formal/2015-06-07, Object Management Group (2015)
73. OMG: OMG Unified Modeling Language (OMG UML) version 2.5.1. Standard formal/17-12-05, Object Management Group (2017)
74. Ponce, F., Soldani, J., Astudillo, H., Brogi, A.: Smells and refactorings for microservices security: a multivocal literature review. J. Syst. Softw. **192**, 111393 (2022). https://doi.org/10.1016/j.jss.2022.111393
75. Rademacher, F.: Genlets for LEMMA's JBG on Software Heritage. https://archive.softwareheritage.org/browse/directory/7dccb79b9804d8d9459c86ba9721e1197f59b865/?origin_url=https://github.com/SeelabFhdo/lemma&path=code%20generators
76. Rademacher, F.: Grammar specification of LEMMA's Domain Data Modeling Language on Software Heritage. https://archive.softwareheritage.org/browse/origin/content/?origin_

url=https://github.com/SeelabFhdo/lemma&path=de.fhdo.lemma.data.datadsl/src/de/fhdo/lemma/data/DataDsl.xtext
77. Rademacher, F.: Grammar specification of LEMMA's Operation Modeling Language on Software Heritage. https://archive.softwareheritage.org/browse/origin/content/?origin_url=https://github.com/SeelabFhdo/lemma&path=de.fhdo.lemma.operationsdsl/src/de/fhdo/lemma/operationsdsl/OperationDsl.xtext
78. Rademacher, F.: Grammar specification of LEMMA's Service Modeling Language on Software Heritage. https://archive.softwareheritage.org/browse/origin/content/?origin_url=https://github.com/SeelabFhdo/lemma&path=de.fhdo.lemma.servicesdsl/src/de/fhdo/lemma/ServiceDsl.xtext
79. Rademacher, F.: Grammar specification of LEMMA's Service Technology Mapping Modeling Language on Software Heritage. https://archive.softwareheritage.org/browse/origin/content/?origin_url=https://github.com/SeelabFhdo/lemma&path=de.fhdo.lemma.technology.mappingdsl/src/de/fhdo/lemma/technology/mappingdsl/MappingDsl.xtext
80. Rademacher, F.: Grammar specification of LEMMA's Technology Modeling Language on Software Heritage. https://archive.softwareheritage.org/browse/origin/content/?origin_url=https://github.com/SeelabFhdo/lemma&path=de.fhdo.lemma.technology.technologydsl/src/de/fhdo/lemma/technology/TechnologyDsl.xtext
81. Rademacher, F.: LEMMA model processing example on Software Heritage. https://archive.softwareheritage.org/browse/origin/directory/?origin_url=https://github.com/SeelabFhdo/lemma&path=examples/model-processing
82. Rademacher, F.: LEMMA's Java Base Generator on Software Heritage. https://archive.softwareheritage.org/browse/directory/7dccb79b9804d8d9459c86ba9721e1197f59b865/?origin_url=https://github.com/SeelabFhdo/lemma&path=code%20generators/de.fhdo.lemma.model_processing.code_generation.java_base
83. Rademacher, F.: LEMMA's Model Processing Framework on Software Heritage. https://archive.softwareheritage.org/browse/origin/directory/?origin_url=https://github.com/SeelabFhdo/lemma&path=de.fhdo.lemma.model_processing
84. Rademacher, F.: LEMMA's static analysis library on Software Heritage. https://archive.softwareheritage.org/browse/directory/7dccb79b9804d8d9459c86ba9721e1197f59b865/?origin_url=https://github.com/SeelabFhdo/lemma&path=de.fhdo.lemma.analyzer.lib
85. Rademacher, F.: LEMMA's static analyzer on Software Heritage. https://archive.softwareheritage.org/browse/directory/7dccb79b9804d8d9459c86ba9721e1197f59b865/?origin_url=https://github.com/SeelabFhdo/lemma&path=de.fhdo.lemma.analyzer
86. Rademacher, F.: Metamodel implementation of LEMMA's Domain Data Modeling Language on Software Heritage. https://archive.softwareheritage.org/browse/origin/content/?origin_url=https://github.com/SeelabFhdo/lemma&path=de.fhdo.lemma.data.datadsl.metamodel/model/DataViewpointModel.xcore
87. Rademacher, F.: Metamodel implementation of LEMMA's Operation Modeling Language on Software Heritage. https://archive.softwareheritage.org/browse/origin/content/?origin_url=https://github.com/SeelabFhdo/lemma&path=de.fhdo.lemma.operationsdsl.metamodel/model/OperationViewpointModel.xcore
88. Rademacher, F.: Metamodel implementation of LEMMA's Service Modeling Language on Software Heritage. https://archive.softwareheritage.org/browse/origin/content/?origin_url=https://github.com/SeelabFhdo/lemma&path=/de.fhdo.lemma.servicedsl.metamodel/model/ServiceViewpointModel.xcore
89. Rademacher, F.: Metamodel implementation of LEMMA's Service Technology Mapping Modeling Language on Software Heritage. https://archive.softwareheritage.org/browse/origin/content/?origin_url=https://github.com/SeelabFhdo/lemma&path=de.fhdo.lemma.technology.mappingdsl.metamodel/model/TechnologyMappingModel.xcore
90. Rademacher, F.: Metamodel implementation of LEMMA's Technology Modeling Language on Software Heritage. https://archive.softwareheritage.org/browse/origin/content/?origin_url=https://github.com/SeelabFhdo/lemma&path=de.fhdo.lemma.technology.technologydsl.metamodel/model/TechnologyDefinitionModel.xcore

91. Rademacher, F.: Service model for the `OrderService` on Software Heritage. https://archive.softwareheritage.org/browse/origin/content/?origin_url=https://github.com/frademacher/dissertation-supplemental-material&path=chapters-5-6-concrete-syntax-example-and-intermediate-models/Order/Order.services
92. Rademacher, F.: An overview of modeling concepts for service-based software architectures. In: Software Engineering Publications. Kasseler Online Bibliothek, Repository und Archiv (KOBRA) (2020). https://doi.org/10.17170/kobra-202008191601
93. Rademacher, F.: A language ecosystem for modeling microservice architecture. Ph.D. Thesis, University of Kassel (2022). https://doi.org/10.17170/kobra-202209306919. https://kobra.uni-kassel.de/handle/123456789/14176
94. Rademacher, F., Peters, M., Sachweh, S.: Design of a domain-specific language based on a technology-independent web service framework. In: Weyns, D., Mirandola, R., Crnkovic, I. (eds.) Software Architecture, pp. 357–371. Springer, Cham (2015). https://doi.org/10.1007/978-3-319-23727-5_29
95. Rademacher, F., Sachweh, S., Zündorf, A.: Aspect-oriented modeling of technology heterogeneity in microservice architecture. In: 2019 IEEE International Conference on Software Architecture (ICSA), pp. 21–30. IEEE, Piscataway (2019). https://doi.org/10.1109/ICSA.2019.00011
96. Rademacher, F., Sachweh, S., Zündorf, A.: Deriving microservice code from underspecified domain models using DevOps-enabled modeling languages and model transformations. In: 2020 46th Euromicro Conference on Software Engineering and Advanced Applications (SEAA), pp. 229–236. IEEE, Piscataway (2020). https://doi.org/10.1109/SEAA51224.2020.00047
97. Rademacher, F., Sachweh, S., Zündorf, A.: A modeling method for systematic architecture reconstruction of microservice-based software systems. In: Nurcan, S., Reinhartz-Berger, I., Soffer, P., Zdravkovic, J. (eds.) Enterprise, Business-Process and Information Systems Modeling, pp. 311–326. Springer, Berlin (2020). https://doi.org/10.1007/978-3-030-49418-6_21
98. Rademacher, F., Sorgalla, J., Wizenty, P., Sachweh, S., Zündorf, A.: Graphical and textual model-driven microservice development. In: Bucchiarone, A., Dragoni, N., Dustdar, S., Lago, P., Mazzara, M., Rivera, V., Sadovykh, A. (eds.) Microservices: Science and Engineering, pp. 147–179. Springer, Berlin (2020). https://doi.org/10.1007/978-3-030-31646-4_7
99. Rademacher, F., Sorgalla, J., Wizenty, P., Trebbau, S.: Towards an extensible approach for generative microservice development and deployment using LEMMA. In: Scandurra, P., Galster, M., Mirandola, R., Weyns, D. (eds.) Software Architecture, pp. 257–280. Springer International Publishing, Cham (2022). https://doi.org/10.1007/978-3-031-15116-3_12
100. Rahman, M.I., Panichella, S., Taibi, D.: A curated dataset of microservices-based systems. In: Joint Proceedings of the Inforte Summer School on Software Maintenance and Evolution, pp. 1–9. CEUR-WS (2019). http://ceur-ws.org/Vol-2520/paper1a.pdf
101. Richards, M.: Software Architecture Patterns, 1st edn. O'Reilly, Sebastopol (2015)
102. Richardson, C.: Microservices Patterns, 1st edn. Manning Publications, Shelter Island (2019)
103. Rumpe, B.: Agile Modeling with UML, 1st edn. Springer, Berlin (2017)
104. Ruscio, D.D., Malavolta, I., Muccini, H., Pelliccione, P., Pierantonio, A.: Developing next generation ADLs through MDE techniques. In: 2010 ACM/IEEE 32nd International Conference on Software Engineering, vol. 1, pp. 85–94. IEEE, Piscataway (2010). https://doi.org/10.1145/1806799.1806816
105. Schauerhuber, A., Schwinger, W., Kapsammer, E., Retschitzegger, W., Wimmer, M., Kappel, G.: A survey on aspect-oriented modeling approaches. Technical Report, Vienna University of Technology (2007)
106. Schermann, G., Cito, J., Leitner, P.: All the services large and micro: Revisiting industrial practice in services computing. In: Norta, A., Gaaloul, W., Gangadharan, G.R., Dam, H.K. (eds.) Service-Oriented Computing – ICSOC 2015 Workshops, pp. 36–47. Springer, Berlin (2016). https://doi.org/10.1007/978-3-662-50539-7_4

107. Sobernig, S., Zdun, U.: Inversion-of-control layer. In: Proceedings of the 15th European Conference on Pattern Languages of Programs, EuroPLoP '10, pp. 1–22. ACM, New York (2010). https://doi.org/10.1145/2328909.2328935
108. [Software] Florian Rademacher: Language Ecosystem for Modeling Microservice Architecture (LEMMA). VCS: https://www.github.com/SeelabFhdo/lemma, SWHID: <swh:1:dir:4ac248661825a16a18a88b976734455f601e0d85;origin=https://github.com/SeelabFhdo/lemma;visit=swh:1:snp:f57caa7209e46735adc66f1cb937a606b4466556; anchor=swh:1:rev:22fd04c6b8a4cb126334db40c331f90ca9730606> (2022)
109. Soldani, J., Tamburri, D.A., Heuvel, W.J.V.D.: The pains and gains of microservices: a systematic grey literature review. J. Syst. Softw. **146**, 215–232 (2018). Elsevier. https://doi.org/10.1016/j.jss.2018.09.082
110. Soliman, M., Riebisch, M., Zdun, U.: Enriching architecture knowledge with technology design decisions. In: 2015 12th Working IEEE/IFIP Conference on Software Architecture, pp. 135–144. IEEE, Piscataway (2015). https://doi.org/10.1109/WICSA.2015.14
111. Soltesz, S., Pötzl, H., Fiuczynski, M.E., Bavier, A., Peterson, L.: Container-based operating system virtualization: A scalable, high-performance alternative to hypervisors. In: Proceedings of the 2nd ACM SIGOPS/EuroSys European Conference on Computer Systems 2007, EuroSys '07, pp. 275–287. ACM, New York (2007). https://doi.org/10.1145/1272996.1273025
112. Sorgalla, J., Rademacher, F., Sachweh, S., Zündorf, A.: Modeling microservice architecture: A comparative experiment towards the effectiveness of two approaches. In: Proceedings of the 35th Annual ACM Symposium on Applied Computing, SAC '20, p. 1506–1509. ACM, New York (2020). https://doi.org/10.1145/3341105.3374065
113. Sorgalla, J., Sachweh, S., Zündorf, A.: Exploring the microservice development process in small and medium-sized organizations. In: Morisio, M., Torchiano, M., Jedlitschka, A. (eds.) Product-Focused Software Process Improvement, pp. 453–460. Springer, Cham (2020). https://doi.org/10.1007/978-3-030-64148-1_28
114. Sorgalla, J., Wizenty, P., Rademacher, F., Sachweh, S., Zündorf, A.: AjiL: Enabling model-driven microservice development. In: Proceedings of the 12th European Conference on Software Architecture: Companion Proceedings, ECSA '18, pp. 1:1–1:4. ACM, New York (2018). https://doi.org/10.1145/3241403.3241406
115. Sorgalla, J., Wizenty, P., Rademacher, F., Sachweh, S., Zündorf, A.: Applying model-driven engineering to stimulate the adoption of devops processes in small and medium-sized development organizations. SN Comput. Sci. **2**(6), 459 (2021). https://doi.org/10.1007/s42979-021-00825-z
116. Steinberg, D., Budinsky, F., Paternostro, M., Merks, E.: EMF: Eclipse Modeling Framework, 2nd edn. Addison-Wesley, Boston (2008)
117. Stoermer, C., Rowe, A., O'Brien, L., Verhoef, C.: Model-centric software architecture reconstruction. Softw. Practice Exper. **36**(4), 333–363 (2006). Wiley. https://doi.org/10.1002/spe.699
118. Taibi, D., Lenarduzzi, V.: On the definition of microservice bad smells. IEEE Softw. **35**(3), 56–62 (2018). IEEE. https://doi.org/10.1109/MS.2018.2141031
119. Taibi, D., Lenarduzzi, V., Pahl, C.: Processes, motivations, and issues for migrating to microservices architectures: an empirical investigation. IEEE Cloud Comput. **4**(5), 22–32 (2017). IEEE. https://doi.org/10.1109/MCC.2017.4250931
120. Terzić, B., Dimitrieski, V., Kordić, S., Milosavljević, G., Luković, I.: Development and evaluation of MicroBuilder: a model-driven tool for the specification of REST microservice software architectures. Enterprise Informat. Syst. **12**(8-9), 1034–1057 (2018). Taylor & Francis. https://doi.org/10.1080/17517575.2018.1460766
121. The Open Group: SOA reference architecture. C119 (2011)
122. Trebbau, S., Wizenty, P., Sachweh, S.: Towards integrating blockchains with microservice architecture using model-driven engineering. In: Gregory, P., Kruchten, P. (eds.) Agile Processes in Software Engineering and Extreme Programming – Workshops, pp. 167–175. Springer International Publishing, Cham (2021). https://doi.org/10.1007/978-3-030-88583-0_16

123. Whittle, J., Hutchinson, J., Rouncefield, M.: The state of practice in model-driven engineering. IEEE Softw. **31**(3), 79–85 (2014). IEEE. https://doi.org/10.1109/MS.2013.65
124. Whittle, J., Hutchinson, J., Rouncefield, M., Burden, H., Heldal, R.: Industrial adoption of model-driven engineering: Are the tools really the problem? In: Model-Driven Engineering Languages and Systems: 16th International Conference, MODELS 2013, Miami, FL, USA, September 29–October 4, 2013. Proceedings 16, pp. 1–17. Springer, Berlin (2013). https://doi.org/10.1007/978-3-642-41533-3_1
125. Wizenty, P., Ponce, F., Rademacher, F., Soldani, J., Astudillo, H., Brogi, A., Sachweh, S.: Towards resolving security smells in microservices, model-driven. In: Proceedings of the 18th International Conference on Software Technologies (ICSOFT 2023). To appear
126. Wizenty, P., Rademacher, F.: Towards viewpoint-based microservice architecture reconstruction. In: Abstracts of the Fourth International Conference on Microservices (Microservices 2022). Microservices Community (2022). https://www.conf-micro.services/2022/papers/paper_16.pdf
127. Wortmann, A., Barais, O., Combemale, B., Wimmer, M.: Modeling languages in industry 4.0: an extended systematic mapping study. Softw. Syst. Model. **19**(1), 67–94 (2020). https://doi.org/10.1007/s10270-019-00757-6
128. Zimmermann, O.: Microservices tenets. Comput. Sci. Res. Develop. **32**(3–4), 301–310 (2017). Springer. https://doi.org/10.1007/s00450-016-0337-0
129. Zimmermann, O., Stocker, M., Lübke, D., Pautasso, C., Zdun, U.: Introduction to microservice API patterns (MAP). In: Cruz-Filipe, L., Giallorenzo, S., Montesi, F., Peressotti, M., Rademacher, F., Sachweh, S. (eds.) Joint Post-proceedings of the First and Second International Conference on Microservices (Microservices 2017/2019), OpenAccess Series in Informatics (OASIcs), vol. 78, pp. 4:1–4:17. Schloss Dagstuhl–Leibniz-Zentrum für Informatik, Dagstuhl, Germany (2020). https://doi.org/10.4230/OASIcs.Microservices.2017-2019.4
130. Zimmermann, O., Stocker, M., Lübke, D., Zdun, U., Pautasso, C.: Patterns for API Design: Simplifying Integration with Loosely Coupled Message Exchanges. Addison-Wesley Signature Series (Vernon). Addison-Wesley Professional, Boston (2022)

Open Access This chapter is licensed under the terms of the Creative Commons Attribution 4.0 International License (http://creativecommons.org/licenses/by/4.0/), which permits use, sharing, adaptation, distribution and reproduction in any medium or format, as long as you give appropriate credit to the original author(s) and the source, provide a link to the Creative Commons licence and indicate if changes were made.

The images or other third party material in this chapter are included in the chapter's Creative Commons licence, unless indicated otherwise in a credit line to the material. If material is not included in the chapter's Creative Commons licence and your intended use is not permitted by statutory regulation or exceeds the permitted use, you will need to obtain permission directly from the copyright holder.

Usefulness of Automatic Static Analysis Tools: Evidence from Four Case Studies

Alexander Trautsch

Abstract Automated Static Analysis Tools (ASATs) are an additional tool available to developers in their pursuit of high-quality software. ASATs match source code against configured rules and produce a warning when a rule is violated. However, the evaluation of the warnings by developers as well as the resolution of warnings requires time. This raises the question of whether we are able to evaluate the usefulness of ASATs empirically. Within this chapter, we present the results of four case studies, which investigate different aspects regarding the impact of ASATs on software quality and the perception of the developers thereof. We present results regarding the evolution of ASAT warnings from a longitudinal study of 54 open-source projects. To evaluate the impact on defects, we present results from two studies. The first study is evaluating predictive models in the context of defect prediction with ASAT-based features. The second study provides a statistical investigation of the differences between changes that induce a defect and all other changes. In order to observe the developer's perspective regarding ASAT warnings and other software quality metrics, we include the results of a study of developer intent, which compares changes where the developers intend to improve the quality of the code base with all other changes to see which quality metrics and ASAT warnings change in which way. We employ methods of empirical software engineering research to investigate these relationships and provide evidence-based information for researchers and practitioners alike. Within our studies, we can show empirically that we are able to measure an impact on quality. However, the effect is surprisingly small. Moreover, our investigation of developer intents yield information about the magnitude of bug fixing as a driver for complexity in software. Our results can help practitioners estimate the possible impact of introducing an ASAT on defects, as well as provide guidelines for managing the complexity of software.

A. Trautsch (✉)
Universität Passau, Passau, Germany
e-mail: alexander.trautsch@uni-passau.de

© The Author(s) 2024
E. Bodden et al. (eds.), *Ernst Denert Award for Software Engineering 2022*,
https://doi.org/10.1007/978-3-031-44412-8_6

1 Introduction

Automated Static Analysis Tools (ASATs) parse source code into internal representations and match these representations against a predefined set of rules. If a rule is matched, a warning is triggered, which shows a position in the source code and the rule that was triggered. Depending on the type of ASAT, the rules range from stylistic issues to patterns of known bugs. Rules can be defined in the configuration of the ASAT. In summary, ASATs are providing a type of automatic inspection of the source code [66].

Within our studies, we predominantly investigate a commonly used static analysis tool for Java: PMD.[1] The reason for this is that PMD has been used for a long time, which allows for a rich source of historical data. It also directly works with the source code instead of the bytecode, which is an advantage as older revisions of open-source projects might not be compilable anymore [60]. PMD also provides a diverse set of rules, which range from code style issues to best practices to known problems. This combination makes PMD an ideal tool for our studies. While ASATs can be helpful, they can have problems with false positives, i.e., warnings about code that is not problematic, which may hinder adoption by developers [10, 26]. This led to many studies concerned with classification of ASATs into potential false positives or actionable warnings, e.g., [19, 29, 31]. While the results of this research were not transferred to practice, the authors of ASATs are always interested in improving the tools by considering bug reports about false positives. However, there may be a different definition of false positive; some studies, e.g., [4, 20, 63] define false positives as every warning, except the ones which the developer believes could lead to significant program misbehavior. Others defined false positives as warnings that were not resolved in a bug fix change after a certain time, e.g., [29], which brings its own validity problems. Ayewah et al. [4] also discuss the issue of false positives and summarize that simply classifying into true and false positives is an oversimplification of the issue. There may be coding style-related warnings that are good to resolve, but may not necessarily lead to errors. Other studies try to find real defects, e.g., [52] or [18]. Thung et al. [52] investigated three open-source projects and linked bug reports to fixes. They found that PMD misses bugs in 3.9% (AspectJ), 15% (Rhino), and 50% (Lucene) of cases. FindBugs (a bug focused ASAT) misses 33.6%, 10% and 71.4%. Habib and Pradel [18] used Defects4J [27] and found that SpotBugs [50] (successor to FindBugs [17]) is able to find 18 of the 594 bugs in the extended Defects4J dataset. These numbers provide some insight into the recall. However, given that we are also interested in warnings that do not necessarily cause a defect, this is not ideal for our approach. Lee et al. [32] provide some numbers for false positives (10% of about 10,000). However, in their study, they only check six in house checks for C/C++, which do not necessarily apply to Java, e.g., check for double-free.

---

[1] https://pmd.github.io.

Regardless of the problem of false positives, many developers still believe that static analysis tools have a positive impact on software quality [11, 61]. This invites the question whether using ASATs provides a net-benefit regarding software quality and how large the benefit might be. Some researchers investigate this impact via predictive models for defects in software, e.g., [33, 38, 41, 43, 45]. This is an angle we also cover in our own research [55]. Other researchers investigate whether they are able to find defects directly, e.g., [18, 52, 62].

However, for predictive models as well as finding defects, validity problems need to be considered. Finding defects, even with full access to the Issue Tracking System (ITS) and Version Control System (VCS), can be problematic. Usually a variant of the Śliwerski Zimmermann Zeller (SZZ) algorithm [48] is used to link defects to bug fixes and subsequently to the bug inducing change, i.e., the change that is responsible for the bug. While the SZZ algorithm provides bug fixes and from there bug-inducing changes, the data that is provided contains noise, e.g., in the form of mislabeled issue types in the ITS [3, 24], faulty links from bug report to bug-fixing or bug-inducing changes [15, 46] or tangled changes, i.e., a bug-fixing change that is tangled with unrelated changes to the code [23, 25, 36].

Most data validity problems require manual investigation of the data to mitigate the noise. Building upon previous work [59], we extended the existing data mining platform SmartSHARK with additional data and features [56] to aid us and other researchers in his endeavor. Using the SmartSHARK mining ecosystem with its many plugins and manual validation frontend, we were able to provide a feature-rich, new dataset for researchers, which also addresses data validity problems. Within our case studies, we applied the results and data of several previous studies, which investigate data validity problems including manually investigating noisy data. We use an improved SZZ variant, which also includes manually validated issue types [22]. In addition, we include manually validated bug-fixing lines to mitigate tangling noise, i.e., unrelated changes alongside a bug fix, from a large investigation into effects of tangling [21].

Within this chapter, we present and combine the results of four large peer-reviewed empirical studies to investigate different aspects of ASATs. We provide empirical data on the evolution of ASAT warnings, impact on defects, as well as the perspective of the developers regarding quality and ASATs. The presented results are acquired over multiple years and use manually validated data where possible to mitigate noise in the data and provide a clearer picture of the results. We are able to present empirical data for a very common case, that of using a well-known static analysis tool (PMD) for the Java programming language and its impact on quality. Within this chapter, we will use PMD and ASAT interchangeably.

Multiple empirical methods are available to researchers to investigate these questions [64]. In the results presented in this chapter, we apply empirical methods to gather evidence in an evidence-based software engineering context. Kitchenham et al. [30] introduced the term evidence-based software engineering by borrowing the idea of it from medicine. In evidence-based medicine, the practitioner takes current research into consideration and weighs the data presented in empirical studies to improve his ability to provide treatments for patients. Evidence-based software engineering aims to do the same for practitioners in software engineering. More concretely, "...to provide the means by which current best evidence from research can be integrated with practical experience and human values in the decision-making process regarding the development and maintenance of software"[30].

To this end, evidence-based software engineering can provide empirical data for practitioners to base their decisions on, e.g., whether to use a certain tool or methodology. In this chapter, we provide evidence for practitioners regarding the use and configuration of ASATs within the results of the studies we combine. In addition to the data provided for research, this gives a very practical insight into the impact of ASATs in a general overview that applies to every practitioner that programs in Java and considers static analysis.

This chapter is based on four peer-reviewed publications [54, 55, 57, 58] and my PhD thesis [53]. The rest of this chapter is organized as follows: Sect. 2 summarizes the results of our studies, while Sect. 3 summarizes limitations of the studies and the data. Section 4 sets our studies into the context of their respective related work. Section 5 summarizes this chapter and provides a short outlook on future work.

2 Results

In this chapter, we will present results together, which are published separately. This allows us to connect to them and emphasize why each of the parts was needed for a better picture of the overall topic. The study subjects of all studies discussed here are shown in Table 1. For the sake of brevity, we do only include short descriptions of the methodology.

In Sect. 2.1, we investigate changes in the evolution of static analysis warnings and how they are correlated with the size of the project or changes in the configuration of the ASAT. In Sect. 2.2, we investigate ways to measure the correlation between ASAT warnings and defects via building defect prediction models using features based on ASAT warnings as well as a statistical comparison of ASAT warning density between bug-inducing and other changes over the lifetime of open source repositories. Section 2.3 observes developers of open-source projects "in the wild" and whether they connect removing static analysis warnings and static source code metrics with quality improvements in the code base.

2.1 Evolution of ASAT Warnings

The first question we ask in our investigation of static analysis tools is whether we have to account for a change over time regarding static analysis warnings. We therefore investigate the change of ASAT warnings over time in multiple open source projects.

Table 1 Study subjects used in our studies and the sections in which they are used

Project	Section 2.1	Section 2.2.1	Section 2.2.2	Section 2.3
ant-ivy	No	Yes	Yes	No
archiva	Yes	Yes	No	Yes
calcite	Yes	Yes	No	Yes
cayenne	Yes	Yes	No	Yes
commons-bcel	Yes	Yes	Yes	Yes
commons-beanutils	Yes	Yes	Yes	Yes
commons-codec	Yes	Yes	Yes	Yes
commons-collections	Yes	Yes	Yes	Yes
commons-compress	Yes	Yes	Yes	Yes
commons-configurations	Yes	Yes	Yes	Yes
commons-dbcp	Yes	Yes	Yes	Yes
commons-digester	Yes	Yes	Yes	Yes
commons-imaging	Yes	No	No	Yes
commons-io	Yes	Yes	Yes	Yes
commons-jcs	Yes	Yes	Yes	Yes
commons-jexl	Yes	Yes	No	Yes
commons-lang	Yes	Yes	Yes	Yes
commons-math	Yes	Yes	Yes	Yes
commons-net	Yes	Yes	Yes	Yes
commons-rdf	Yes	No	No	Yes
commons-scxml	Yes	Yes	Yes	Yes
commons-validator	Yes	Yes	Yes	Yes
commons-vfs	Yes	Yes	Yes	Yes
deltaspike	No	Yes	No	No
eagle	Yes	Yes	No	Yes
falcon	Yes	No	No	Yes
flume	Yes	No	No	Yes
giraph	Yes	Yes	Yes	Yes
gora	Yes	Yes	Yes	Yes
helix	Yes	No	No	Yes
httpcomponents-client	Yes	No	No	Yes
httpcomponents-core	Yes	No	No	Yes
jena	Yes	No	No	Yes
jspwiki	Yes	Yes	No	Yes
knox	Yes	Yes	No	Yes
kylin	Yes	Yes	No	Yes
lens	Yes	Yes	No	Yes
mahout	Yes	Yes	No	Yes
manifoldcf	Yes	Yes	No	Yes
mina-sshd	Yes	No	No	Yes

(continued)

Table 1 (continued)

Project	Section 2.1	Section 2.2.1	Section 2.2.2	Section 2.3
nutch	No	Yes	No	No
opennlp	No	Yes	Yes	No
parquet-mr	No	Yes	Yes	No
pdfbox	Yes	No	No	Yes
phoenix	Yes	No	No	Yes
ranger	Yes	No	No	Yes
roller	Yes	No	No	Yes
santuario-java	Yes	Yes	Yes	Yes
storm	Yes	No	No	Yes
streams	Yes	No	No	Yes
struts	Yes	No	No	Yes
systemml	Yes	Yes	No	Yes
tez	Yes	No	No	Yes
tika	Yes	Yes	No	Yes
wss4j	Yes	Yes	Yes	Yes
zeppelin	Yes	No	No	Yes

Table 2 Correlation coefficients and *p*-values between LLOC and the number of static analysis warnings. Adapted from Trautsch et al. [54], used under Creative Commons CC-BY license

Method	Coefficient	*P*-value
Spearman's ρ	0.57509	**<0.0001**
Kendall's τ	0.71654	**<0.0001**

Statistically significant *p*-values are bolded

First, however, is the question of whether the size of the project correlates with the number of ASAT warnings. We therefore correlate the changes in ASAT warnings with the Logical Lines of Code (LLOC), i.e., the number of lines of code without comments and empty lines.

Table 2 shows the correlation between the number of ASAT warnings and the size of the project in LLOC for Spearman's ρ [49] and Kendall's τ [28]. Both are non-parametric correlation metrics, which are appropriate for our data. The results show that the number of static analysis warnings grow as the size of the open-source project is growing. If we look at the number of warnings per LLOC of the system $wd(s) = \frac{\#warnings}{LLOC}$ as warning density, we find that it is decreasing.

Table 3 shows the averaged results over all years of project history. We can see that warning density is decreasing. Over all study subjects, 3.5 ASAT warnings per 1k LLoC are resolved per year. If we only measure subjects and years in which PMD is included in the build, we measure a number of 2.3 ASAT warnings. We only measure full years in which PMD was included, not years in which it was introduced into the project because all measurements were per year; this means we may be missing the cleanup phase after the introduction of an ASAT. Even though

Table 3 Mean changes per year for all study subjects. Adapted from Trautsch et al. [54], used under Creative Commons CC-BY license

Method	Change per year per kLLoC
Mean warning density	−3.5035
Mean warning density after PMD introduction	−2.2913

we measure a value of 2.3, we still find that the majority of study subjects retain a positive trend of ASAT warning evolution a year after they introduced PMD into the build process.

2.2 Impact on Defects

As we are interested in whether PMD has an impact on software quality, we investigate defects as the "de facto standard measure of software quality" [16]. We investigate different views with respect to defects. Section 2.2.1 summarizes results from a study that investigates feature sets for predictive models to investigate whether features previously not considered, e.g., based on static analysis warnings and static source code metrics, can improve the prediction of defects. Section 2.2.2 compares bug-inducing changes, i.e., changes which require a bug fix later, with all other changes, therefore, shedding light on whether static analysis warnings are more common in these kinds of changes.

2.2.1 Predictive Models

A large branch of research that investigates the relationship between defects and metrics in the form of process metrics, e.g., number of changes, and static source code metrics, e.g., cyclomatic complexity, is categorized as defect prediction research. Within this category, predictive models are built, which aim to predict faulty code at different granularity using data collected about the code or the process of developing the code. Pascarella et al. [40] introduced a fine-grained just-in-time defect prediction model, which is a good fit for our study, as it is concerned with changes on a file level instead of change level or release level. However, it is only investigating change features on a per-file basis. Therefore, we extend this approach with additional features to investigate the impact of source code metrics and ASAT warnings through the lens of change-based defect prediction research. We build predictive models with different sets of features and evaluate them to compare their performance including different labeling strategies.

As shown in the previous section, static analysis warnings are resolved over time, on average. Therefore, we introduce features that take this into account to investigate ASAT warnings as part of the features for the predictive models. To achieve this, we do not simply use the sum of ASAT warnings as it increases in most cases or the

Table 4 Feature sets used in the predictive models. ©2020 IEEE. Adapted, with permission, from Trautsch et al. [55]

Name	Feature set description
combined	All features combined
jit	Change features commonly used in just-in-time defect prediction adapted for a fine-grained scenario by Pascarella et al. [40]
static	Static source code metrics by OpenStaticAnalyzer. A full list is available online[a]
pmd	Static analysis warnings by PMD also collected via OpenStaticAnalyzer. A full list is available online[a]

[a] See footnote 2

Table 5 Additional warning density based features introduced in our case study. ©2020 IEEE. Adapted, with permission, from Trautsch et al. [55]

Name	Formula	Description
wd(s)	$wd(s)_t$	The warning density (wd) of the system (s) at the current change (t)
swd(f)	$\sum_t wd(f)_t - wd(s)_t$	The cumulative difference between warning density of the file and the system over all changes (t) up to the current change
swd(a)	$\sum_t wd(a)_t - wd(a)_{t-1}$	The cumulative sum of the changes in warning density by the author (a)

warning density as it declines in most cases. We calculate the difference between the warning density of the current file and the rest of the system at that point in time as a feature for the predictive models.

Table 4 shows a short description of the feature sets used in the model evaluations. The study makes heavy use of OpenStaticAnalyzer[2] via the SmartSHARK [56, 59] infrastructure. Moreover, we also use two common defect labeling strategies used in research, ad-hoc SZZ, which is only based on keywords within the commit message to identify bug fixes, and ITS SZZ, which requires a direct link between the ITS and the bug fix commit as well as the correct, manually validated issue type, i.e., bug instead of enhancement.

Within this study, we use model performance metrics based on the confusion matrix, true positives, TP; false positives, FP; false negatives, FN; and true negatives, TN. We aggregate them as precision $\frac{TP}{TP+FP}$, recall $\frac{TP}{TP+FN}$, and a combination F-measure $\frac{2 \cdot precision \cdot recall}{precision+recall}$. In addition, we use AUC, the area under the Receiver Operating Characteristic (ROC) curve, which is the false-positive rate against the true-positive rate.

Table 5 shows aggregated warning density-based features in addition to the sum of static analysis warnings simply aggregated by their warning type already contained in the pmd feature set. As we have seen in Sect. 2.1, warning density is decreasing, so we may encounter time effects. Therefore, we aggregate warning

---

[2] https://www.sourcemeter.com/resources/java/.

density via differences between the file and the system or aggregate the sum of the differences per author.

Figure 1 shows the model performance metrics F-measure and AUC for all feature sets and labeling strategies. Complementary to the critical distance diagram in Fig. 1, we include Table 6. We can see that the combined feature set is ranked first with a significant distance to the second rank except for F-measure with the ITS SZZ

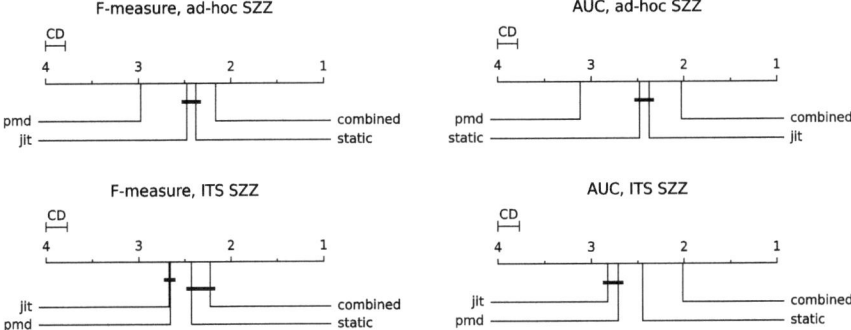

Fig. 1 Ranking of model performance metrics in an interval approach. ©2020 IEEE. Adapted, with permission, from Trautsch et al. [55]

Table 6 Ranking of model performance metrics, median (MED), mean absolute error (MAD), confidence interval (CI), effect size; effect size magnitudes are negligible (n), small (s), medium (m), large (l). Bolding denotes a statistically significant difference to the first rank. ©2020 IEEE. Adapted, with permission, from Trautsch et al. [55]

			Ad-hoc SZZ		
	Feature	MED	MAD	CI	Effect size
AUC	combined	0.707	0.121	[0.685, 0.732]	0.000 (n)
	jit	0.695	0.136	[0.664, 0.716]	**0.078** (n)
	static	0.681	0.126	[0.657, 0.709]	**0.110** (n)
	pmd	0.625	0.123	[0.597, 0.645]	**0.351** (n)
	Feature	MED	MAD	CI	Effect size
F-Measure	combined	0.350	0.236	[0.304, 0.400]	−0.000 (n)
	static	0.333	0.225	[0.286, 0.382]	**0.015** (n)
	jit	0.320	0.250	[0.273, 0.370]	**0.063** (n)
	pmd	0.272	0.227	[0.233, 0.320]	**0.158** (s)
			ITS SZZ		
	Feature	MED	MAD	CI	Effect size
AUC	combined	0.759	0.170	[0.730, 0.795]	0.000 (n)
	static	0.733	0.162	[0.703, 0.773]	**0.088** (n)
	pmd	0.697	0.186	[0.657, 0.727]	**0.202** (s)
	jit	0.672	0.199	[0.632, 0.716]	**0.247** (s)
	Feature	MED	MAD	CI	Effect size
F-Measure	combined	0.086	0.128	[0.049, 0.126]	0.000 (n)
	static	0.091	0.135	[0.055, 0.127]	−0.011 (n)
	pmd	0.062	0.091	[0.029, 0.100]	**0.057** (n)
	jit	0.054	0.080	[0.000, 0.087]	**0.119** (n)

labeling approach. This shows that we are able to improve the fine-grained just-in-time defect prediction approach introduced by Pascarella et al. [40], which only considers jit features with additional features over multiple labeling approaches.

If we only consider a comparison between static and the aggregated ASAT warnings, we find that the combined set is ranked first in both labeling approaches for AUC, while only the static set is ranked first in F-Measure. However, the distance between both is not significant, and the number of features is vastly different (207 static source code features vs. 3 aggregated ASAT features). In addition, we calculated the feature importance for the two models used in the study, a regularized logistic regression model and a Random forest model. We found that for the ITS SZZ labeling approach as well as the ad-hoc SZZ labeling approach, the aggregated warning density metrics $wd(s)$, $swd(f)$ and $swd(a)$ were in the top 10 most important features.

Overall, our research points to the predictive power of the additional features, especially static source code features, which can enhance just-in-time defect prediction approaches, e.g., Rosen et al. [47] or Yan et al. [65].

2.2.2 Statistical Observation

In Sect. 2.2.1, we did get some hints that adding features based on ASAT warnings can improve predictive models, however, only slightly. In a more direct investigation of this phenomenon, we specifically look at differences between bug-inducing changes in files and all other changes in files over the lifetime of a repository.

We aggregate the different warning types by summation on a per-file basis as described in Table 7. In addition, we also discern between two sets of rules for the ASAT. If nothing is added to the description, we use all rules available; if (default) is added, we only use the default rules. This categorization increases the amount of information while at the same time mitigating the risk of subgroup analysis. Figure 2 shows negative values for both $fd(f)$ and $dfd(f)$; this shows that we can still see an effect of decreasing warning density with differences in warning densities. However, we can also see that bug-inducing changes have a slightly higher warning density for default warning. When looking into the data, we can see that files changed reduce warning density over time, while files not changed often retain a higher warning density.

Figure 3 and Table 8 shows the final results and statistical tests for the comparison between bug-inducing changes and other file changes for all study subjects. We can

Table 7 Warning density based metrics compared in this section

Name	Formula	Description
$fd(f)$	$wd(f)_t - wd(s)_t$	The difference in warning density between the file f and the system at current change
$dfd(f)$	$\sum_{j=1}^{j=t} \frac{wd(f)_j - wd(s)_j}{t-j+1}$	The linearly discounted cumulative warning density of the file and the system up to the current change t

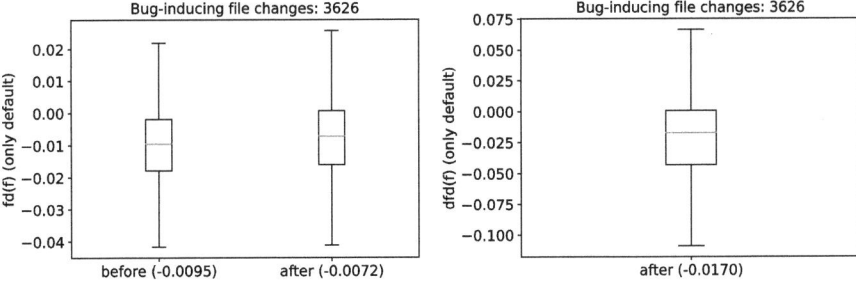

Fig. 2 Box plot of $fd(f)$ and $dfd(f)$ for only default warnings of all bug-inducing files before and after the bug-inducing change, median value in parentheses. Fliers are omitted. From Trautsch et al. [58], used under Creative Commons CC-BY license

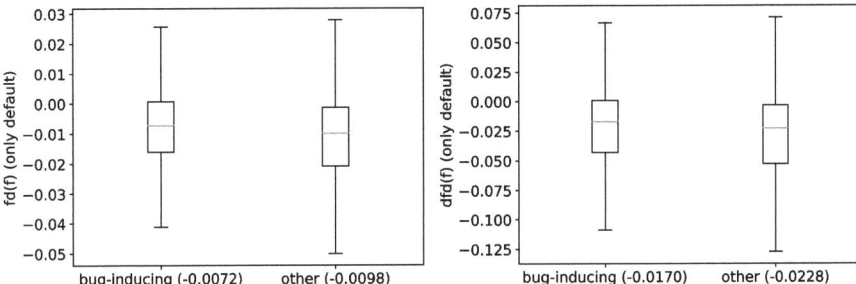

Fig. 3 Box plots of $fd(f)$ and $dfd(f)$ for only default warnings of all bug-inducing changes and all other file changes, median value in parentheses. Fliers are omitted. Adapted from Trautsch et al. [58], used under Creative Commons CC-BY license

Table 8 Median values, Mann-Whitney U test p-values, and effect sizes for all warning density metrics. From Trautsch et al. [58], used under Creative Commons CC-BY license

WD Metric	Median other	Median bug inducing	P-value	Effect size
$fd(f)$	−0.0440	−0.0300	<**0.0001**	0.05 (n)
$fd(f)$ (default)	−0.0098	−0.0072	<**0.0001**	0.10 (n)
$dfd(f)$	−0.0948	−0.0661	0.0247	–
$dfd(f)$ (default)	−0.0228	−0.0170	<**0.0001**	0.07 (n)

Statistically significant p-values are bolded

see that while the difference is statistically significant, the effect size is negligible for all. If we only look at default warnings, we see that the effect size is slightly higher. This indicates that with our metrics, there is a difference in warning density between bug-inducing changes and all other changes, even though it is likely very small. In addition, using the default rules provided increases the effect size and is statistically significant in all measured metrics. This means that the configuration of rules has an impact and is something practitioners and researchers should consider.

2.3 Perception of the Developers

In our investigation of static analysis warnings, we also want to look at whether developers are really perceiving ASAT warnings as quality improving. To achieve this, we are looking into changes where the developer intends to improve the quality, either by fixing a bug (corrective) or an internal quality improvement (perfective) e.g., by refactoring, cleanup, or simplifications. We decided to name the categories perfective and corrective after Swanson [8] to ease the readability. To determine the intent of the developers, two researchers manually classified a random sample of 2,533 commit messages into these categories. This data was then used to fine-tune a BERT [12] large language model and to evaluate its performance. The fine-tuned model is then used to classify the rest of the commit messages into these categories. After this categorization, we are comparing the differences between these categories to see whether ASAT warnings are removed when developers intend to improve the quality of the codebase.

In addition to ASAT warnings, we also compare these categories of changes via other software quality metrics from the most recent version [6] of a software quality model [5]. This includes complexity metrics such as cyclomatic complexity [35] and object-oriented metrics after Chidamber and Kemerer [9]. Table 9 shows all software quality metrics used in this section as well as a short description. In this section, the ASAT warnings are aggregated by their severity rating, analogous to the quality model [6].

2.3.1 Size of Perfective and Corrective Changes

As a first step, we are interested in whether we can see differences in perfective and corrective changes regarding the size of the change. Previous work finds that corrective and perfective changes are smaller than other changes [1, 37, 42]. We can also see that this is the case in our own data in Table 10. Our data shows that the difference is statistically significant for the number of lines added and deleted even though the effect size is small.

Figure 4 visualizes the differences between all changes, only perfective changes and corrective changes. We can see that corrective changes add less lines than other changes, while perfective changes remove more lines of code than other changes.

Due to these differences in size between the categories of changes, we will correct for size using the number of changed lines going forward, analogous to using warning density in previous results. However, we can already note that our results replicate previous research, which suggests that our study setup and data collection are valid.

Table 9 Static source code metrics and static analysis warning severities used in this results section. Adapted from Trautsch et al. [57], used under Creative Commons CC-BY license

Name and description	Abbrev.
Cyclomatic Complexity [35]	
The number of independent control-flow paths	McCC
Logical Lines of Code	
Number of lines in a file without comments and empty lines	LLOC
Nesting Level else-if	
Maximum of nesting level in a file	NLE
Number of parameters in a method	
The sum of all parameters of all methods in a file	NUMPAR
Clone Coverage	
Ratio of code covered by duplicates	CC
Comment lines of code	
Sum of commented lines	CLOC
Comment density	
Ratio of CLOC to LLOC	CD
API Documentation	
Number of documented public methods, +1 if class is documented	AD
Number of Ancestors	
Number of classes, interfaces, enums from which the class is inherited	NOA
Coupling between object classes	
Number of used classes (inheritance, function call, type reference)	CBO
Number of Incoming	
Invocations Other methods that call the current class	NII
Minor static analysis warnings	
E.g., brace rules, naming conventions	Minor
Major static analysis warnings	
E.g., type resolution rules, unnecessary/unused code rules	Major
Critical static analysis warnings	
E.g., equals for string comparison, catching null pointer exceptions	Critical

Table 10 Statistical test results of comparing perfective and corrective commits to non-perfective and non-corrective, Mann-Whitney U test p-values, and effect size with category (n is negligible, s is small). Statistically significant p-values are in bold. Adapted from Trautsch et al. [57], used under Creative Commons CC-BY license

	Perfective		Corrective	
Metric	P-value	Effect size	P-value	Effect size
#lines added	**<0.0001**	0.20 (s)	**<0.0001**	0.21 (s)
#lines deleted	**<0.0001**	0.15 (s)	**<0.0001**	0.16 (s)
#files modified	0.2081	–	**<0.0001**	0.22 (s)
#hunks	**<0.0001**	0.01 (n)	**<0.0001**	0.22 (s)

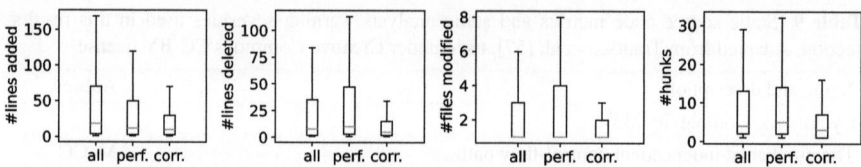

Fig. 4 Commit size distribution over all projects for all perfective and corrective commits. Fliers are omitted. From Trautsch et al. [57], used under Creative Commons CC-BY license

2.3.2 Differences in Perfective and Corrective Changes

While the size is important to determine whether we need to account for different sizes between our categories, the more important question we ask in this section is whether there are differences between perfective, corrective, and all other changes. More to the point, we are interested in whether ASAT warnings are reduced in perfective and corrective changes and whether we can compare the magnitude of this effect with other traditional source code quality metrics (see Table 9). This comparison should yield insights into whether developers regard ASAT warnings as important to quality by exploring whether the developers remove the warnings when they intend to improve the quality of the source code.

Figure 5 shows the differences between all changes, only perfective and only corrective changes. We can already see that corrective changes tend to be more complex when we look at the McCC and NLE metrics, for example. We can also see that perfective changes are less complex as shown in multiple software quality metrics, e.g., McCC, NLE, CBO. These results are somewhat expected, however, the magnitude of the effect for corrective changes and complexity was not expected when setting up the study. While we expected that corrective changes would increase the complexity, we did not expect such a magnitude especially when correcting for size and in comparison to all changes, which also include types of change that we would expect a high complexity from, e.g., feature additions. Having done a visual analysis of the distributions of all groups, we are interested in the differences between perfective, corrective, and their counterparts, e.g., perfective against all non-perfective changes, especially whether they are statistically significantly different and the effect size of the differences.

Table 11 shows the differences between perfective, corrective, and their counterparts over the full history of all study subjects. We can see that static analysis warnings are removed in perfective as well as in corrective changes. While the effect size is higher in perfective changes, this hints at evidence that developers in fact do remove static analysis warnings or improve the code that generated the warnings when they intend to improve source code quality.

Table 11 emphasizes, for us, an unexpected result of the study. McCC, LLOC, and NLE are not reduced in corrective commits when compared with all other non-corrective commits. While we did not expect complexity and size to be reduced in corrective changes, the comparison here is one of statistical dominance over all other changes, including feature additions. This means that corrective changes are

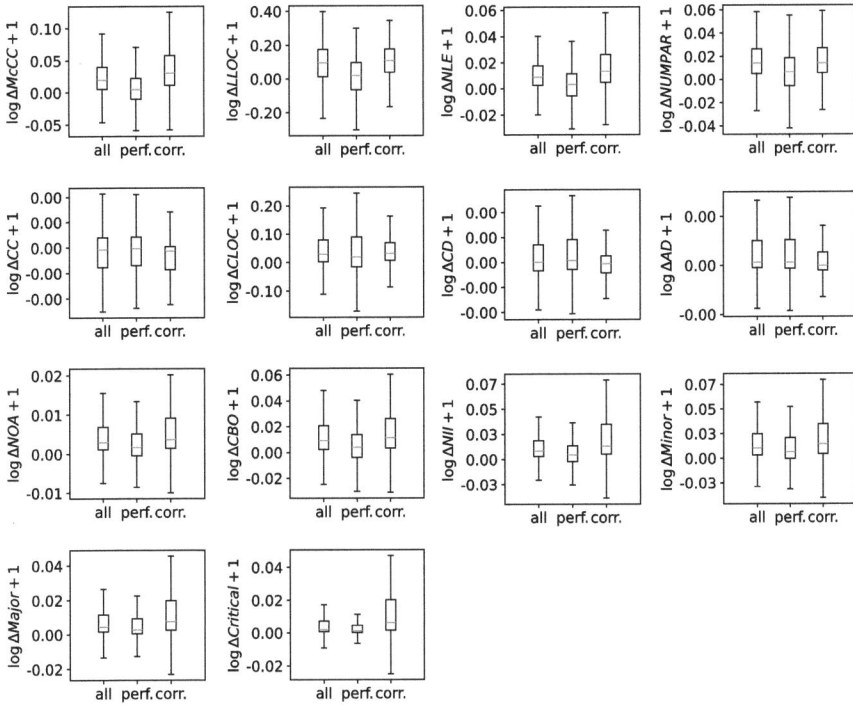

Fig. 5 Static source code metric value changes in all perfective and corrective commits divided by changed lines. Fliers are omitted. From Trautsch et al. [57], used under Creative Commons CC-BY license

Table 11 Statistical test results of comparing perfective and corrective commits to non-perfective and non-corrective commits, Mann-Whitney U test *p*-values, and effect size with category (*n* is negligible, *s* is small, *m* is medium). Statistically significant *p*-values are in bold. All values are normalized for changed lines. Adapted from Trautsch et al. [57], used under Creative Commons CC-BY license

Metric	Perfective		Corrective	
	P-value	Effect size	*P*-value	Effect size
McCC	**<0.0001**	0.39 (m)	1.0000	–
LLOC	**<0.0001**	0.45 (m)	1.0000	–
NLE	**<0.0001**	0.27 (s)	1.0000	–
NUMPAR	**<0.0001**	0.25 (s)	**<0.0001**	0.09 (n)
CC	1.0000	–	**<0.0001**	0.12 (s)
CLOC	**<0.0001**	0.16 (s)	**<0.0001**	0.05 (n)
CD	1.0000	–	**<0.0001**	0.16 (s)
AD	**<0.0001**	0.02 (n)	**<0.0001**	0.08 (n)
NOA	**<0.0001**	0.08 (n)	**<0.0001**	0.07 (n)
CBO	**<0.0001**	0.19 (s)	**<0.0001**	0.06 (n)
NII	**<0.0001**	0.19 (s)	**<0.0001**	0.02 (n)
Minor	**<0.0001**	0.19 (s)	**<0.0001**	0.05 (n)
Major	**<0.0001**	0.12 (s)	**<0.0001**	0.05 (n)
Critical	**<0.0001**	0.05 (n)	**<0.0001**	0.03 (n)

not less complex or smaller than all other changes even when corrected for size via changed lines.

2.3.3 State Before Perfective and Corrective Changes

After we have investigated the differences in Sect. 2.3.2, we also want to investigate the state of the changed files before the changes were applied. This gives us the information which types of files with regard to software quality metrics and static analysis warnings are the target of perfective or corrective changes. Figure 6 shows the distribution of all metrics before any change, perfective change, or corrective change is applied. We can see some results we would have expected, e.g., the cyclomatic complexity is higher before a corrective change is applied. We can also see that other complexity metrics are slightly higher, e.g., CBO, NOA, NLE, as well as the different severities of static analysis warnings.

Nevertheless, we also see some results we did not expect. For example, the files which are the target of perfective changes are on average less complex and smaller even before the change is applied. Table 12 gives the median of the changes. If we

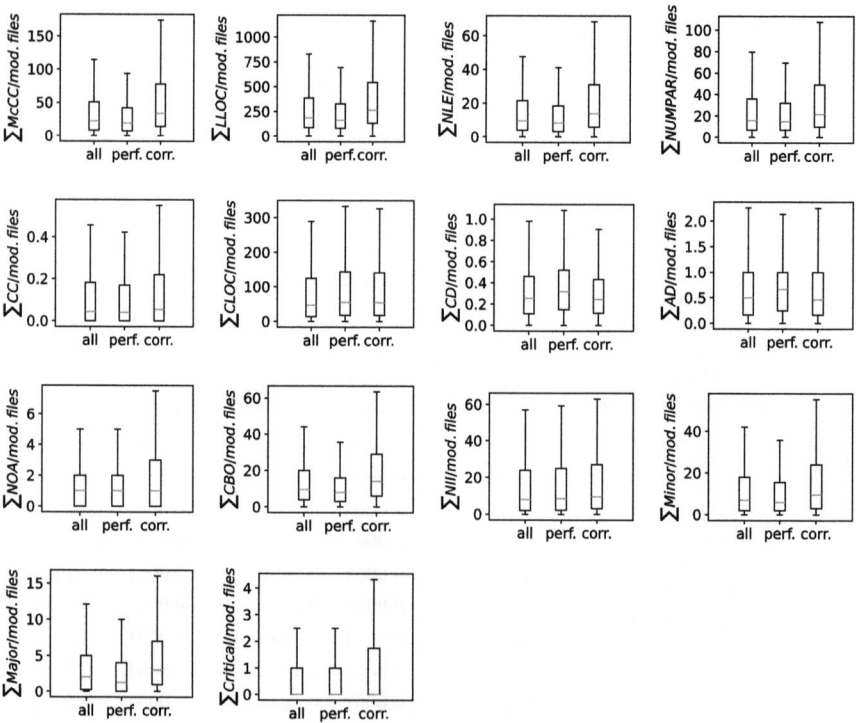

Fig. 6 Static source code metrics divided by the number of changed files before the change is applied. Fliers are omitted. From Trautsch et al. [57], used under Creative Commons CC-BY license

Table 12 Median metric values per file before the change is applied. From Trautsch et al. [57], used under Creative Commons CC-BY license

Metric	All	Perfective	Corrective
McCC	21.78	18.78	33.23
LLOC	186.98	163.75	264.18
NLE	9.60	8.33	14.00
NUMPAR	16.06	15.00	22.00
CC	0.04	0.04	0.05
CLOC	46.25	55.00	54.00
CD	0.25	0.32	0.25
AD	0.50	0.67	0.46
NOA	1.00	1.00	1.00
CBO	9.67	8.00	14.00
NII	8.00	8.50	9.50
Minor	7.00	6.00	9.67
Major	2.00	1.25	3.00
Critical	0.00	0.00	0.00

Table 13 Statistical test results for perfective and corrective commits regarding their average metrics before the change, Mann-Whitney U test p-values, and effect size with category (n is negligible, s is small, m is medium). Statistically significant p-values are in bold. Adapted from Trautsch et al. [57], used under Creative Commons CC-BY license

Metric	Perfective		Corrective	
	P-value	Effect size	P-value	Effect size
McCC	**<0.0001**	0.05 (n)	**<0.0001**	0.08 (n)
LLOC	**<0.0001**	0.05 (n)	**<0.0001**	0.05 (n)
NLE	**<0.0001**	0.04 (n)	**<0.0001**	0.07 (n)
NUMPAR	0.6367	–	0.0218	–
CC	**<0.0001**	0.01 (n)	0.0011	–
CLOC	**<0.0001**	0.12 (s)	**<0.0001**	0.06 (n)
CD	**<0.0001**	0.15 (s)	**<0.0001**	0.15 (s)
AD	**<0.0001**	0.17 (s)	**<0.0001**	0.15 (s)
NOA	0.5109	–	**<0.0001**	0.02 (n)
CBO	**<0.0001**	0.09 (n)	**<0.0001**	0.07 (n)
NII	**<0.0001**	0.05 (n)	**<0.0001**	0.04 (n)
Minor	**<0.0001**	0.04 (n)	**<0.0001**	0.02 (n)
Major	**<0.0001**	0.09 (n)	**<0.0001**	0.04 (n)
Critical	**<0.0001**	0.05 (n)	**<0.0001**	0.03 (n)

combine these with the results presented in Sect. 2.3.2, this means that complex files are more often the target of bug-fixing operation. However, bug fixing in the form of corrective changes also increases the complexity of the file. Moreover, we have shown that complex files are not necessarily the target of perfective changes. This combination yields the unfortunate result that files only get more complex and that we need the focus perfective improvements more on the complex files than on the simpler files like it is shown in our data now.

In addition to the visualization of the distribution in Fig. 6 and medians in Table 12, we provide statistical test results in Table 13. These show that while the differences are statistically significant, the effect size is negligible to small in all cases.

3 Limitations

We acknowledge several limitations in the presented results and studies. Our results are focused on PMD for Java as the ASAT of choice due to its broad use, age, excellent documentation, and ability to work with source code directly. A different ASAT as well as a different type of language, e.g., interpreted, may yield completely different results. We only used an ASAT for a compiled language. Using an ASAT for an interpreted language, e.g., JavaScript with JLint, could yield a larger effect on defects, as the compiling step for Java already takes care of a lot of source of errors. This view is shared by Beller et al. [7] as mentioned in their results.

Moreover, due to the nature of our work, we only include open-source projects. While open-source projects provide a convenient source of data, it may also influence the results, and investigating closed-source industry projects may yield different results. In addition, we are only able to investigate software repository data. If a developer uses an ASAT offline or within the IDE, which is not also in the build configuration, we are not able to detect it. However, this would only decrease the measurable effect instead of increasing the risk of overestimating our findings.

Data validity is necessarily limited by the available time and personnel for study. Some aspects require manual validation, e.g., issue types in the ITS, lines which contribute toward the bug fix or the intent of the developer as expressed in the commit message. In the data for our studies, we mitigate this by including the best currently available manually validated data either directly in the study, e.g., for developer intents [57], for issue types [22], or data from a large labeling study regarding tangling for bug fix lines [21].

4 Related Work

Multiple researchers investigated ASATs over time. In this section, we summarize their work and how it relates to our studies. Due to the different viewpoints, we divide the related work into different categories. Section 4.1 contains related work regarding the evolution of static analysis warnings. Section 4.2 contains related work regarding the impact of ASATs or ASAT warnings on defects. Section 4.3 contains related work regarding the perspective of developers on ASATs.

4.1 Evolution

Beller et al. [7] investigate the state of static analysis tools. They explore how ASATs are used in open-source projects in different programming languages and how their rules evolve. They found that about 60% of the most popular projects make use of ASATs, dynamically typed languages profit more from ASATs, and that default rules seem to be a good fit for most projects. In our work, we are also investigating rule changes. However, we are more interested in the actual warnings that an ASAT produces. In contrast to Beller et al. [7], we retroactively run an ASAT for each revision of our study subjects to investigate the actual warnings produced.

Marcilio et al. [34] investigate resolution times of ASAT warnings and developer engagement on the example of SonarQube.[3] While they do not provide information about general trends in the paper, we were able to use the provided replication kit to reproduce our results of increasing number of warnings in most projects. The data does not contain a size measure, so we were not able to reproduce warning on density-based results.

Some ASATs contain rules that are focused on security. Di Penta et al. [13] study the evolution of three open-source projects regarding the warnings produced by three security ASATs. The authors used vulnerability density and found that they were not able to discern a general trend of reducing density. In contrast to Di Penta et al. [13], our results contain a reducing warning density trend. However, we explore a general-purpose ASAT, which is not focused on security warnings, which might explain this difference.

Aloraini et al. [2] investigate security ASATs over two snapshots, one at 2012 and one at 2017 of 116 open-source projects. The authors also come to the conclusion that warning density is constant, which is in contrast to our own non-security focused results. This hints at a possible difference between security warnings and general-purpose warnings regarding their removal trends.

4.2 Defects

ASATs are investigated in many different ways regarding possible defects that can be identified in research. One avenue of investigation is whether ASATs can identify existing defects as part of their warnings. Thung et al. [52] manually validate all lines responsible for a bug for 439 bugs. The authors note the difficulties of this approach regarding tangling but were able to identify all lines for 200 of the 438 bugs. After this, the authors were able to execute static analysis tools to investigate whether the tools do find these bugs fully (all lines) or partially. When combining three ASATs, the authors find that between 1.9% and 50% of bugs are missed on three open-source projects with large variations between projects. In addition, the authors find that PMD and FindBugs perform best, but note that their warnings are very generic.

Habib and Pradel [18] conduct a similar study with an extension[4] of the Defects4J [27] dataset. The authors investigate three ASATs and the question whether they are able to indicate each bug from the dataset. The authors found that only 27 of 594 bugs were found by at least one of the ASATs. Due to our

---

[3] https://www.sonarqube.org.

[4] https://github.com/rjust/defects4j/pull/112.

usage of SmartSHARK [59] and the large-scale study it enabled [21], we are able to investigate 1,723 bugs for which all lines were manually validated and agreed upon by least three researchers. In contrast to both studies, we are concerned with general trends and whether we are able to measure a net-benefit of a general-purpose ASAT over multiple years of project evolution.

A different avenue of investigation is an indirect exploration of extending predictive models with data from ASATs. Nagappan and Ball [38] explore predicting defect density with static analysis warnings in a case study with Microsoft. They find that static analysis warnings can be used to predict defect prone modules in which to focus quality assurance efforts. In contrast to Nagappan and Ball [38], we investigate an open-source general-purpose ASAT and open-source projects.

Plosch et al. [41] investigate correlations between ASAT warnings and the number of bugs in each file for three releases of Eclipse JDT. The authors find that PMD performs better than FindBugs with correlation values between 0.25 and 0.34, which is a weak to slightly moderate correlation.

Rahman et al. [45] compare the ASATs FindBugs and PMD with a logistic defect prediction model. They analyze 34 releases from 5 open-source projects and find that while FindBugs outperforms the predictive model PMD does not. However, the reported precision is low in all cases. The authors find that they were not able to improve their predictive model with additional data from the ASATs, which is in contrast to our own findings. The reason for this, aside from the data and age of releases, could be that we create aggregated features from ASAT warnings, which Rahman et al. [45] do not.

While Rahman et al. [45] used a release-level defect prediction approach, Querel and Rigby [43] investigate whether they can improve an existing just-in-time defect prediction approach implemented in commit guru [47]. The authors add ASAT warnings as features to the just-in-time defect prediction model. Their results indicate that they were able to improve the predictive model. A later study [44] finds that the magnitude of the effect of ASAT warnings is likely small. Our own results replicate this outcome with different data and models. This indicates that there may be a correlation between bugs and static analysis warnings, even for a general-purpose ASAT such as PMD even if it is likely small.

4.3 Developers

The perspective of the developers on source code quality improvements is investigated in numerous studies. We focus in this section on studies which extracted the intent of the developers to increase quality and after the change measured an effect on software quality attributes. Stroggylos and Spinellis [51] investigate intended refactorings via commit messages and measured a change via several source code metrics. The authors find that refactoring often decreases source code quality metrics, i.e., the intent of the developer does not match the resulting measurements.

Fakhoury et al. [14] compare the intent of developers to increase the readability in the code base with the change of readability measured with an existing readability model. The authors show that the intent of the developers is not matched by the readability model. The readability improvement perceived by the developers is not matched by the results of the measurements by the readability model.

Pantiuchina et al. [39] compare the intent of developers to increase certain software quality metrics with actual measurement of these metrics. The authors also find that the intent of the developer is not captured by the value change of the software quality metric. In contrast to Pantiuchina et al. [39], Fakhoury et al. [14], and Stroggylos and Spinellis [51], our study measures a more generic improvement intent by the developer. Refactoring, readability, and the mention of static source code metric improvement are part of our classification schema. Moreover, we include ASAT warnings as part of the measurement of the outcome of the change. All of the studies mentioned in this section measure a mismatch between intent of developer and actual measurement. This can mean that the intent was misunderstood, the change was badly implemented, or that the measured metrics or models used may not be as accurate as assumed. In our work, we show that most of the changes for perfective quality improvements actually match the measurements as expected. Corrective quality improvements did yield unexpected results however.

5 Summary

In this section, we summarize the chapter and link our results from Sect. 2 together with the results briefly discussed in the related work in Sect. 4 in a loose qualitative meta-analysis. Within this chapter, we have presented results of several large studies of ASATs and static software metrics associated with quality. We are using empirical methods, statistical analysis, and large-scale studies to produce empirical data and ultimately evidence to be used by researchers and practitioners. Estimating the usefulness of static analysis tools can help practitioners select tooling based on empirical evidence; this is the idea behind evidence-based software engineering. Moreover, general trends or lessons extracted from research can improve software development processes, i.e., an indication on where to focus perfective maintenance within a software project.

We use our extended version [56] of the SmartSHARK mining ecosystem [59] to mine and validate large amounts of open-source software development data. The data is used to investigate different aspects of ASATs and their impact on software quality from different perspectives. With the help of SmartSHARK, we conducted several large studies that required manual validation [21, 22, 57] that were enabled by our implementations inside the SmartSHARK frontend. In addition to the replication kits of each publication, all of the raw data is made public for other researchers or practitioners on the SmartSHARK website.[5]

---

[5] https://smartshark.github.io/dbreleases/.

We can show that while the sum of static analysis warnings is steadily increasing and correlated to the number of LLOC, the warning density is decreasing in most of our study subjects. A steady increase of the number of static analysis warnings is also found in previous research [34], however not explicitly mentioned in the paper. Our results contain a decrease in warning density; overall, each project resolves about 3.5 ASAT warnings per kLLOC per year, which means that if we think of warning density as an indicator of source code quality, source code quality improves over time.

While we are the first to report warning density for a general-purpose ASAT, Aloraini et al. [2] and Di Penta et al. [13] found no decrease in warning density for security-focused ASATs. A reason for this could be a difference in removal effort between general-purpose ASAT warnings and security-focused ASAT warnings. Regardless, our findings indicate that we have to account for changes in general warning density of open-source projects for longitudinal studies, which utilize source code evolution data.

Our investigation into the impact of ASATs on quality from the perspective of predictive models as well as statistical comparisons yields a surprisingly small effect. However, this small effect is replicated by other researchers for predictive models [44] or simple correlation measures [41], increasing the evidence toward a small effect of ASATs on defects. In addition, our research indicates that a subset of rules provides a larger effect size, which hints toward differences in rules regarding their impact.

Previous work has shown that the perception of source code quality by the developers and the actual measurements of static source code quality metrics does not always match. In our research, we found that ASAT warnings are not only associated with quality by developers in questionnaires as in [10, 61] but that static analysis warnings are in fact reduced when developers intend to improve code quality. We measured an effect that is not as high as static source code metrics commonly associated with quality, e.g., McCC or CBO. In the course of this study, we also noticed a small effect where corrective changes increase complexity of already complex files, but perfective changes, which reduce complexity, are only applied on already less complex files.

Combining our results, we can draw several conclusions for practitioners. The number of ASAT warnings is going to increase with the size of the code base. Adopting a metric-like warning density for Continuous Integration (CI) systems can therefore be a more helpful measure for a general overview. We presented data on the impact on defects, which can help practitioners weight the benefits against the cost of introducing and maintaining ASATs. While our results only point to a very small effect on defects, there may still be more positive influence of ASATs not part of our study, e.g., readability of code. Our results also show a higher effect for the default subset of warnings, indicating that this configuration is a good starting point when using PMD for Java.

Fixing a bug is a complex operation, while maintenance that reduces complexity is predominantly focused on less complex parts of the code. To dissolve this contradiction, maintenance activities should be focused on files that were part of a

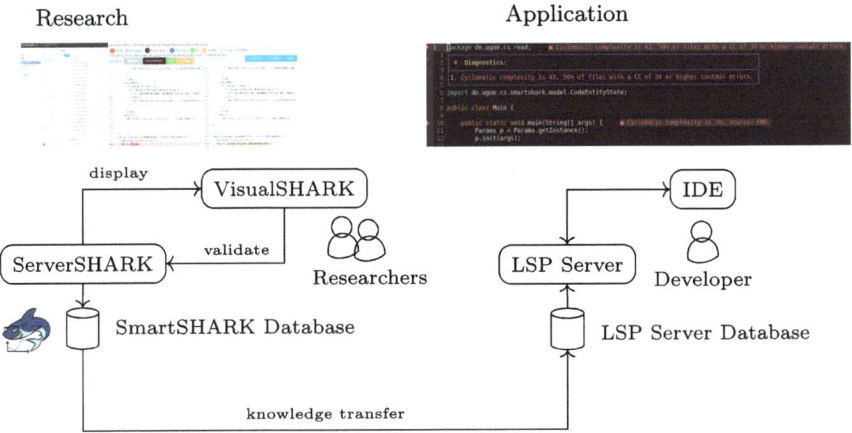

Fig. 7 Knowledge transfer from studies to practitioners

bug-fixing operation. Another solution would be to reserve resources for perfective maintenance on overly complex files; these could be indicated by tooling using thresholds from our research. This would reduce complexity and can also lead to a reduced number of bugs as indicated in our research.

The SmartSHARK mining infrastructure and the data collected can be further utilized by researchers for all topics that rely on software repository data as well as manual validation via web frontend. We will continue to support and enhance this platform in the future.

Given the results of our empirical studies and the implementations required to conduct them, we are able to proceed in various directions. Our research can be utilized inside the IDE via Language Server Protocol (LSP) integration. Figure 7 depicts such a scenario in which the data acquired from research is transferred to the practitioner. This allows thresholds from research, e.g., complexity or types of ASAT warnings, to be displayed while working on the source code of a file and show hints and recommendations to the developer.

References

1. Alali, A., Kagdi, H., Maletic, J.I.: What's a typical commit? A characterization of open source software repositories. In: 2008 16th IEEE International Conference on Program Comprehension, pp. 182–191 (2008). https://doi.org/10.1109/ICPC.2008.24
2. Aloraini, B., Nagappan, M., German, D.M., Hayashi, S., Higo, Y.: An empirical study of security warnings from static application security testing tools. J. Syst. Softw. **158**, 110427 (2019). ISSN 0164-1212. https://doi.org/10.1016/j.jss.2019.110427. http://www.sciencedirect.com/science/article/pii/S0164121219302018
3. Antoniol, G., Ayari, K., Di Penta, M., Khomh, F., Guéhéneuc, Y.-G.: Is it a bug or an enhancement?: A text-based approach to classify change requests. In: Proceedings of the 2008

Conference of the Center for Advanced Studies on Collaborative Research: Meeting of Minds, CASCON '08, pp. 23:304–23:318. ACM, New York (2008). https://doi.org/10.1145/1463788. 1463819. http://doi.acm.org/10.1145/1463788.1463819
4. Ayewah, N., Pugh, W., David Morgenthaler, J., Penix, J., Zhou, Y.Q.: Evaluating static analysis defect warnings on production software. In: Proceedings of the 7th ACM SIGPLAN-SIGSOFT Workshop on Program Analysis for Software Tools and Engineering, PASTE '07, pp. 1–8. Association for Computing Machinery, New York (2007). ISBN 9781595935953. https://doi.org/10.1145/1251535.1251536
5. Bakota, T., Hegedűs, P., Körtvélyesi, P., Ferenc, R., Gyimóthy, T.: A probabilistic software quality model. In: 2011 27th IEEE International Conference on Software Maintenance (ICSM), pp. 243–252 (2011). https://doi.org/10.1109/ICSM.2011.6080791
6. Bakota, T., Hegedűs, P., Siket, I., Ladányi, G., Ferenc, R.: Qualitygate sourceaudit: a tool for assessing the technical quality of software. In: 2014 Software Evolution Week – IEEE Conference on Software Maintenance, Reengineering, and Reverse Engineering (CSMR-WCRE), pp. 440–445 (2014). https://doi.org/10.1109/CSMR-WCRE.2014.6747214
7. Beller, M., Bholanath, R., McIntosh, S., Zaidman, A.: Analyzing the state of static analysis: a large-scale evaluation in open source software. In: 2016 IEEE 23rd International Conference on Software Analysis, Evolution, and Reengineering (SANER), vol. 1, pp. 470–481 (2016). https://doi.org/10.1109/SANER.2016.105
8. Burton Swanson, E.: The dimensions of maintenance. In: Proceedings of the 2nd International Conference on Software Engineering, ICSE '76, pp. 492–497. IEEE Computer Society Press, Washington (1976)
9. Chidamber, S.R., Kemerer, C.F.: A metrics suite for object oriented design. IEEE Trans. Softw. Eng. **20**(6), 476–493 (1994). ISSN 0098-5589. https://doi.org/10.1109/32.295895
10. Christakis, M., Bird, C.: What developers want and need from program analysis: an empirical study. In: Proceedings of the 31st IEEE/ACM International Conference on Automated Software Engineering, ASE 2016, pp. 332–343. ACM, New York (2016). ISBN 978-1-4503-3845-5. https://doi.org/10.1145/2970276.2970347. http://doi.acm.org/10.1145/2970276.2970347
11. Devanbu, P., Zimmermann, T., Bird, C.: Belief evidence in empirical software engineering. In: 2016 IEEE/ACM 38th International Conference on Software Engineering (ICSE), pp. 108–119 (2016). https://doi.org/10.1145/2884781.2884812
12. Devlin, J., Chang, M.-W., Lee, K., Toutanova, K.: BERT: pre-training of deep bidirectional transformers for language understanding. CoRR, abs/1810.04805 (2018). http://arxiv.org/abs/1810.04805
13. Di Penta, M., Cerulo, L., Aversano, L.: The life and death of statically detected vulnerabilities: an empirical study. Inform. Softw. Technol. **51**(10), 1469–1484 (2009). ISSN 0950-5849. https://doi.org/10.1016/j.infsof.2009.04.013. http://www.sciencedirect.com/science/article/pii/S0950584909000500. Source Code Analysis and Manipulation, SCAM 2008
14. Fakhoury, S., Roy, D., Hassan, A., Arnaoudova, V.: Improving source code readability: theory and practice. In: 2019 IEEE/ACM 27th International Conference on Program Comprehension (ICPC), pp. 2–12 (2019). https://doi.org/10.1109/ICPC.2019.00014
15. Fan, Y., Xia, X., Alencar da Costa, D., Lo, D., Hassan, A.E., Li, S.: The impact of changes mislabeled by SZZ on just-in-time defect prediction. IEEE Trans. Softw. Eng. 1–1 (2019). https://doi.org/10.1109/TSE.2019.2929761
16. Fenton, N., Bieman, J.: Software Metrics: A Rigorous and Practical Approach, 3rd edn. CRC Press, Inc., Boca Raton (2014). ISBN 1439838224, 9781439838228
17. FindBugs: Findbugs (2018). http://findbugs.sourceforge.net/
18. Habib, A., Pradel, M.: How many of all bugs do we find? A study of static bug detectors. In: Proceedings of the 33rd ACM/IEEE International Conference on Automated Software Engineering, ASE 2018, pp. 317–328. ACM, New York (2018). ISBN 978-1-4503-5937-5. https://doi.org/10.1145/3238147.3238213. http://doi.acm.org/10.1145/3238147.3238213
19. Heckman, S., Williams, L.: A model building process for identifying actionable static analysis alerts. In: 2009 International Conference on Software Testing Verification and Validation, pp. 161–170 (2009). https://doi.org/10.1109/ICST.2009.45

20. Heckman, S., Williams, L.: A systematic literature review of actionable alert identification techniques for automated static code analysis. Inf. Softw. Technol. **53**(4), 363–387 (2011). ISSN 0950-5849. https://doi.org/10.1016/j.infsof.2010.12.007
21. Herbold, S., Trautsch, A., Ledel, B., Aghamohammadi, A., Ghaleb, T.A., Chahal, K.K., Bossenmaier, T., Nagaria, B., Makedonski, P., Ahmadabadi, M.N., Szabados, K., Spieker, H., Madeja, M., Hoy, N., Lenarduzzi, V., Wang, S., Rodríguez-Pérez, G., Colomo-Palacios, R., Verdecchia, R., Singh, P., Qin, Y., Chakroborti, D., Davis, W., Walunj, V., Wu, H., Marcilio, D., Alam, O., Aldaeej, A., Amit, I., Turhan, B., Eismann, S., Wickert, A.-K., Malavolta, I., Sulir, M., Fard, F., Henley, A.Z., Kourtzanidis, S., Tuzun, E., Treude, C., Shamasbi, S.M., Pashchenko, I., Wyrich, M., Davis, J., Serebrenik, A., Albrecht, E., Aktas, E.U., Strüber, D., Erbel, J.: A fine-grained data set and analysis of tangling in bug fixing commits. Empirical Softw. Eng. **27**(6), 125 (2022). ISSN 1573-7616. https://doi.org/10.1007/s10664-021-10083-5
22. Herbold, S., Trautsch, A., Trautsch, F., Ledel, B.: Problems with SZZ and features: an empirical study of the state of practice of defect prediction data collection. Empirical Softw. Eng. **27**(2), 42 (2022). ISSN 1573-7616. https://doi.org/10.1007/s10664-021-10092-4
23. Herzig, K., Zeller, A.: The impact of tangled code changes. In: Proceedings of the 10th Working Conference on Mining Software Repositories, MSR '13, pp. 121–130. IEEE Press, Piscataway (2013). ISBN 9781467329361
24. Herzig, K., Just, S., Zeller, A.: It's not a bug, it's a feature: How misclassification impacts bug prediction. In: Proceedings of the International Conference on Software Engineering, ICSE '13, pp. 392–401. IEEE Press, Piscataway (2013). ISBN 978-1-4673-3076-3. http://dl.acm.org/citation.cfm?id=2486788.2486840
25. Herzig, K., Just, S., Zeller, A.: The impact of tangled code changes on defect prediction models. Empirical Softw. Eng. 1–34 (2016). https://www.microsoft.com/en-us/research/publication/the-impact-of-tangled-code-changes-on-defect-prediction-models/
26. Johnson, B., Song, Y., Murphy-Hill, E.., Bowdidge, R.: Why don't software developers use static analysis tools to find bugs? In: Proceedings of the 2013 International Conference on Software Engineering, ICSE '13, pp. 672–681. IEEE Press, Piscataway (2013). ISBN 978-1-4673-3076-3. http://dl.acm.org/citation.cfm?id=2486788.2486877
27. Just, R., Jalali, D., Ernst, M.D.: Defects4j: a database of existing faults to enable controlled testing studies for Java programs. In: Proceedings of the 2014 International Symposium on Software Testing and Analysis, ISSTA 2014, pp. 437–440. Association for Computing Machinery, New York (2014). ISBN 9781450326452. https://doi.org/10.1145/2610384.2628055
28. Kendall, M.G.: Rank Correlation Methods. Charles Griffin & Co. Ltd., London (1955)
29. Kim, S., Ernst, M.D.: Which warnings should i fix first? In: Proceedings of the the 6th Joint Meeting of the European Software Engineering Conference and the ACM SIGSOFT Symposium on The Foundations of Software Engineering, ESEC-FSE '07, pp. 45–54. ACM, New York (2007). ISBN 978-1-59593-811-4. https://doi.org/10.1145/1287624.1287633
30. Kitchenham, B.A., Dyba, T., Jorgensen, M.: Evidence-based software engineering. In: Proceedings of the 26th International Conference on Software Engineering, ICSE '04, pp. 273–281. IEEE Computer Society, Washington (2004). ISBN 0-7695-2163-0. http://dl.acm.org/citation.cfm?id=998675.999432
31. Koc, U., Saadatpanah, P., Foster, J.S., Porter, A.A.: Learning a classifier for false positive error reports emitted by static code analysis tools. In: Proceedings of the 1st ACM SIGPLAN International Workshop on Machine Learning and Programming Languages, pp. 35–42 (2017). ISBN 978-1-4503-5071-6. https://doi.org/10.1145/3088525.3088675
32. Lee, S., Hong, S., Yi, J., Kim, T., C.-J. Kim, Yoo, S.: Classifying false positive static checker alarms in continuous integration using convolutional neural networks. In: 2019 12th IEEE Conference on Software Testing, Validation and Verification (ICST), pp. 391–401 (2019). https://doi.org/10.1109/ICST.2019.00048
33. Lenarduzzi, V., Lomio, F., Huttunen, H., Taibi, D.: Are sonarqube rules inducing bugs? In: 2020 IEEE 27th International Conference on Software Analysis, Evolution and Reengineering (SANER), pp. 501–511 (2020)

34. Marcilio, D., Bonifácio, R., Monteiro, E., Canedo, E., Luz, W., Pinto, G.: Are static analysis violations really fixed?: A closer look at realistic usage of sonarqube. In: Proceedings of the 27th International Conference on Program Comprehension, ICPC '19, pp. 209–219. IEEE, Piscataway Press (2019). https://doi.org/10.1109/ICPC.2019.00040
35. McCabe, T.J.: A complexity measure. IEEE Trans. Softw. Eng. **2**(4), 308–320 (1976). ISSN 0098-5589. https://doi.org/10.1109/TSE.1976.233837
36. Mills, C., Pantiuchina, J., Parra, E., Bavota, G., Haiduc, S.: Are bug reports enough for text retrieval-based bug localization? In: 2018 IEEE International Conference on Software Maintenance and Evolution (ICSME), pp. 381–392 (2018). https://doi.org/10.1109/ICSME.2018.00046
37. Mockus, Votta: Identifying reasons for software changes using historic databases. In: Proceedings 2000 International Conference on Software Maintenance, pp. 120–130 (2000). https://doi.org/10.1109/ICSM.2000.883028
38. Nagappan, N., Ball, T.: Static analysis tools as early indicators of pre-release defect density. In: Proceedings of the 27th International Conference on Software Engineering, ICSE '05, pp. 580–586. ACM, New York (2005). ISBN 1-58113-963-2. https://doi.org/10.1145/1062455.1062558. http://doi.acm.org/10.1145/1062455.1062558
39. Pantiuchina, J., Lanza, M., Bavota, G.: Improving code: the (mis) perception of quality metrics. In: 2018 IEEE International Conference on Software Maintenance and Evolution (ICSME), pp. 80–91 (2018). https://doi.org/10.1109/ICSME.2018.00017
40. Pascarella, L., Palomba, F., Bacchelli, A.: Fine-grained just-in-time defect prediction. J. Syst. Softw. **150**, 22–36 (2019). ISSN 0164-1212. https://doi.org/10.1016/j.jss.2018.12.001. http://www.sciencedirect.com/science/article/pii/S0164121218302656
41. Plosch, R., Gruber, H., Hentschel, A., Pomberger, G., Schiffer, S.: On the relation between external software quality and static code analysis. In: 2008 32nd Annual IEEE Software Engineering Workshop, pp. 169–174 (2008). https://doi.org/10.1109/SEW.2008.17
42. Purushothaman, R., Perry, D.E.: Toward understanding the rhetoric of small source code changes. IEEE Trans. Softw. Eng. **31**(6), 511–526 (2005). https://doi.org/10.1109/TSE.2005.74
43. Querel, L.-P., Rigby, P.C.: Warningsguru: Integrating statistical bug models with static analysis to provide timely and specific bug warnings. In: Proceedings of the 2018 26th ACM Joint Meeting on European Software Engineering Conference and Symposium on the Foundations of Software Engineering, ESEC/FSE 2018, pp. 892–895. Association for Computing Machinery, New York (2018). ISBN 9781450355735. https://doi.org/10.1145/3236024.3264599
44. Querel, L.-P., Rigby, P.C.: Warning-introducing commits vs bug-introducing commits: a tool, statistical models, and a preliminary user study. In: 29th IEEE/ACM International Conference on Program Comprehension, ICPC 2021, Madrid, May 20–21 (2021), pp. 433–443. IEEE, Piscataway (2021). https://doi.org/10.1109/ICPC52881.2021.00051
45. Rahman, F., Khatri, S., Barr, E.T., Devanbu, P.: Comparing static bug finders and statistical prediction. In: Proceedings of the 36th International Conference on Software Engineering, ICSE 2014, pp. 424–434. ACM, New York (2014). ISBN 978-1-4503-2756-5. https://doi.org/10.1145/2568225.2568269. http://doi.acm.org/10.1145/2568225.2568269
46. Rosa, G., Pascarella, L., Scalabrino, S., Tufano, R., Bavota, G., Lanza, M., Oliveto, R.: Evaluating SZZ implementations through a developer-informed oracle. In: 43rd IEEE/ACM International Conference on Software Engineering, ICSE 2021, Madrid, 22–30 May 2021, pp. 436–447 (2021). https://doi.org/10.1109/ICSE43902.2021.00049
47. Rosen, C., Grawi, B., Shihab, E.: Commit guru: analytics and risk prediction of software commits. In: Proceedings of the 2015 10th Joint Meeting on Foundations of Software Engineering, ESEC/FSE 2015, pp. 966–969. Association for Computing Machinery, New York (2015). ISBN 9781450336758. https://doi.org/10.1145/2786805.2803183
48. Śliwerski, J., Zimmermann, T., Zeller, A.: When do changes induce fixes? SIGSOFT Softw. Eng. Notes **30**(4), 1–5 (2005). ISSN 0163-5948. https://doi.org/10.1145/1082983.1083147
49. Spearman, C.: The proof and measurement of association between two things. Am. J. Psychol. **15**, 88–103 (1904)

50. SpotBugs: Spotbugs (2020). https://spotbugs.github.io/
51. Stroggylos, K., Spinellis, D.: Refactoring–does it improve software quality? In: Fifth International Workshop on Software Quality (WoSQ'07: ICSE Workshops 2007), pp. 10–10 (2007). https://doi.org/10.1109/WOSQ.2007.11
52. Thung, F., Lucia, Lo, D., Jiang, L., Rahman, F., Devanbu, P.T.: To what extent could we detect field defects? An empirical study of false negatives in static bug finding tools. In: 2012 Proceedings of the 27th IEEE/ACM International Conference on Automated Software Engineering, pp. 50–59 (2012). https://doi.org/10.1145/2351676.2351685
53. Trautsch, A.: Automated Static Analysis Tools: A Multidimensional View on Software Quality Evolution. PhD thesis, Georg-August-Universität Göttingen (2022)
54. Trautsch, A., Herbold, S., Grabowski, J.: A longitudinal study of static analysis warning evolution and the effects of PMD on software quality in apache open source projects. Empirical Softw. Eng. **25**(6), 5137–5192 (2020). ISSN 1573-7616. https://doi.org/10.1007/s10664-020-09880-1
55. Trautsch, A., Herbold, S., Grabowski, J.: Static source code metrics and static analysis warnings for fine-grained just-in-time defect prediction. In: 2020 IEEE International Conference on Software Maintenance and Evolution (ICSME), pp. 127–138 (2020). https://doi.org/10.1109/ICSME46990.2020.00022
56. Trautsch, A., Trautsch, F., Herbold, S., Ledel, B., Grabowski, J.: The smartSHARK ecosystem for software repository mining. In: 42nd International Conference on Software Engineering (ICSE 2020 Demos) (2020). https://arxiv.org/abs/2001.01606
57. Trautsch, A., Erbel, J., Herbold, S., Grabowski, J.: What really changes when developers intend to improve their source code: a commit-level study of static metric value and static analysis warning changes. Empirical Softw. Eng. **28**(2), 30 (2023). ISSN 1573-7616. https://doi.org/10.1007/s10664-022-10257-9
58. Trautsch, A., Herbold, S., Grabowski, J.: Are automated static analysis tools worth it? An investigation into relative warning density and external software quality on the example of apache open source projects. Empirical Softw. Eng. **28**(3), 66 (2023). ISSN 1573-7616. https://doi.org/10.1007/s10664-023-10301-2
59. Trautsch, F., Herbold, S., Makedonski, P., Grabowski, J.: Addressing problems with replicability and validity of repository mining studies through a smart data platform. Empirical Softw. Eng. (2017). https://doi.org/10.1007/s10664-017-9537-x
60. Tufano, M., Palomba, F., Bavota, G., Di Penta, M., Oliveto, R., De Lucia, A., Poshyvanyk, D.: There and back again: can you compile that snapshot? J. Softw. Evol. Process **29**(4), e1838 (2017). http://dblp.uni-trier.de/db/journals/smr/smr29.html#TufanoPBPOLP17
61. Vassallo, C., Panichella, S., Palomba, F., Proksch, S., Gall, H.C., Zaidman, A.: How developers engage with static analysis tools in different contexts. Empirical Softw. Eng. **25**(2), 1419–1457 (2019). https://doi.org/10.1007/s10664-019-09750-5
62. Vetro, A., Morisio, M., Torchiano, M.: An empirical validation of findbugs issues related to defects. In: 15th Annual Conference on Evaluation Assessment in Software Engineering (EASE 2011), pp. 144–153 (2011). https://doi.org/10.1049/ic.2011.0018
63. Wagner, S., Jürjens, J., Koller, C., Trischberger, P.: Comparing bug finding tools with reviews and tests. In: Khendek, F., Dssouli, R., (eds.) Testing of Communicating Systems, pp. 40–55. Springer, Berlin (2005). ISBN 978-3-540-32076-0
64. Wohlin, C., Runeson, P., Höst, M., Ohlsson, M.C., Regnell, B., Wesslén, A.: Experimentation in Software Engineering. Springer Science & Business Media, Berlin (2012)
65. Yan, M., Xia, X., Fan, Y., Lo, D., Hassan, A.E., Zhang, X.: Effort-aware just-in-time defect identification in practice: A case study at alibaba. In: Proceedings of the 28th ACM Joint Meeting on European Software Engineering Conference and Symposium on the Foundations of Software Engineering, ESEC/FSE 2020, pp. 1308–1319. Association for Computing Machinery, New York (2020). ISBN 9781450370431. https://doi.org/10.1145/3368089.3417048
66. Zheng, J., Williams, L., Nagappan, N., Snipes, W., Hudepohl, J.P., Vouk, M.A.: On the value of static analysis for fault detection in software. IEEE Trans. Softw. Eng. **32**(4), 240–253 (2006). https://doi.org/10.1109/TSE.2006.38

Open Access This chapter is licensed under the terms of the Creative Commons Attribution 4.0 International License (http://creativecommons.org/licenses/by/4.0/), which permits use, sharing, adaptation, distribution and reproduction in any medium or format, as long as you give appropriate credit to the original author(s) and the source, provide a link to the Creative Commons licence and indicate if changes were made.

The images or other third party material in this chapter are included in the chapter's Creative Commons licence, unless indicated otherwise in a credit line to the material. If material is not included in the chapter's Creative Commons licence and your intended use is not permitted by statutory regulation or exceeds the permitted use, you will need to obtain permission directly from the copyright holder.

If you have any concerns about our products,
you can contact us on
ProductSafety@springernature.com

In case Publisher is established outside the EU,
the EU authorized representative is:
**Springer Nature Customer Service Center GmbH
Europaplatz 3, 69115 Heidelberg, Germany**

Printed by Libri Plureos GmbH
in Hamburg, Germany